D1163391

THE JEWISH WOMAN IN AMERICA:

TWO FEMALE IMMIGRANT GENERATIONS 1820-1929

OTHER BOOKS BY THE AUTHOR

JEWS IN RELATION TO THE CULTURAL MILIEU OF THE
GERMANS IN AMERICA UP TO THE EIGHTEEN EIGHTIES
NEW YORK 1947

THE JEWS IN AMERICAN ALASKA (1867–1880)
NEW YORK 1953

THE JEWS OF CALIFORNIA
FROM THE DISCOVERY OF GOLD UP TO 1880
NEW YORK 1960

THE JEW IN THE OLD AMERICAN FOLKLORE
NEW YORK 1961

JEW AND MORMON
HISTORIC GROUP RELATIONS AND RELIGIOUS OUTLOOK
NEW YORK 1963

JEW AND IRISH
HISTORIC GROUP RELATIONS AND IMMIGRATION
NEW YORK 1966

GESCHICHTE DES NIEDEREN JÜDISCHENVOLKES
IN DEUTSCHLAND
EINE STUDIE ÜBER HISTORISCHES GAUNERTUM, BETTELWESEN
UND VAGANTENTUM
NEW YORK 1968

THE GERMAN JEW IN AMERICA
AN ANNOTATED BIBLIOGRAPHY INCLUDING BOOKS, PAMPHLETS
AND ARTICLES OF SPECIAL INTEREST
NEW YORK 1968

STUDIES IN JUDAICA AMERICANA
NEW YORK 1970

JEW AND ITALIAN: HISTORIC GROUP RELATIONS
AND THE NEW IMMIGRATION (1881–1924)
NEW YORK 1971

THE JEW IN EARLY AMERICAN WIT AND
GRAPHIC HUMOR
NEW YORK 1973

THE JEWISH WOMAN IN AMERICA:

TWO FEMALE IMMIGRANT GENERATIONS 1820-1929

VOLUME II
The German Jewish Woman

by Rudolf Glanz

KTAV PUBLISHING HOUSE, INC.
and
NATIONAL COUNCIL OF JEWISH WOMEN

**Library of Congress Cataloging in Publication Data
(Revised)**

Glanz, Rudolf.
    The Jewish woman in America.

    Bibliography: v. 1, p.   , v. 2, p.
    CONTENTS: v. 1. The Eastern European Jewish
woman.—v. 2. The German Jewish woman.
    1. Jews in the United States. 2. Women, Jewish. 3.
Jews—Migrations. 4. United States—Emigration and
immigration. I. Title.
E184.J5G493   973'.04'924   75-29350
ISBN 0-87068-462-0 (v. 1)

MANUFACTURED IN THE UNITED STATES OF AMERICA

Table of Contents

Preface

In historical studies of the Atlantic migrations from Europe to America, the fate of its female generations is not clearly differentiated in any way—neither in its general nor in its individual and ethnic aspects. Similarly ignored is the fate of the woman immigrant who settled in the New World, her role in building its ethnic society and, especially, in creating her own female world, originating in the immigrant people from which she sprang. To fill the gap, this study presents examples of the two generations of Jewish women immigrants: the German and the Russian, who were destined together to build up American Jewry and give it its présent form.

Although the emigration of the two groups continued unabated during the life of its generation, the major portion of their problems soon gravitated away from the sphere of emigration to the process of adjustment to the new continent. The new community of Russian Jews, then in progress, played the greater role in this process, with its two thorough transformations through its two mass immigrations. The Sephardic Jews, who were the original nucleus of American Jewry in colonial times, were transformed by the German Jewish immigration in the same way as the overwhelmingly German Jewish community was later transformed into a new community by the immigration of the Russian Jews. If the descendents of the then immigrating generation took an increasingly greater share in this transformation, nevertheless, during the entire period of its existence the preceding immigrant generation remained the sustaining power in the process of building the new community. This was especially true among the German Jews until 1880 and also in the period of the New Immigration until 1924 holding on longer in the earlier period because the creation of families and family life among the German Jewish immigrants came about largely after their immigration, and because, generally, descendents were born in America. In contrast, the majority of the Russian Jewish emigrants

had already established their families in Europe and brought a generation of numerous children with them to America, with new children
born to these families shortly after settling here. Thus, the proportion
of Russia-born to native-born children among the immigrants was only
slowly reduced during the coming years.

As a consequence, the influence of the Russian Jews on American
Jewry was seen longer, actually until the gates were closed to immigration. This influence was established by the immigrants themselves, and
not by their descendents, especially as their immigration continued, and
they settled in America with their genuine folk culture, their own religious traditions, and their own cultural life carried on in their own
language—Yiddish. Furthermore, in the cultural institutions created in
this language, as the Yiddish press, book publishing, theater, and social,
organizations were active economically, culturally, and even purely
philanthropically.

These facts, demonstrable for any period of free immigration, justify
the undertaking of considering the history of the two immigrant groups
in their relevant periods—1815-1880 and 1881-1924—as seen, on the
one hand, with all the formations of their independent group life, and
in the relations of one group with the other; and, on the other hand,
in the effect of both groups on the achievement of the final result—a
united American Jewry, insofar as it existed already in 1924. Only the
independent development of the American-born descendents of both
groups remains outside of this study, since only in this way can the independence of problems to be dealt with be secured. Occasionally, the
common problem of youth, involving immigrated as well as native-born
children, may throw light on a facet of our understanding, as in describing the taking care of immigrants in institutions, or even in demon-
strating mixed marriage between the two groups or with Gentiles. All
these sidelights, however, should not cause us to deviate from our principal task of making a conclusive judgment on the state of the immigrant
generations.

Everything that has been said above holds generally true for the
female immigrants as well as for the male. But the process of adjustment
to the American scene and to intercourse with other ethnic groups of
the same period of immigration was an entirely different one for the

two groups. The German Jewish group could continue their cultural life in the milieu of the German immigrants of the same period; the Russian Jewish group, with few exceptions, was far removed from any contact with any Slavic immigrant group, be it from Central Europe or further East. In the world of German Jewish women, there existed a peculiar restriction in respect to the cultural German milieu which cultivated mainly men's organizations, like Turnvereins (gymnastic) and glee clubs, many allowing only men to its membership, participation of women existing only modestly in the sector of German school organizations.

Embedded in the growth of the German female society, was the position of a special immigrant group from the Germanized Polish district of Poznan—in German, Posen. The Poseners were Jews of the last region the Germans acquired from the East and were not yet fully accepted as members in the consciousness of German Jewry at the time the Jews emigrated from southern and western sections of Germany. Preparations of the Posener emigrants were hardly observed. And also not observed was a special sentiment of their women for emigration. In this sentiment the Jewish female youth excelled in the other German countries. "Prussia," which meant mostly the Poseners (Herzogthümer) in terms of Jewish emigration, was psychologically far from the average German Jew in the process of emigration. Nevertheless, we know that the emigration from the Grand Duchy of Posen was accomplished mainly by its youthful element and that, in many cases, Poseners arrived in America as young married couples.

It was important for the adaptation of this new female element into the German Jewish feminine milieu in America that the Poseners had already been thoroughly trained in the German schools of Prussian Poland. The history of education in the province of Posen demonstrates that in the great Jewish communities there, such as the city of Posen, Lissa (Polish—Leszno), and followed by the smaller communities, private schools for Jewish girls were already established at a time when given, in part, by women teachers. Heppner, Dr. A. u. J. Herzberg. *Aus* public schools still did not exist there. Instruction in these schools was *Vergangenheit und Gegenwart der Juden in den Posener Landen*. Koschmin, 1904-1928, p. 603 (Lissa and Posen); p. 689 (Pinne); p. 883

(Rackwitz). Konapka, Otto, "Das Privatschulwesen der Stadt Posen unter besonderer Berücksichtigung der Erziehungsanstalten für das weibliche Geschlecht," *Zeitschrift . . . Provinz Posen,* vol. 26(1911), pp. 243-309, p. 248 (year 1835), p. 250 (1839). All in all, the education received by the girls in Posen and brought with them to America was pretty much on a par with what Jewish girls in the Jewish schools in German countries elsewhere received. In Posen, as also in Bavaria, "Jüdisch Schreiben" was taught because it was just as important there for communication of remaining parents with their emigrated children as it was in Bavaria. The crest years of the emigration from Posen started two decades later than that of the Bavarian Jews, from 1860 on, and Prussian school instruction so many years later was rather more thorough than that of Bavaria so long before.

The picture of the Jewish emigrating family from Posen at that time and the place of the woman in it was not so different from that of the German Jewish woman in the same situation: in economic life the help-mate of her husband, her problems in establishing a new household in America were basically the same. The mobility of her new family was the same: in the Far West and in the Middle West they were merchant pioneers in new places; on the Atlantic, however, in the big cities, they were often the drudging pathmakers for the later arrivals. The Posener's knowledge of German facilitated also an economical nearness to the Germans in America.

Introduction

From the beginning, the new American society that sprang from the trans-Atlantic migration of European peoples, had to concede a new role to its female generations that contrasted essentially with the customary serfdom of the woman in the European mother-countries. Family building and social mores went hand-in-hand with the hard necessities of a new reality on a new continent. Here, woman had to meet specific challenges of pioneering that did not exist in the static life of women in Europe, especially of its peasant nations.

This position of the generations of pioneering immigrant women had to be acknowledged, at first only on life terms, outside the framework of customary law brought over from Europe. However, legal rights followed as soon as customary law succumbed to the actual conditions of women's life in the New World.

The new Jewish center created in America in the course of the nineteenth century included two female immigrant generations. Whatever of Judaism existed in America previously was represented by a small static group, dependent in their religious interests on European Jewish communities and only slightly moved by the spiritual currents within European Jewry. In this group, the Jewish woman occupied only her traditional place in the life of the Jewish family. The real forces leading to the creation of an American Israel, later of such importance for Jewish people of the whole world, didn't lie with this group. They were, rather, the result of the great Atlantic migrations which brought to this country two essentially different generations of female immigrants separated from one another by a life's span, the German Jewish and Russian Jewish woman.

The German Jewish immigration coincides with the westward movement and the opening of the interior of the American continent that was accomplished by the pioneer family. The female who followed her husband to the West was assigned a life under entirely novel conditions. The same life-style was the fortune of the German Jewess who followed her pioneering merchant husband to the West, under entirely new conditions if we view it from the historical observation point of the traditional life of Jewish women. She had lived predominantly in old, long established small communities in the German countries, taking over her conventional functions in the Jewish family learned from her mother. On the side, she had also helped her husband in his economic struggle.[1] Now, on the new continent, she had to occupy a function first, in the building up of a new economy and society and then, in addition, to found a new family on new soil.

On the other hand, from an American point of view, the influx of an urban female element, as represented by the German Jewish immigration, was a unique appearance among all the other female immigrants of rural background. The rise of German Jewish men from their original status as pioneering merchants to a settled life as part of the merchant class in the rapidly growing cities, catapulted this female element to unforeseen heights in an urban "society" that was shaping up there. Reviewing the achievement of the German Jewish woman in the course of a single generation, we must conclude that it matched the progress of her husband in every way.

This middle class further created a distinct feminine sphere in a society which was upper middle class throughout by its economic achievement. From this middle class later arose the fighters for women's rights and the active participants in all progressive social work in America.

Totally unlike the path of the German Jewess was the way taken by the Russian Jewish woman of a subsequent immigration. Her rise was made possible only by her influx into the new industrial proletariat of America. This rise, however, coincided with the revolutionary change already in progress in the position of women in the new industrial society of America. In this period, all the new possibilities for women started, which were later to bring her forward as the bearer of new rights—the woman's rights movement had begun. News of the new rights of women in America, especially of the voting rights exercised there in states of the Union before they were acquired in European countries, filled Europe with awe. The news encouraged the partisans of womans' suffrage in Europe, and especially in England. America became the great example. In the same way, reports were received of the dignified social position of the woman in America, especially as the teacher of the children of both sexes. Their echo appeared also in the European Jewish community where there arose numerous supporters of woman's suffrage.[2] Among new Jewish female emigrants therefore the consciousness arose that America would be for them a new world in every respect.

The female Russian Jewish workers remained outside of the consolidated German Jewish class; only patronized by them, they had to find their own way in creating their own life as a new youthful society. Her own feminine sphere grew slowly for the Russian Jewess, and she finally developed a modest middle class of her own, in time fighting for women's rights in unison with the German Jewish women.

The resulting women's societies, both German and Russian, stood in opposition to one another at a distance of several decades since their founding, and with a future further apart for some decades more before they could, at least partly, merge.

These female generations of the two so different Jewish immigrations and their societies form the theme of this study.

CHAPTER ONE

American Jewry and Female Immigration

American Jewry of to-day is a far cry from what it was in the times that its immigration streams from the outside could form its character; it is, in an overwhelming majority, native-born. The tiny rivulets streaming from dissolving European Jewish communities since the end of the Second World War or their gathered remnants made no mark on the American Jewish community, however fruitful the religious currents originating within these European communities might have been for American Jewry. Thus, it is only during the nineteenth century and its aftermath—until the closing of the immigration gates (1924)—that immigrant waves could affect the form of Jewish society. Aside from legal and economic conditions, Jewish immigration received its initial impetus from the European revolutions as well as the Russian pogroms of that century.

Circumstances unique to Jewish immigration, and not matched by any other ethnic immigrant group, brought about the consolidation of one individual immigration wave, the German Jewish, to a closed society during the life-span of only one generation. This society consisted essentially of a well-adjusted upper middle class of merchants in the cities of America. Insofar as the activities of these German Jews did not simply belong to the cultural milieu of the Germans in America, this German Jewish society was considered to represent all American Jewry vis-à-vis the native American population. Facing it, the weaker remnant of Sephardic Jewry existing since colonial times, was given only limited attention because it built up only a few new communities in the nation, and none in the West. In addition, the German Jewish society was secluded from the net of congregations and the organizational life of Russian Jews, having started in America long before the beginning of the mass immigration spurred by the pogroms in Russia. In fact, nowhere among the spiritual leaders of this German Jewry, not among their rabbis, did an interpreter arise to explain this Russian Jewish immigrant life to the gentiles. A Yankee of many generations, Hutchins Hapgood had to be the mentor to open to the gentile world the spiritual values of the immigrant life found in Yiddish literature, the press, and the theater as well as in its social movements.[1] There were exceptions to this failure of the German Jew in regard to the Russian Jewish community, such as some of their enlightened personalities like Emil Hirsch, who recognized, in time, that the Russian Jews would, in the end, form the bulk of American Israel. In the early years of his confrontation with the Russian Jewish ghetto in America, Emil G. Hirsch shared the sentiments of the German Jews to the "Russians."

Prejudice against Yiddish, the Yiddish press, Yiddish literature, and the Yiddish theater was common among German Jews. It was rooted partly in classconscious snobbery and partly, perhaps unconsciously, in the earlier times of the period of Enlightenment when German Jews liquidated the remnants of the old Jewish folk language as a step toward assimilation with the gentile majority. Keenly felt by the German immigrant generations was the economic and educational gap between themselves and the Eastern Jew who spoke Yiddish. Often, in fact, this was the factor that determined the attitude to Yiddish of upper-class Russian Jews as well.

Emil Hirsch, in a memorial to Liebman Adler proclaimed:

> It was he who reclaimed them [the Jews of his native town of Staats-Lengsfeld in Thüringen] from the use of the hybrid jargon that passed among them in those days for German; . . .[2]

For Hirsch this was "a social revolution, yea, a regeneration of the whole Jewish community."

The inclusion of this German Jewish society into the general sphere of American society was a relatively easy process. Social rules of its elite appeared noticeable, its personal examples of thrift and success remarkable, and its family life exemplary. Insofar as Jewish society and family life was the achievement of the Jewish woman, she stood as its representative in the limelight of the American world. In many respects she was felt to be an example worthy of emulation. The American world met this Jewish woman in the circuit of social behavior and especially manners, as well as in her traditional religious position in Jewry.

As to society life and manners, one has to consider that the America of the nineteenth century was still in search of most of its social rules, therefore a firmly consolidated orientation of an ethnic group in these very things couldn't help but make a perceptible and favorable impression. This was even true in the German-Jewish female world. Not only was the dignified position of the German Jewess in relation to religious tradition recognized, but also that she had been, at least partly, shaped through Western European cultural traditions. At that time, America looked outward to Western Europe for a solid set of society rules. Although Jewish female emigrants hailed from many stations of life in the old homeland, the number of well-educated persons among them was considerable.

Furthermore, the relative economic independence of the German Jewish woman is pointed out by observers who are intent to show its difference from the sad fate of the American female wage earner. Stress is laid on the fact that the Jewish husband avoided, wherever possible, permitting his wife to work as someone else's employee.

The existence of such an independent class of women and their sympathies, became helpful wherever the fight for women's rights was an issue in America. And this helpfulness was not dependent on the number of partisans for a political women's movement to be recruited from this class. As all modern movements, the one for women's rights was in need of a periphery of sympathizers and quite a number of supporting voices rose from this camp at the right time. This circumstance was fully acknowledged by the American woman's press.

Even more outstanding was the participation of the upper middle class woman, now risen to financial security, in other reform movements of America. Many of them who were social workers in the broadest meaning of the term, voluntary or professional, belonged largely to the second generation of German Jewish parents and were native-born. Only in a few exceptional cases, did Jewesses who had been born in Germany or in Central Europe reach this position.[3]

A real class of Jewish female wage-earners appeared only with the

Russian Jewish catastrophe—immigration. A youthful generation of women arrived with their families who immediately were forced into the labor market; this contingent was augmented in time by Russian Jewish immigrant girls who grew up in this country. The Russian Jewish family, and especially the women, remained strangers to German Jewish society for a long time, an alienation that increased in instances when the Russian Jewish girls left their traditional ways of life behind them and enrolled in the radical movements of America.

The Jewish working girl earned her living, like so many Russian Jewish men, in the factories of the German Jew, and contributed her share to the experiences of the Jewish working class in America,[4] and her later contributions to the American trade union movement were formed by these experiences. The days when the Russian Jewish working girl was noticeably patronized by organized circles of German Jewish women and their newly created institutions, lay still in the future. In this initial phase of her life in America the Russian Jewish girl had to find herself in her own cultural milieu, of which the socialist movement was the strongest factor. Her early years were saturated with the promise of a new time; new mores, social intercourse between the sexes, leisure time spent in sport, study, and creative activities bear witness to the new forces unleashed by this new generation.

They were very far from the social norms and forms of life of the German Jewish women's world. The idols of this new generation became the modern figures of the female social worker and teacher. However, a new situation was in the process of developing because the same figures were also becoming the idols of a new generation of young German Jewish women. A bridge was built in this way between the two youth generations of such different parents. In the course of time, the German Jewish youth generation produced the greater number of female social workers whom the Jewish working girl was destined to seek out everywhere for help and understanding. In time, the rapprochement between the young women of the two great Jewish groups drew them together into a very close relationship as the Russian girl was trained in social work by the German Jewish girl, and exercised her new profession in collaboration with her in Jewish institutions. In this way the ground for the American Israel of the women's world was laid.

This process, however took time, and was, at the end of the nineteenth century, still largely unfulfilled. But there were already signs of the beginnings of an understanding for the Russian Jew in the German Jewish women's world. We can find traces of this new feeling in the Jewish educational field, where the Sunday schools directed by German Jewish women brought them, perforce, into closer contact with Russian immigrant life by way of their pupils.[5]

CHAPTER TWO

The Woman of the German Jewish Emigration

Contemporary reporting in the Jewish press about the ongoing emigration was limited, and for understandable reasons. However obvious its motives might be and however brisk its preparations, caution was in order. Despite the great hopes for a better future for the emigrating masses, a certainty remained that Jewish communities would continue to exist in Germany. Helping emigrants should not be decried as being an unpatriotic attitude on the part of the Jews remaining in Germany. Only the rudiments of news, at the time already known to everybody, showed up in the Jewish press.

The scope of the emigration and the share of the female element in it, was recognizable to everyone in spite of the scarcity of news. Naturally, the biggest impression was made on the environment by the defection of whole family groups, men, women and children of both sexes depleting small Jewish communities completely in a short time:

> Ichenhausen in Württemberg, June 16 [1839]
> . . . Today . . . six fathers of families with their wives and children, all told 44 persons of the Mosaic faith, left home to find a new fatherland in far-off America. . . . Such departures leave a visible void in the local community from whose midst 100 persons have left so far, and have already or will soon settle in the free United States of America.[1]

6

Or another description:

Ellwangen, May 11

This day, we saw passing through here a wholly singular company of emigrants to North America. The whole company consisted entirely of Jews from nearby Oberdorf, in the superior bailiwick of Neresheim. As a rule, we observe among emigrants an extreme shortage of conveyances and clothing and a poor appearance in general. Here, we saw affluence in everything; an elegant omnibus conveyed the group to the point of embarkation; everyone, especially the Jewish girls in the party, were smartly dressed and presented a cheerful and lively appearance. The group carries with it a *Torah* written on parchment, which they solemnly consecrated in the synagogue at Oberdorf before their departure. The emigrants, twelve in number, are following their kinsmen and acquaintances, who preceded them a number of years ago, and who encouraged them to seek the yearned-for promised land in North America, where their co-religionists are not (as in most German states) deprived of their natural and civil rights because they cling to the faith of their fathers. . . .[2]

Early experience had taught that in a majority of cases individual emigrants, and not whole families, would leave. However, this emigration of individuals would be planned and prepared for by their families in many cases.

On the basis, to be sure, of only fragmentary sources, we are able to state the proportion of female emigration, at least in a few cases, and at the same time discover the proportion of individual emigrants compared to whole families that emigrated. Furthermore, comparative figures of individually emigrating men and women emerge.

For the period covered (1830-1870), the registration of Jebenhausen, Württemberg, contains the largest number of emigrants.[3] It lists, among the 317 persons who were emigrating to North America, 297 whose families and full names are known to us. Of these, eighteen were individually emigrating women, of whom sixteen were young girls. The number of all individually emigrating persons listed was 207, of whom 189 were therefore men.

An entirely different list was compiled through scholarly efforts of Adolph Kober, covering the entire Jewish emigration from Württemberg between 1848 and 1855. During these years, 640 Jews registered as emigrants through the medium of 300 administrative files (*Auswanderungs-akten*). Of the applicants, 316 were men and 64 women. Of this number, 190 men and 49 women were individual emigrants.[4]

A further source that has not until now been exploited, are the passenger lists of the ships coming into American ports. From the passenger lists of the major immigration ports, we are often able to enumerate all the bearers of an individual family name according to sex. For example, of the thirty-four Einsteins who arrived at the ports of Boston, New York, Philadelphia, and Baltimore, eleven were women, and six were individually emigrating persons.[5]

In the much larger, typical German Jewish name group of the Oppenheimers, we find, among 60 passengers who landed in New York and Baltimore, that 24 were women. Women of marriageable age usually immigrated individually.[6] Of the 47 Oppenheimers who landed at these two ports, 13 were women, and of the 83 Rothschilds (New York and Baltimore), 29 were women.

In Bavaria, the main emigrating territory of the early years of German Jewish emigration, the figures for all emigrants—Jewish and non-Jewish—were about equal for men and women: 12,806 men and 11,701 women between 1835 and 1839.[7]

We may assume an approximately similar proportion of the sexes among the Jewish emigrants from Bavaria. There were a variety of motives that led to making Bavaria a center of emigration for Jews; several are of specific importance for the Jewish woman.

1. Marriage as a Motive for Emigration

Actual restrictions existed in most of the German territories regarding marriage among Jews. For example, Bavaria provides a prototype of this situation:

As is known, the register (*Matrikel*) makes it little short of impossible for young Israelites to set up housekeping in Bavaria; often their heads are plentifully adorned with gray hairs before they receive permission to set up house and can, therefore, think of marriage.[8]

The Bavarian *Matrikel,* giving the right to settle to only one son as the heir of his father existed for nearly fifty years after the *Juden Edikt* of 1813. A woman could acquire the right to settle only by marriage, a marriage which was taxed heavily; thus, the government was interested only in the marriage of rich girls from abroad with an only son with a right to settle. This explains the high interest of girls in emigration.[9]

Despite all this, the Jewish population in Bavaria multiplied. At the beginning of the big emigration in 1822, it numbered 53,402 souls and did not decrease until the middle of the century, notwithstanding the emigration.[10]

Due to the marriage restrictions upon young men, the young women participated in the fever of emigration right from the start, with high hopes. They had before them the example of many engaged couples as well as the news of marriage ceremonies performed while still on board ship or immediately after arrival in America. There were numerous reports in the Jewish press of young girls traveling with groups of emigrants.[11] Under these circumstances, help to emigrating girls was regarded by Jewish communities as direct assistance to the bride in the spirit of the ancient Jewish tradition.[12]

In comparison with other emigrating peoples, the great drawing power exerted on young Jewish women by the possibility of marriage was peculiar to them and was not found among the women of other emigrating groups. A gentile journalist made this observation at a time that German Jews were not yet numerous in America:

In consequence of the obstacles which the Bavarian government has thrown in the way of marriages among Jews, by requiring the possession of a sum of money by the contracting parties and a large fee for license, no less than nine couples of that persuasion, the men all mechanics, have arrived here to be married under our laws and to reside here in the future. The confidence and constancy manifested by the young women in venturing across the ocean with their lovers to a new world where Hymen's torch burns bright and free, is worthy of the best days of ancient days, when seven years was deemed light servitude for a good wife. One of the females is a capital engraver of visiting cards. . . .[13]

Occasionally, a marriage was concluded between emigrants aboard ship. A belated report of such a wedding between a Jewess from Hamburg and a Jew from Bavaria that followed Jewish marriage law, with Jews as witnesses, was published in a Jewish newspaper in Germany.[14]

Young married couples from Bavaria were conspicuous in synagogue life. Thus writes a woman observer visiting the new synagogue in Attorney Street at the occasion of its consecration: The congregation of the new synagogue are German emigrants, driven from Bavaria, the Duchy of Baden, etc., by oppressive laws. One of these laws forbade Jews to marry; and among the emigrants were many betrothed couples, who married as soon as they landed on our shores; trusting their future support to the God of Jacob.[15]

2. The Female "After-Pull" in the Wake of Immigration

The case of the single female who emigrated as an individual is also significant from another point of view. When an emigration sister left other brothers and sisters behind, she often drew them after her at a later date. These cases were especially interesting in cases where sisters followed one another to America, whereas brothers remained, or where unmarried sisters came to America later and the married ones, stayed on in Germany. There were also cases where there were only sisters in a family, the most curious of them a sister who drew her other five sisters after her to America.[16]

The role of the daughter as the first-born child becomes especially important in bringing brothers and sisters to America.[17]

This pulling-after of brothers and sisters is indeed the most significant feature of the German Jewish immigration to America. From the viewpoint of the history of the Jewish family, the size of the family, age and sex of its children at the moment the first member of the family starts out from home, the order in which male and female children follow according to their birthdates, are the most important human factors of the emigration movement. These factors must be considered if the pull of the first emigrating family member on those following after him is to be explained reasonably.

3. The Preparation for Emigration

Young Jewish men in Germany had already received training in certain professions chosen with a view to their usefulness to a prospective emigrant. The occupational preparation of the girls, however, was limited to what was considered to be general women's handiwork as it was taught in girls' schools and in the girls' classes of general schools, primarily sewing. And, whereas special organizations were formed for the purpose of instructing boys in the trades stressing that this meant preparation for emigration, there was nothing of a similar nature to prepare the girls. Nevertheless, Jewish girls, aside from tailoring, received private instruction in specific female trades like millinery and the results of this training showed up later in the business directories of American cities.

One emigration aspect of girls' education that was not stressed officially was, nevertheless, clear in the Jewish communities. A great part of the youthful generation of women had to use later the received industrial training abroad. To them, the emigration of girls appeared as a necessity, since the multiplication of the Jewish population in the German countries of the nineteenth century had created a large pool of Jewish girls who were not cared for. Moral dangers that cropped up in such a situation had even occupied the Jewish community much earlier. The rise of a class of Jewish female domestic servants in the big cities and the prostitutes recruited from it dates from as far back as the eighteenth century. Actually attempts at "industrial" education for girls had already begun at that time. The special industrial school (*Industrieschule*) for girls asserted itself successfully in bigger communities in the early nineteenth century,[18] where special schools were founded for poor girls with a primitive curriculum meant to prepare them for some occupation. For instance, a report of 1839 informs us about the *Armen-Mädchen Anstalt* (poor girls' institute) in Berlin with an enrollment that year of ninety-four pupils:

> It fulfills its purpose which is mainly to detach the girls from their lives of misery by giving them a solid elementary instruction and acting as a possible influence on their morality. . . . Instruction is restricted to the most necessary things, comprising ordinary elementary subjects and female handiwork, and, in addition, also Hebrew reading and religious instruction. . . .
>
> Very useful is the regulation that the pupils make hand-worked objects to order and under supervision. . . . All such work is checked against the names of the pupils who have done the work as is also all the money the pupils earned from their work.[19]

Industrial education was also carried on forcefully in the girls' classes of the general Jewish community schools. In the *Karl-Schule* in Frankfurt-am-Main, handiwork instruction, limited to what was considered women's work, was given in knitting, sewing, needlework, drawing, lacemaking, embroidery, spinning, laundering, ironing, and cooking ("stricken, nähen, Nadel-und Kunstzeichnen, Spitzenpflicken, sticken, waschen, bügeln, und kochen").[20]

In Halberstadt, the girls' class was given thirty hours of weekly instruction, of which fifteen hours were given over to training in this kind of handiwork.[21] In the industrial school of Schwarzkosteletz, the afternoons of the girls' classes were given over to the same kind of instruction.[22] The advertisement of a new girls' school in Prague announces instruction in handiwork such as knitting, sewing, making nets, all kinds of embroidering, knotting, crocheting, and dressmaking.[23]

No wonder that the emigrating Jewish girl expected economic collaboration with her mate in America! Reviewing the occupational preparations of the emigrating girls, it may be said that they went on in the quiet frame of a general girls' education in the Jewish communities that might not have been as aware of emigration of the young women as that of the men. The latter, in the course of their lives, would have been destined to become the backbone of the future community. There was also no certainty as to the success of the newly started women's education which still had to prove itself on a new continent.

The education of these girls preceding their industrial training differed in different areas.

In the earliest group of German Jewish female immigrants the elementary-school level was the highest any of them had attained. Those were the daughters of the Bavarian small communities whose fathers were artisans, agriculturists, or petty merchants. We have adequate data on the schools in these communities, in which the girls often remained in school longer than the boys, who were, at an early age, bound over by their fathers into apprenticeship or were needed by them to help in the fields or in trades.

The *Judenreglement* (Jewish statute) of June 10, 1813 states that: "the frequenting of the German public schools is imposed on Jewish youth, the Jews are permitted, along with the public schools, to establish schools of their own if they employ educated and examined teachers." [24]

On the basis of this ordinance, the Bavarian Jews established their own schools according to the size of their communities which united elementary school with religious school or were only religious schools. In both, girls were educated together with boys. In 1828, the organization of these schools, in general, already on a higher level so that "for instance in the *Rezatkreis* (district of Rezat) in 1839 fifty-three school communities existed, with sixteen united schools, and thirty-nine religious schools in which 1,676 boys and girls were instructed on weekdays."

From the Jewish press[25] we learn the location of the fifty-three school communities where it is said that the biggest of all these communities, Fürth, had 143 pupils in the boys' school and 118 girls as students in the girls' school. In the districts of Mittelfranken, Schwaben, Neuburg, and Oberfranken, as also in Unterfranken, the Pfalz and Oberpfalz, united schools existed everywhere in which girls were also instructed.[26]

In the well-informed Jewish press, the Bavarian Jews were recognized as willing to make sacrifices for the education of their children: "One

has only to go to the big cities and to the rural communities to be convinced of the enormous sums the Jewish father with scarcest means ex-
pends on the spiritual training of his children." [27]

But even in this early Bavarian group there were a number of girls
from cities who had received a better education in more advanced
schools. Thus, among a group of eleven women born in Germany who
were Jewish social workers in America, there was one who received a
higher education and, finally, a teacher's diploma from the Teachers'
Seminary in Memmingen in Bavaria where she was born. [28]

By the time Jewish emigration from the German south began to spread
further, to western, central and to northern German areas, the women
were already hailing, in large measure, from cities where many of them
had already received better instruction in advanced schools. These were
the women who became prominent in future organizations of women in
America, such as the *Treue Schwestern* ("Loyal Sisters"), the first female order, and also in the women's divisions of the German Masonic
lodges. The Jewish women who were teachers in the German American
schools also had their origin in this emigration from the cities. [29] Such
well-educated women soon achieved influence in the women's clubs of
the American cities. By their concentration in social work in the National Council of Jewish Women, they attained general esteem. [30]

In concluding, it may also be said that a stock of religiously as well
as generally educated German Jewish women decided the forms of intercourse in Jewish society in America. Nevertheless, certain critics never
tire of trying to hold up a prototype of these early Bavarian women immigrants before the world as having little education and a great many
shortcomings.

The Jewish communities of German countries which, in general, held
to the principle of avoiding public discussion of the emigrating process,
were even more taciturn in respect to the girls. Only later, when the
after-pull of young women emigrants was already noticeable in the
communities, did a new chapter begin. A more intimate page opened in
Jewish community life when its families were extended across the ocean
in the persons of the newly founded emigrant families that settled in the
New World.

However, all the new conditions of life created for the Jewish woman by emigration had not eliminated the traditional forms of parental care for their daughters. Insofar as we have data at all about the emigrants' financial state, we find that providing a daughter's dowry in support of her future married life in America was not forgotten. It was a part of the capital sums men brought with them for the purpose of establishing businesses. In the only source mentioning the sums emigrating women brought along with them individually, we find that the most frequently named amount of money was one to two hundred fl., apparently the most a family in a small community blessed with small children could scratch together for a daughter's portion. However, larger sums marked down as dowries are also mentioned.[31] In one case, a Jewish community's contribution for a poor girl is given.[32]

American help for the influx of women was not general during the German Jewish emigration. Individual Jewish women's organizations of New York mention female immigrants as protégées, for instance, at a time when it was an important port of entry for immigrants. It was quite different when the Russian Jewish immigration took place, and work had to be found for women from the start.[33]

Chapter Three

German Jewish Family Life

a) Marriages of Emigrants

The painful consciousness of the marriage restrictions in Germany accompanied the young emigrant woman to her new home. Reports from the Fatherland constantly reiterate: "In Fürth, they say, more than twenty candidates for marriage are marked for one vacant *matrikel*." [1]

The Jewish press points out, from its beginning, that in contrast to the German gentiles who emigrated to America, in the German Jewish emigration there were "far more single persons than families. From this one might also draw a conclusion as to the motives for emigration. The Jewish emigration appears to be due less to greed for gain than to the consciousness of being unable in any other way to achieve independence or to found a family." [2] This founding of a family was surely the primary motive of the girls, for whom economic independence was not in the foreground of their imagined future life.

A typical example of the contrasting ambitions in life of the young men as against the young women emigrants, is described in a paper describing the occasion of a meeting between two friends on the quay of San Francisco, the boy having become a ship's captain: "The girl grew up and a year ago she became the wife of a sincere and able man who owns a well-founded business in this city." [3]

In contrast to this state of affairs, news of the adjustment of young families to the new country reached the Fatherland in abundance and was soon coupled with descriptions of the life of women in America stressing her dignified position in American society and the Jewish husband's concern and care for her in an atmosphere of plenty. [4] Numerous combinations for possible marriages overseas formed the substance of family correspondences, and the feminine sphere in the New World was given new contents. New economic possibilities arose by marrying into the family of the owners of new businesses, where the new partner married the sister of the owner. In the course of these frequently occurring marriages, existing family units widened as did associations from old native regions in which all partners hailed from the same native district. This situation is evident from the history of many Jewish business firms as well as from the memories of Jewish merchant pioneers.

Thus, the reverse of the European marriage for money, the financially successful emigrant became a much-sought-after subject of matrimony wherever he undertook the search for a fitting mate in the old homeland. The final result was that the marriage bond in the New World became just as strong as in the old Jewish community. Marriage remained the clear purpose in life for female Jewish youth in spite of all the changes in the women's world in America. At the end of the century it remained as true as at its beginning: "Marriage is the foremost aim of the American Jewess, as it was of her grandmother. . . ." [5] For a century, emigration had become the practical medium to achieve the married state.

b) The Traditional Image of Jewish Family Life

Whatever new situations the German Jewish emigrant could have anticipated finding in America, they couldn't have lain in the family area. All he counted on in this direction was the possibility of founding a family in the traditional Jewish way.

Objective circumstances immediately lifted this expectation to the highest social level, because the excellent reputation of traditional Jewish family life had hurriedly preceded him to America. This good reputation that was held in Europe by friend and foe alike, was a commonplace in America, living on in public opinion as well as in literature even before the Jewish masses had set foot on the new continent. Later decades of actual observation of Jewish marriages in America fortified this opinion, mainly the view of the dignified position of the Jewish wife. Voices in this respect are impressive especially when a woman testifies to it:

"Their treatment of one another is Godlike, charitable, and admirable . . ." [6]

In Jewish self-assessment the same point is made in full awareness: "Socially we also have our peculiarity, a distinctive feature: our domestic hearth is indescribable, it is an Eden of this world." [7]

A further detail of Jewish married life is reported in America on the ground of multiple experience: A Jewish husband will do everything to keep his wife from industrial employment; thus she will not become a competitor of males in search for jobs: "Their women are not street-walkers and serfs, clamoring for masculine positions, nor are their men afraid to marry through the nonsupporting plea." [8]

Miscegenation which was widespread in the South and, in many cases, also among Jewish men during colonial times, gained no hold on the German Jewish immigrant. The groundswell of abolitionist sentiment in the German American cultural milieu was his as well. And, certainly, his abhorrence of the white slavemasters' breeding of new slaves also had a religious basis excluding this kind of illegitimate sexual intercourse, although we find no public discussion of this theme in the Jewish press. Of course, the denial of the legitimacy of "breeding rights was sometimes transformed into a religious theme even by adherents of slavery, as divinely ordained, which the Mormons did who discussed it openly." [9] The few Jews who came out for slavery as a Biblical institution, also refrained from defending the "breeding rights" of white slave owners.

c) The Young Jewish Immigrant Family

The transplantation of the German Jewish youth generation to the New World took place in the century which became decisive for the evolution of the American family. In this, the nineteenth century, industrialization and urbanization at last established the modern position of women. It was this period that finally saw the great sectional barrier to uniform family life, miscegenation in the South, actually overcome.

In the midst of social and political changes, the Jewish woman established her traditional position as mistress of the house and educator of her children in the New World. In addition, in the process of economic adjustment to his new country, incomparably more consolidated middle-class families arose among Jewish immigrants than among any other ethnic immigrant groups, where women, and even children, remained workers for a long time. Often, they found work in the development of industrial sites only with the employment of whole families, children included. In contrast to the position of the wives of Jewish husbands who refused to send their wives into the work market, the dependent woman's work in other ethnic groups was the precondition of their success. With this, however, they had only transplanted the European status of their women to the new world. Characteristic examples of such dependent woman's work, as observed in America, carry the contrast to the Jewish woman even to situations in individual industries and factory surroundings:

> . . . The Jewess, too, is never known to be engaged in shoebinding or other industrial employment. . . . More than all this, she is never too poor to marry, whilst the beautiful New England factory girl must shrink from a "proposal," if she pauses to consider the life of slavery to which, by marriage, [she] subjects herself.[10]

The comparison becomes even sharper when the proposed-to girl receives wages "from a Jew clothing establishment."

This characteristic feature of the Jewish woman became true again at a later time, when masses of Russian Jewish working girls appeared in the clothing industry. After marriage, in accordance with their husband's wishes, they quit industrial work: "The Jew will not permit his wife to work in a factory, and insists upon sending his children to school. . . ."[11]

According to contemporary opinion, a main result of the individual success of the German Jewish immigrant is his ability to provide for old parents, mostly still resident in the old country. Marital bliss played a great role in this respect and the success of some of the children could effect this: ". . . seven sons and four daughters. . . . Of them one died suddenly in Chicago, and a second, twenty years old, was killed in the Civil War. The children, except the youngest daughter, all live in America and created a carefree old age for their parents."[12] Help to relatives in Europe on a broad scale is registered early.[13]

Aside from the consolidation of Jewish communities through new immigrant marriages, there lived also a number of young unmarried men contributing little to the upkeep of Jewish congregations there. This situation developed frequently in the various phases of the opening of Western territories. In time, however, this changed, too, by their subsequent marriage.

A small irregularity in the family picture consisted in the fact that husbands of broken marriages in the old homeland emigrated. Even the arrival of Jewish men from countries where polygamy was still legal, could give Jewish authorities a headache. For instance, Rabbi Felsenthal stated in a rabbinical conference in 1869: ". . . There were already several cases where men from Eastern Europe, perhaps even from Western Europe, deserted their wives and came to America. They then remarried without a dissolution of their former marriage." [14]

The individual experience of American rabbis in this respect, from earlier years had already familiarized them with the sorry state of deserted wives. Isaac M. Wise lists the fifty-ninth case of this kind in the *Israelite* with the following words: "The desertion of hapless women by faithless husbands among a certain class of people. Some come from Europe where they have wife and children; after they have received a few dollars from the conversion society in England, they marry here also, only to desert again their deceived wives. Lately, we had the fifty-ninth case in this category under consideration, a woman of Chicago. . . ." [15]

Occasional irregularities, however, as they existed in some cases, had no importance against the sound instinct of the young immigrant generation which was fully strengthened by the continuing Jewish family tradition.

d) Home as the Sphere of the Jewish Woman

In the young families' first struggles on American soil that were destined to be decisive for the fate of a whole immigrant generation, homemaking was at the forefront. Woman had to hold this front to secure economical success for her husband. We possess sufficient biographical testimony describing the difficulties of managing the household of these beginners, especially under frontier conditions. These testimonies, however, also give us a portrayal of the Jewish womans' joy in life, of the pleasure with which she used her husband's even modest achievements to beautify her home, and of her gratitude for everything. The same

witnesses also note her sacrifice, childbearing under difficult circumstances, welding the family bond ever stronger.[16] Homemaking absorbed
the feminine sphere so completely that a social sphere of woman was almost non-existent outside it. There was, therefore, no theory as yet about
the womanly domain because, according to common concepts of man
and woman, homemaking was woman's sole activity. This aspect of the
Jewish home was also, to a great extent, removed from the public eye
and even from Jewish self-observation. There was still no real society
page in the Jewish press. Our orientation about the functioning of the
Jewish home, insofar as we hear appraising voices at all, does not find
its origin until the time when this state of affairs was no longer unde-
batable. Then, there already existed male criticism of the feminine sphere
that was answered by the criticism of the females. Finally, there was
even self-criticism by the women and an assessment of their own position. Such emanations from the female part of Jewish society appear
then also strongly under the influence of contemporary American movements, especially the demands of the modern woman's rights movement. However, common to both men and women, is the fact that the
power of their convictions flows, to a great extent, from elegiac memory.
The good things of old times are remembered, if a man is talking:

"The good old fashion.

    . . . It is cheap to ridicule "kitchen-Judaism,"—but in those days,
and we speak now of two decades ago in this country, the Jew
never suffered the shame of being expelled from hotels, nor was
the charge of Atheism levelled at him. For the Jewess made the
home the dearest spot on earth to her family, she never thought
of flaunting her diamonds and costly dresses at late breakfasts in
summer hotels, nor did she attend races on her Sabbath, nor vie
with the most vulgar and ostentatious people of other
creeds. . . ." [17]

An appropriate statement of what a man of the old school expects
from the feminine sphere combines with the good advice to young men
who want to take on themselves a bond for life:

A man wants less ceremony and more cordiality. He likes to
feel at home—. . . Home life.

There is nothing more beautiful than Jewish home life, and no
one appreciates it more than the average young man—but it must
be a social home, not a fashionable one. I know an old lady who
was said to have married off her nine daughters by having young men
drop in to her Friday night suppers. . . . All true men love domestic
life. . . .[18]

Challenged in this way by male criticism, women saw the modern
situation in a different way, as an innner contradiction between two
worlds with different demands on female education, and further complicated by the position of the Jewish woman in the general life of American
women. As an American woman, the Jewess had to fulfill the demands
of self-dependence advanced by the American woman in her surroundings.
Especially in the West, where women worked, fought, built, and struggled
to create better lives side-by-side with men, the injustice of their position
weighed heavily on women. The Jewish woman actually lived between two
worlds, firmly anchored in Jewish family tradition on the one hand, and
on the other, seeking the new with all her soul. Self-defense was transformed to accusation once the Jewish woman surveyed her position and
finally assessed the man's outlook on it:

Her parents, being frequently imbued with continental notions,
condemn self-dependence in their daughters, and harp on the
necessity of being settled for life. . . . We are continually informed
that to converse on other subjects is to be a "bluestocking," and
that such women never marry. Intelligent men will not scruple
to say that they want a wife who will make a good housekeeper,
and will raise their children industriously; that when they come
home, tired out, they don't care to talk "ologies," but would like a
good meal. Are remarks of this kind calculated to encourage a girl
in her studies? Surely, a sound education cannot be incompatible
with good housekeeping! . . . a girl may dress with taste, may have
her peculiar notions about the (self-styled) "lord of creation," may

enjoy the drama, and express her views on the latest romance, and yet not be at all frivolous.[19]

e) Childbearing and Raising a Family

Unrestricted marital bliss in the sense of the oldest Jewish family tradition remained the essential character of the marriage bond of this new immigrant generation. This basic character of the Jewish marriage was acknowledged unreservedly by non-Jews as well who were referred in this to Jewish tradition. This is notable for the time after the Civil War, when newer conceptions arose as to the desirability of extensive childbearing and the thought of avoiding pregnancy was leading to new practices in the female world. Still, to the Jewish family at that time was attributed the old acknowledgment in circles which fought aloud for similiar principles: ". . . criminal abortion . . . was universally practiced among all the nations of antiquity, the Jews alone excepted. . . . That one reason would be almost if not quite sufficient to justify choosing the Jews as a peculiar people, notwithstanding their proverbial stiffneckedness. The Latter-Day Saints are, if not the only people, at least the people who, as a community, most strenuously oppose all abuse of the laws of life, and therefore may justly be termed a peculiar people. . . ." [20]

The large numbers of children in the average family during this period, revealed in family histories, testifies that there was only one concept of the purpose of marriage. We have reasons, even without detailed statistics, to believe that infant mortality among the German Jewish immigrants was lower than in the general population of the same localities and regions. This is especially true of the West, with its enormous rate of infant mortality.[21] Maternal care of small children was partially responsible as well as the average prosperity of the Jewish merchant family.

The Jewish woman's readiness to bear children, even under the difficult conditions of living in the West and the mobility of the Jewish merchant family, was never denied. The new restriction of the family size that appeared in Europe as a consequence of the rise of an upper class, remained an unknown phenomenon in America for the greater part of the nineteenth century. Although most of the Jewish merchant families achieved prosperity, the number of children did not decline according to the wealth of the parents. America leveled the size of these families as it had leveled their average economic and social statuses. Complaints about an unwillingness to support big families became loud only at the end of the century and may be, at least unconsciously, a reaction to the demands of the modern women's movement. In certain places, the smaller family size was already visible as we may learn from a sarcastic commentary in San Francisco (1887):

> . . . Our *mohelim* [circumcisers] complain bitterly of hard times. They say that Jewesses have learned American tricks and that the injunction of *perijah v'rebiyah* [be fruitful and multiply] is totally ignored. In fact, they claim that with double the population of Jews since 1870, there are not half as many births as then, and the poor cutters and trimmers will have to adopt another profession.[22]

The Jewish young mother had no help in solving the educational problems that accompanied the process of child rearing. Not much was heard of in public about this, but it was recognized that a child's fundamental impressions as well as his moral discipline in life were entirely dependent on his relationship with his mother. Responsibility for the final results of the child's training for life was assigned to the mother, and his education was regarded as "home work" like her other duties at home. Women were barely represented, if at all, on the staffs of Jewish schools—except later in Sunday Schools—and nearly nonexistent on school boards. Everything was expected from the home:

American Jewess at Home

> . . . you have yet another son, and his whole ambition is "to get in the store." Do not thwart him, let him go, but teach him the higher aims and ends of trade. Show him how a merchant, successful by means of honest, upright industry, clear-headed wisdom, of broad views of progress and improvement, of sterling integrity,

may stand among the princes of the land. Point out to him how he may be a power among his fellow-men, holding the prosperity of many families in his hands; but teach him, not to abuse his strength. Let him be just to all, from high to low, from the strong to the weak, but to the weak let his justice be tempered with mercy. Impress on him that in proportion to his station, wealth, and power, shall he be held responsible for his duty to humanity: "Of him who has much, much shall be required."

This is an education that must be given *at home.* . . .[25]

Such an appeal to education at home depicts everything the mother is supposed to have contributed to the already finished education of the grown-up child. Significantly, it was only the son whose future morale was problematic, the girl's was understood to be the result of simply emulating her mother's life.

The only thing discussed in public in respect to the child's education by his mother was the subject of the child's language. As soon as he left his parents' home for formal training in school a language problem arose. German had remained as the parents' language. Often, it was even the old folk-language of the German Jews spoken by his parents to each other that the child heard and that was impressed on him.[24] Fear that the child's poor speech might hamper him in life gripped many a parent. Thus, a special appeal appeared in the Jewish women's press, because most of what the child hears in his parents' house, is spoken by his mother.[25]

There is a great difference between the condition of the Russian Jewish child and the secure state of the German Jewish child who was supposed to be introduced into the economic and social world only after his mother's finishing touches had been applied and after having been furnished with the necessary moral maxims. Interested observers of the new Russian immigrant family point out that among them the child learns economic functions from his mother and also receives a complete orientation as to the important things in life. A description by a muckraker describes his experience in appraising this Jewish child-hood.[26]

CHAPTER FOUR

Social Life and Communication

a) Social Intercourse and the Feminine Sphere

During colonial times, and continuing to the beginning of the Old Immigration, a broadminded intercourse of Jew and gentile existed in their social forms of communication in which the Jewess played a visible role. Travelers and contemporary observers have remarked on such instances as inviting Jewesses to family celebrations of gentiles.[1] The appearance of Jewish women at grand public affairs provoked the amazement of a Hessian officer who was certainly in a position to compare social facts of this kind with the situation prevailing in Germany.[2] These authors to a man stress the fact that the Jewess of that period kept up with and matched the contemporary gentile woman in respect to her appearance. The same Hessian reports: ". . . Their [the Jews] womenfolk wear the same French attire as the women of other religion."[3]

Such broad tradition, however, was suited to a time when only a small number of Jewish families, most of them belonging to an economic upper class, lived in colonial America. The situation changed with the arrival of great numbers of young Jewish people from Central Europe, without means, whose traditions were on another level than that of the older merchant class. The new immigrant lived without social contact with the old Jewish settlers, and only rarely with gentiles. This lack of connection with gentiles holds true for both phases of the German Jewish immigration: the first economic adjustment to the new country, and the later consolidated Jewish merchant class that developed from these immigrants. By the time of the appearance of the latter group, the world of the gentiles had already created their society of exclusivity, exhibited foremost in their attitudes to the Jew in clubs and resorts.[4] This exclusion manifested itself in rigidly adhered to social rules and, according to explanations that were given about it by feminine sources which unwillingly illuminated the situation, gentile ladies played their part in this exclusion by applying it to Jewish women:

> Are Jews ever received in good society outside of their own?
> Do Americans ever associate with Jews outside of business? Do
> American ladies call on Jewish ladies and receive them at their
> houses? If they do I am not aware of it; on the contrary, I know
> that they do not, and would turn up their noses if they should
> meet them on terms of social equality; the Constitution and fundamental laws of this country notwithstanding.[5]

The exclusion of the Jewess from the visiting list of gentile woman— not to mention keeping her out of the gentile's home circle—brought the intercourse of Jewish and gentile men down to the purely economic level in the men's world. There, all necessary contacts with Jews were made outside of the clubs, the sole social milieu of the men.

However, the voice of a Jewish critic at the Golden Gate lays the exclusion of men from gentile society at least partly at the door of the Jews' bad manners shown in their lack of gallantry to their women:

"When some of our millionaire Jews was invited by a Christian gentleman to a banquet, the Jew took his wife home at midnight, without having ordered a carriage, walking no less than a mile and a half in order to reach his home. It is enough to disgust a Chinaman. . . ." [6]

With the arrival of a second generation of these immigrants, the impeded social intercourse became, for the first time, a problem of a native-born Jewish youth. Traces of the problem can be found in the juvenile press of the country. In public institutions frequented by Jew and gentile together, at that time already more important, the young Jewess appears already subjected to the assessment of the young women's world of the gentiles. Exclusion of the Jewess from young gentiles' social circles goes without saying: "She is a Jewish girl." [7] could be a decisive argument in the course of an initiation into a literary society and was not very different from blackballing in a club.[8] Nevertheless, literary meetings were also taking place at the same time, where Jew and gentile mingled. Insofar as these contacts did not lead to social invitations in the homes of the gentiles, they had no importance for the Jewish home. Furthermore, if the Jewess intended to create an atmosphere in which the sexes could meet for the purpose of finding partners in matrimony, the home circle had to be Jewish.

In pioneering days, when Jewish women opened their homes to the families of friends, they were still remote from the social problems of the times and even further removed from the kind of Jewish youth problems that emerged later. Such problems were destined to invade her home until she became familiarized with them. Her life was also removed from all the burgeonings of that women's society life which later also permeated the Jewish home through the new problems of the self-dependent woman as well as through a new family etiquette of society life.

The Jewess had only sought to facilitate a more beautiful life for her husband through sociability with other families, and that she thereby created a feminine sphere of all Jewish society life in America was her privilege partly accomplished through her freedom from the pressures of earning a living. The idea of "Society," however, hadn't any attraction for her for a very long time. When, later, in the few cases of enormous wealth, it could have interested her, she was already shut out of "High Society" due to its self-selective principle of exclusion.

All these circumstances brought about an inversion of Jewish femininity which finally made her society different from that of gentiles. This is as true in the general directions of intercourse as in its mere externals. Even these externals, imitating many ways the social forms of the surroundings, nevertheless do not lose their relationship to the specific situation of Jewish femininity, and were, therefore, not far from social reality. Certainly, the Jewess's religious life at home went on as always, expressed in the usual ritual things observed by the Jewish housewife and mother, and was a far cry from any ostentatious show for the world outside. The criticism that on her walk to the synagogue the Jewess was "hiding [her] plain prayer-book under a lace handkerchief" was certainly unjustified.[9]

The Jewish woman scrutinized test cases of gentile exclusivity, such as "Judge Hilton's refusal to receive Mr. Seligman and family at the Grand Union Hotel at Saratoga some years ago, or of Mr. Corbin's

What are you giving us? (*Puck*, Vol. 4, 1878/79, No. 94, p. 1).

order not to admit Jews to certain places on Coney Island. . . ." [10] with sharpened senses. It may be concluded, then, that the Jewess made much more logical deductions from this exclusion and reached clearer and more far-reaching conclusions than her husband who was preoccupied with the hard necessities of business life and more apt to indulge in wishful thinking. That she was so certain of her picture of gentile surroundings brought her, however, security in her own world and full satisfaction with her creations in the social sphere. Finally, however, when in the last decades of the century the demands of the modern woman's movement was approaching fulfillment and promising equality of women with men, her enthusiasm was boundless. In some ways she fitted into this modern world, although for her many things appeared somewhat different than it did to other modern women.

b) From Home Circle to At Home

The earliest beginnings of socialization in the immigrant's home that went beyond the close family circle only, was more likely to occur when persons who were close to each other in the old homeland lived as neighbors in the sprouting small Jewish communities of America. The informal meeting at the family table united old friends and relatives. It was furthered by the fact that many communities consisted of a group of persons, often branches of the same family, who had already lived in the same community in Germany. In that case, community matters were the natural basis of conversation, and religious family celebrations, like weddings and circumcisions, brought together the same people. Hanukkah and Purim were social gatherings spent in homes, whereby the many unmarried males, present in all communities, played their peculiar role.

For a long time, the outdoor pastimes of the American sporting scene, especially hunting, did interest a small number of Jewish men. After the day's work was over the informal and the formal visit in the restful home circle of the Jewish family was the center of interest for men and women alike. It may be added here that card playing at the family table was a favored diversion from daily tensions. This resulted in a division of the home circle: the ready card table for the men and the *Klatsch* corner for the women.[11] In later years, this peaceful scene of the men's card table and the women's *Klatsch* corner was not often seen any more. The women formed their own card games at home, with or without the men. Isaac M. Wise found this situation in New York before it was imitated in the West: "The next evil are the cards, the terrible cards which form the principal amusement of both male and female." [12] Nevertheless, the home circle remained intact, the lady of the house was its master and she was viewed as its symbol. Again, we may permit memories to speak for themselves:

"There was a time when a Jewish matron was proud of her home, and gloried in making it a gathering place of comfort, hospitality, and sociability." [12]

The home circle was open then, the custom of *"at home days"* had not yet been instituted, announcing that only certain days were for visiting. Whoever belonged to this home circle came informally, and no rules existed for when visiting was permitted. Not attending to special forms of visiting was also generously conceded to other acquaintances whose visit at the house could not have been foreseen: "There was a time when visits were ever unceremonious; if a lady was not out or indisposed, she was ready to receive visitors at any time, and the more the merrier. Gentlemen did not find it necessary to keep a visiting calendar, with the days of the month marked as such and such a lady's visiting day, and one's acquaintances limited to those who gave regular formal receptions. . . ." [13]

Because of the lack of ceremony, visiting was a natural expression of feelings wherever hearths were close by and romance was the goal of the visit. In such cases, old remembrances tell us of the solemn serenity of a visit which was in itself unceremonious:

> The visit once was a matter which involved much serious deliberation. There was conscience about it. There was religion in the air with which the swain approached the object of his attentions. It was not lightly assumed and lightly dismissed, but was deemed a high and holy privilege. And the soberness on one side was equaled by the grace and picturesqueness on the other—the lady regarding

it as mark of chivalrous devotion, to be rewarded by all her witchery of manner and studied charm of personal beauty.[14]

The experienced world of a whole generation of young immigrants in a new world was not so easily forgotten through a mere change of habits; so much still hung on vivid memories that criticism could spring from such remembrance: ". . . modern society has reason to bewail the difference between visiting now and in these sunny days of our sires, or even within more recent days." [15] For a long time, open house to the greatest number of welcome visitors was offered on Purim, although demands of decorum and limits of the abilities of the lady of the house slowly induced an advisable reduction of hospitality:

Purim is a merry festival, but it need not degenerate into a "free and easy."—Families who receive hospitality cannot be criticised if they close the doors to strangers, and families who admit all comers without questioning their degree of intimacy, have themselves to blame if discreet critics judge them harshly for their questionable conduct. Purim receptions regulated by the rules that ladies and gentlemen understand, are extremely fascinating and entertaining, and we know no social affairs that can give equal enjoyment to as many people; but there should be no imposing on good nature, and fathers and mothers are wise in insisting on a limit to the numbers of visitors.[16]

Recognition of the "Society" concept little by little spurred all the changes in the forms of sociability that lessened the significance of the home circle. "Society" appears as a power from without, demanding something from the inner man, his homelife, family table, and open house for friends, forcing everything into new forms that stressed her omnipotence and breaking her staff over anyone who resisted her. All divergent opinions, however deeply rooted in the traditional forms of Jewish society, are forced into silence: "Society, it is true, regards with suspicion all who refuse their allegiance, and with contempt the few who assail its pretensions." [17] The new goddess also had her admirers in

Jewish houses, and made herself 'at home" there. All social life must now serve her exclusively, independent of friendly emotions and only as an image of Society and exactly under the rules Society set. Announcing visiting days, the 'at home" meant preparation for a Society event, not an inner preparedness for social communication:

At home

One might say with perfect propriety that most families are at least at home when they are professedly "at home." They may be occupying their parlors in state costume, with all the brilliant accessories of lights, music and general illusion. Their object, however, is hardly to display the beauty and charm of home life, but to pay their debt to society; nor do they aim at impressing any other fact than their perfect ability to give a "reception," or a "kettledrum," or a "social dance and midnight supper." [18]

c) Formal Visiting

"At home," or open house on certain announced visiting days, managed to live out its precarious existence during approximately two decades (1860-1880) and then subsided to social criticism. The cause of its final demise was that preparations for an unknown number of visitors in proper style were not easy to make. On the other hand, there was also an impediment on the visitor's side, who was not sure whom he would meet at the open house. The first difficulty was met by parties arranged for a given number of visitors, the second, by formal visiting where the visitor could rightfully expect to be the center of his host's attention.

The tendency against continuing to receive guests at an "open house" was so strong that it could not survive even for traditional feast days, and its decay struck at Purim in the same way as the civil New Year's celebrations in Jewish homes. The visits of masked celebrants in fancy dress expressing an intimacy not proper to occasional visitors, offended against the new concept of restricted visiting. The Jewish press mirrors this tendency of the subsiding sentiment for the frolicsome pastime that was maintained only because it was once customary: ". . . no one should think of visiting in mask any family upon whom, for obvious reasons, he would not call on other occasions in ordinary costume. . . ."[19] Pranks of merrymaking young people on Purim, which were already customary during the Middle Ages and which also occurred later elsewhere, were certainly not absent in America as well.[20] However, the rising rejection of the holidaymaking of Purim and of the customary open house didn't stem from moral considerations in America as it had among the forefathers. It was based on an entirely new criterion, the decorum of Society, and, above all, the uncompromising opposition to any social meetings not strictly subjected to Society rules. It goes without saying that here too, as at all times, the depravity of the youth generation, the first raised in America, is pointed out and given as the reason for ending the open house on Purim:

> . . . *Purim* was a very dull affair this year among our people. The more respectable Jews have become heartily tired of the nuisance. The American youngsters, both Jews and Christians—they are in partnership on that occasion—raise the very deuce on Purim night, and but few houses were open to them this season in consequence. It is something like the New Year's calls, which have been abused so much of late that respectable people are afraid to keep "open house," for fear that the hoodlums will take advantage of their hospitality. . . . Let us give up the *Purim* business altogether. . . . It was a splendid thing in the good old times, with the good young people; but, nowadays, when the boys learn to drink before they know how to spell—let's give it up.[21]

This manifestation from the Far West is remarkable if only because it confirms again, as in so many other cases, that Jewish "Society" there followed the lead of the Atlantic Coast social dictates. But it is even more remarkable that, at the same time, open house on the secular New Year's Day is criticized, in this case, however, for the second reason, because it cannot satisfy the visitor's need for recognition of the importance of his visit:

There is a decline in New Year's visits in this city, and there need be no regret at the growing desuetude of a peculiar custom. Those who made preparations to receive a long list and received mainly formal cards, may have this consolation that young gentlemen prefer visiting on other days than New Year's when there is less formality in conversation and more real enjoyment for all parties. Time was when a fashionable lady entertained simply over a hundred visitors in the course of three or four hours; but it does not appear that on Thursday last any house, however numerous the ladies in attendance, witnessed that number of genuine arrivals.[22]

The trial period of the "at home" went by quickly, cracks in the new institution appeared, and criticism of it came early. Aside from the understandable consequence that visits on other days were excluded, the disadvantage to nonconforming feminine circles was only too telling: ". . . upon ladies who have named no special evening there is little expectation of calls being made." [23] On the other hand, social pressures to conform proved insufficient in this case because obviously the new institution was, in itself, unable to solve the problem put up to it. It was soon noted that "at homes" couldn't essentially raise the dignity of visiting at all. The social seismograph registered this at the right time:

Without going back more than a decade or two, a grievous change cannot fail to be noticed even in metropolitan circles. Whether our young men have lost their sense of chivalrous devotion, or our young women their power of inspiring it, whatever be the reasons, the fact cannot be denied that visiting is but rarely indulged in, and is usually regarded as a bore by one sex at least, and only paid as a formal quittance.[24]

Insofar as the courses of this social crisis, touching the Jewish home in such a sensitive way are considered, the changes of living conditions are not overlooked:

Of course, purely local causes are largely to blame for this state of affairs. The size of the city, the pressure of business, the rise of the clubs, the attractions of theatre and concert-hall are not to be underestimated. Add to this social gossip, which so often misconstrues attentions and makes young men reluctant to call; and a sufficient number of reasons will be found partly to excuse the little zeal which they, excepting young buds of tender years, display for visiting.[25]

Once in the possession of the correct diagnosis, various thoughts about therapy arise. The most natural appear to be those demanding an inner change in Society—first the insights, then the prospects:

> It seems difficult to return to the sociability of former times, unless our fashionables utterly discard present practices or be themselves discarded for people who want to make and keep friends, rather than to exhibit a collection of engraved cards and to judge people by the dinners or balls to which they are occasionally invited.[26]

Self-purification or a sound cleansing, both prescriptions for reform of Society, should mean either restitution of a former ideal state or creation of a new beautiful milieu—dependent only on one's direction of nostalgic feelings. Those who hope for restitution, see some hopeful instances even at that time:

> Now, of course, there are families whose "at home" is delightfully homelike, and whose grace, culture and refinement wonderfully stimulate and charm. Yet these exceptions are so few as to make one regret that a little more independent spirit is not manifested by society's leaders, and a less servile disposition to ape what is fashionable, even if it be frivolous, uncomfortable and absurd.[27]

However, all in all the "at home" crisis is seen by the restitutionists as the great chance to exercise, for the first time, full criticism of all nasty social developments, to lay open situations and to state, in general, what "Society" should look like. No ways are given by which the wished-for state could be achieved:

Now being "at home" ought to express something more tangible and satisfactory. Society, it is true, regards with suspicion all who refuse their allegiance, and with contempt the few who assail its pretensions. Generally, the social reformer lacks tact, is too sweeping in his denunciation, is possibly coarse and often unjust in his arraignment, and succeeds in destroying himself rather than the abuses against which he rails. Yet one, without desiring in the least to play so ambitious and unenviable a role as a social reformer, might justly take exception to certain social whims, and plead for a purer and more wholesome atmosphere. Why does society publish the fact of its being at home, and send out dainty cards to that effect, when people are least themselves on such occasions? You cannot tell their thoughts, their aims, their aspirations, their good or bad qualities. Their dialogue may be as inviting as *tutti-frutti,* and as varied as *gemischtes compot;* but you wish to talk to people nowadays, not Mrs. Jarley's Wax Works. The dresses, the jewels, the bows and smiles may be fascinating in the extreme: but you want to associate with soul, not pasteboard, and you resent the heated atmosphere and flippant, intolerable nothingness, which leads to nothingness *pour passer le temps.* . . . There may be the graceful dance for the younger folk, but there should be exercise for other faculties beside those of locomotion and digestion. But no change can be expected until society has a truer standard of measurement than the length of the train or the balance at the banker's, and feels it a greater honor to entertain a select few than to worship a motley crowd.[28]

Emotional effusions of this kind allow only a difficult stand to the would-be practical reformer. However, he draws courage from the general needs of American society which teach him that the situation among the American gentiles doesn't look any different, therefore Jewish society may set its hope on the forces transforming American Society:

So far as our Jewish society is concerned, it does not differ from
the same general social grade. It would be a happy thought, if
some of its leaders would take the initiative and give it a truer
and solider character, one worthier of earnest and thoughtful Israelites.[29]

It is a woman speaking here and she combines her statement with a
hopeful vision for a new feminine sphere. This sphere would come about
by turning antiquated forms into a new cultural version of intercourse.
This, naturally, would take time to achieve; the transition, however, to
the new state of things would fulfill a special task, to give Jewish woman
real refinement:

The ideal "at home" of which mention was made in the last
issue, where one might have an hour or two's quiet restful chat,
and meet intelligent people whose conversation would be a stimulus
and an education, is not by any means so difficult of realization.
But this whole question is one which presents various puzzling
phases, and until refinement, not wealth, is made the badge of
distinction, society will drift along as now, and the independent
few must perforce form their own circles and model them after
their own tastes.[30]

European models for such pioneering work of the Jewish woman were
not lacking. Although the cry for the "salon" is not yet heard in these
words, the watchword to create a sphere of refinement in one's own
home is given utterance. The European models gave wings to fancy,
and the woman thus speaking publicly in the Jewish press had to be
taken as a representative figure of a new society-trend of Jewish women
in America and her words as a challenge:

The *Salon* has yet to make its appearance, which shall inspire
our young people with chivalrous devotion to their faith, and from
which they shall go forth refined and strengthened by the grace,
culture, and enthusiasm of the American Jewess. Of such a type,
our city boasts not a few: their fault is their reluctance to step

forward. They are unobtrusive, timid, negative, when they should
be bold, confident, positive.

Schemes for reforming society are visionary. Let each in his or
her own circle do modest work, and quietly strive to infuse more
sincerity and truth. The aggregate result would be gratifying.

Carom.[31]

But whatever was dreamed of for the elect upper crust of women
and, whatever refinement could beautify their homes, the fact remained
that "Society" created problems for most Jewish homes that were not
to be solved in a jiffy. Only in long, painful stages could a new social
status vivendi emerge to fit the new situations. The main problem, however, in all these stages of society, was the social intercourse of the sexes
directed with a view to its prospect for matrimony.

d) The Party

The dwindling significance of formal visiting on certain days, made
more visible by the nonconformance of many households, was solved
for a time by the house party. In the house party, "Society's" entree into
the Jewish home appears to have been completed according to all signs:
It became the center of social intercourse, continued to follow the rules
for invitation and participation, and combined with the concept of *saison*
created by Society for the purpose of regulating its events. Only the program of the party was not yet certain since there were no authoritative
models for it. Hesitation in the decisions of what to offer at the party,
expresses the fact that the transition from homelife to "Society" was
still not cleared up. A stage of experimenting with this new institution
was beginning and, later, when the party took on its already rigid forms,
criticism of its newly discovered deficiencies followed.

Discussing the party experiment, the Jewish press revealed a good
portion of self-irony in describing the helplessness of the lady of the
house confronted with her new task. For the sphere of the party should
be social, but at the same time also informal, and personal conversation
should take place side by side with entertainment. The party should,
furthermore, stand a comparison with other social events because it had

to be evaluated as an event of the *saison*. Competition in inventing a glittering program for the party was natural:

Hints for Sociables

These generally consist of a few dances, a German, and a supper, varying in elegance and elaborateness. . . . Now and then engage a professional reader or lecturer for half an hour, and let a discussion follow, which shall give the heel and toe some rest and the brain a little activity. Let the members assemble occasionally in visiting costume, and not alway in full dress. . . .[32]

But none of these hints could lead to authoritative models because there were no socially leading houses. Finally, there were also no personalities as arbiters elegantiarum as there was, for instance, in the person of McAllister for the gentiles. Thus, Jewish "Society" drifted, leaderless, in this stage of experimenting. Anything at all possible might be expected for the new *saison,* and the philosophical observer could always indulge in new suggestions, that is, before he became a critic. One thing, however, for him was certain: The party had become a headache for society people and needed continuous refreshing and retouching to be kept alive:

It is to be hoped that a new departure will be made in sociables. These are plants which require considerable care in their nurture, and rarely survive the first winter. They flower very quickly, but fade just as speedily, leaving naught but a badge or german favor behind. A fortune awaits the genius who will invent something original in sociables. The monthly or semi-monthly dress parades, under that name, rarely promote sociability.[33]

Where imagination was lacking, the surest thing that remained to rely on were visible signs easily understandable to the visitor: the wealth of the host and luxury. These things could be offered to the guests without any particular imaginative power on the part of the hostess, too. Indeed, Jewish Society, in its parties, went in this direction in imitation of the highlights of the gentile society *saison*. Although there was no social ladder to climb by way of succeedingly more important invitations to Jewish houses, nevertheless there conviction soon reigned that the more the display of luxury at a party, the higher was the social status of the hospitable house. In a short time, expenditure and luxury became the characteristics of the party and this process continued still further and further:

> Yet no one has yet been able to stem the extravagance that pre-vails at parties, weddings, banquets, etc. No one need object to the fancy that leads wealthy people to secure the choicest emblems and to spend hundreds of dollars on the luxuries of floral decoration; but when fashion decrees that every invitation to a "party" should be followed by the gift of a handsome bouquet or basket to the hostess and additional emblems to her daughters, it is time that young men who have souls above fashion's behests should spurn the custom and brave the conquences.[34]

Even more than for the necessity of lifting the soul, was it advisable to shun the financial consequences of this fashion, because it was expected that expenditure had to be matched by expenditure:

"The nights of the sociables are nearly to a close, and soon the gallant young men who have been so hospitably received by the young ladies, in succession, dined, wined, germaned, and theatre-partied will be expected to return the compliment by entertainments of a gorgeous character. Caterers will be importuned for the most luscious and delicate dishes, engravers will be cross-examined to produce the most elegant *menus,* and jewelers will be ransacked to discover gifts that shall be brilliant beyond question, yet not too costly for the gallant young men's exchequers . . ." [35]

Confronted in this way with the economic situation of the young men for whom the sociables were arranged, the doubts that Society could realize its goal through the party led to a crisis, and from there to open criticism was only a step:

> "Social entertainments are no longer fashionable unless the host or hostess gives presents or favors to the guests before leaving. By

attending every party to which she is invited, a lady nowadays may collect, in the course of a season, enough souvenirs to fill a good sized room with ornaments to last a lifetime. . . ."[36]

Expenditure not only stamps the entire Society life, but creates unsound conditions as well, for people whose income didn't allow it were forced to fall in line with Society habits:

> It is undoubtedly true that there is more lavish expenditure in luxuries in this city now than ever before, and the expenditure is frequently on the part of people who are criminal in thus drawing their narrow means or running into debt to keep in the path of a silly fashion.[37]

There is no lack of satire and mockery of current fashion in this account of the conditions: "If it were only fashionable to distribute articles of value to gentlemen, such as gloves, suspenders, studs, dress suits, and ulsters, we think our young men would be more eager to court society and accept invitations." [38] Finally, should the lady of the house wish to shun the labor of shipping, "cash presents" or "bank checks payable to bearer" would do it.[39]

Whether satire or in deep earnest, the result was the same for Society life; the party was no solution to its problems and visiting still remained the big question. The final effect of the party experiment was viewed by the informed observer as a decisive stroke against visiting itself: ". . . young men have ceased visiting. They seem to find the attraction of drink, billiards and cards, stronger than that of society ." [40]

At the end of the German Jewish period, the world of the young generation of men appeared to have fallen out of the Jewish feminine sphere without any hope of ever being regained. Only an entirely new relationship between the sexes would later give a new meaning to the Jewish home and social intercourse in it.

CHAPTER FIVE

Social Mores and Society Arts

Because she was cut off from gentile society life, the Jewess could not simply follow their lead in establishing social rules. Besides, gentile society was, at that time, itself in search of a valid etiquette.[1] As to Jewish Society, it had no superior class to lay down rules of etiquette. There existed, on the whole, only one leveled, consolidated German Jewish society. Thus the German Jewess was forced to fall back on herself. She was helped in her inventions by a kind of self-exploration which confronted old Jewish tradition in Germany with the needs of her situation in the new country and was at her finest in this confrontation, preserving her essential German Jewish cultural heritage by leaning towards the models of the Jewish upper-crust society in Germany that was crystallizing at that time.

There, side by side with rude antisemitism, Jewish salons existed in which sensitive communication between Jews and gentiles was encouraged. Noted Jewish women represented this other world. But aside from these models, there was much in the traditional Jewish world in Germany that was close to her own concept of how the sexes of the young generation should meet. Parental warp in utilizing the old ways to establish marriages appeared valuable to her for the parent generation generally, and for her maternal role in it, it seemed just indispensable. All in all, there were enough things in which a developing Jewish sociality had to differ from the gentile, while others were vitally necessary to the Jewish woman.

Raised to a comfortable existence from the difficulties of adjusting to a new country, the Jewess found that picking her way through the complicated landscape of unfamiliar social mores was not easy, and blind trust in a strange etiquette with which she had not grown up was not to her liking. However, as soon as she became a mother with marriageable daughters, the task of finding husbands for them fell to her and she saw mores primarily from this viewpoint of the initiation of marriage through the dignified meeting of the young Society partners of both sexes. Managing the household had to fit economic circumstances in the same way as the need to introduce her daughters into social life. She carried her burdens with dignity, without, it should be noted, receiving any serious support in this task from her husband, occupied with his business. Occasionally we learn of her worries through the insights of third persons. These worries often gave her personality a melancholy tinge—and she was the only member of the Jewish family who had this appearance since the Jewish woman of that generation was not by nature a "Society lady." [2] Her low origin was later to be held against her when her inclination to an exaggerated love of luxury was observed.[3] However, this could not affect her true being which revealed itself only in the utmost concern and care for her daughters. In the end, she was quite successful in marrying them off in the way she wished. For a peculiar Jewish social sphere developed around these marriage problems in which her thoughts about the appropriate intercourse of young women with men were mirrored. At the last, her daughters followed in her ways, the *chroniques scandaleuses* not often having occasion to notice them.

The attitude of the German Jewish mother toward her sons is not so well documented. Paradoxically, it seemed to her that at the same age at which her grown-up daughters became her main worry, her sons slipped away from her and came under the influence of their fathers. The insignificance of the maternal influence is mirrored in the increasing number of mixed marriages on the part of her sons.

The Jewish press followed her struggle, not only with an understanding for her personal role, but with sympathy also for the changing conditions in the feminine world. Therefore, the press is, at the same time, the keeper of traditional Jewish community life in respect to womanhood, and the self-styled critic of events in the feminine world. At last the Jewish newspapers took on a new function: To show how a woman's world appears through the eyes of women, especially of cultured women. With this, the man-made press escapes the odium of male arrogance. This is especially the case in discussions about the necessity for women's refinement, in which criticism uttered in the press flowed from the pen of other women.

a) Conversation and the Salon

In the philosophical consideration of any region of life, the question of what constitutes value is soon recognized as the basic problem. "Society" is moved by the same question: Which aspects of its values should be considered worthy of cultivation and by what means should the worthlessness of the existing state of things be set aside, and "Society" be given a more meaningful existence? This question arises first as a practical need from the failure of the already old and tried new forms of intercourse. On the other hand, there also existed the voice of conscience in the Jewish community. Very little in the impulses or attitudes of the young Jewish males reflected this voice, and the burden of conscience fell on Jewish women who feared the breakdown of sociality. As the remarkable consequence of this state of affairs, it can be stated that it was the Jewish woman who took the lead in this basic question of evaluating forms of social intercourse and of creating a concept of societal arts. This is all the more remarkable since no general standards had been gained from social intercourse with gentiles. Indeed, all decisions had to be made by attention to her own inner voice; but this voice—analytic as well as inspirational—led her also to the outside world and to an analysis of her own social status that she made herself. Her full explanation of the circumstances of the status of the American Jewess is given in addition:

> The tone of social life among our American Israelites has not reached that elevation of refinement which we have every right to expect as a distinguishing feature. On the contrary, much that is rough and coarse will have to be eliminated from its midst before we can hope to stand in on an equal footing in this respect with our Christian neighbors, who seem to know and observe the rules and by-laws of etiquettes so much better than the equally educated and intelligent Hebrew. . . . Throughout the United States has gone forth a cry of indignation at the "social ostracism" inflicted

upon the Jewish citizens of the country. Can we wonder that this
is so, when we attend the various reunions among the Israelites,
and notice the amount of weeding out that will be necessary before
we can stand in a circle entirely composed of cultivated ladies
and gentlemen? . . .[4]

From the recognition of these undesirable traits and the acceptance
of their unworthiness, arose the consciousness of the values that had to
be created and also the feminine cry for these values even if their realization could come only in the next generation: "The exercise of a purify-
ing and refining influence is needed, and we look with confidence to
have this want supplied by the generation of Jewish girls who have graduated or will do so, between 1880 and 1885. . . ."[5]

To be sure, there were no American Jewish models of representatives
of the societal arts, but the achievement of Jewish elite personalities on
the old continent held out a hope of success in America. That hope was
that in the end, riches and material achievement would draw to it the
arts able to give Society essence and effect its success. At this point, it
was especially encouraging that the brilliant Jewish standard bearers
of Europe were also known in the world of American gentiles and admired by them as well. Furthermore, the role played by the Jewish woman in this societal representation of famous Jewish families in
Europe was pointed out by interested observers:

> There are the wealthy Jews [in Paris] like the Rothschilds, who
> are much to be commended for their recognition of the supremacy
> of art and letters. They have become the protectors of these classes
> commercially, and their intelligent wives have made their *salons*
> delightful, by bringing in men of culture and talent.[6]

The new hopes, therefore, appeared in the first line as that of
the Jewess in America, fortified, in addition by deliberation on the demo-
cratic character of the country. The promise was apparent that this
refinement would set in in much broader circles than in Europe because
Jewish well-being and individual success had such a much broader basis
in America. Therefore there could also be grades in this newly rising

Society and the idea of the formation of an elite that would give the tone to it was not excluded: "There must be grades in all things, and it is of how the best should be that I write." [7]

This best result of grading, or forming an elite, the thoughtful female critic and would-be reformer naturally reserves to the circles close to her. Nevertheless, she is objective enough to describe the essence of the life of such a Society elite and its appearance in such an unmistakable way, that any Jewish woman could strive for its achievement in her own circle. It is neither more nor less than the establishment of a salon according to American conditions:

> One of the signs of a nation's exuberant civilization is its *salons,* where literature, in its many branches, takes the place of the scandal that may be relegated to a lower sphere. Is it not time for our ladies to declare and enforce a law that their parlors shall not serve as a debating hall for the discussion of servants and cooking? Nor as a dissecting room in which characters take the place of corpses—and are as merciless taken apart, with every imperfection held up to public view! In their stead, discuss letters, politics, religion, art. [8]

In the men's world, at least, this feature of the feminine circle of dissecting reputations had been a subject of their attention since the beginning of time, only the more well-meaning observers observing this feature rather as a safety valve for Society:

> But the chief feature of the community is the Ladies Kaffee Klatsch, a meeting held weekly for charitable purposes, and for— eating. It is an old institution, and has often contributed to funds for the Orphan Asylum, the Russian refugees, the poor of Louisville and of Bowling Green. It also acts as a safety valve, allowing the excess of gossip accumulated during the week to escape without danger. [9]

However, it couldn't be denied that the transition to this newly required essence of Society would meet with nearly insurmountable difficulties in the case of the elite, because of the perfectionism insisted upon in her task:

> As yet, it is hardly to be expected, that Jewish society should be able to boast of possessing such a charmed circle—above all other circles! Jewish development is yet young in America, itself the youngest of nations. But I write with the hope that each day will see some progress made toward the desired end. To reach this objective point, it is but necessary that some one of our fair ladies of fashion should make the move.[10]

Her thought is here not of the societal arts in the sense of *l'art pour l'art,* but in the framework of a general refinement of Jewish women by these arts, applied to her house as a concept of the cultivation of living. At the same time, this cultivation should also bring into being her social Americanization, and, to a certain degree, the assimilation of her home on the model of that of the cultivated gentile woman in America.

b) The Results of Refinement

In her endeavors to open new paths, the reformer chooses a new point of departure: For the first time she no longer chooses particular phenomena for her criticism, she starts with but a general picture of what Jewish "Society" in America is. Against this image she presents her vision of what it should be, and what should finally become of it:

Society as it is

> It is a fact, sorrowfully conceded, that Jewish Society is not what it should be. It is simply a mixture of handsomely dressed, fashionably attired persons of both sexes. Something more than this is necessary to make our gatherings creditable to a race that is as noted for its intellect as for its antiquity. Our men of brains keep away from all such meetings; the few brilliant women we have are seldom found there, because certain elements are wanting that should be inherent in elegant circles. Repose of manner, polish, re-

finement, conversation in lieu of gossip, ideas instead of scandal, dress made subservient to the woman, not the wearer eclipsed by her attire—all these are component parts of polite society. Do we find them among the general run of American Israelites? Unfortunately, we do not.[11]

Only this deplorable situation, the want of everything societal arts can offer, has led to a state of matters in visiting from which there is no way out. Responsibility for this falls on the lady of the house who did not instruct her daughters to make the reception in the house attractive to young men:

> . . . it must surely be the fault of the mothers who raised them, of the sisters around them, of the ladies who are so willing to receive them. Men visit for entertainment, to pass the time pleasantly, to fill up a few idle hours, that if not so employed might be put to worse uses. They are eminently social, hedge[d] in with too much ceremony, they will break all bonds and seek other companionship more congenial to their peculiar tastes. They do not care for dress and jewelry, but really enjoy meeting a lady in plain attire, where she can be judged of, and is not altogether composed of silk, satin and diamonds. Nor do they relish the formality of set evenings for their reception, when in regular costume and general discomfort they pay their respects to their hostess, indulging in mild platitudes about the weather, the opera and the styles. . . .[12]

And turning directly to the young women, they are reproached with a lack of intellectualism:

"Our girls seldom engage in intellectual imployment. They sew, embroider, crochet—keeping time to their needles with many a tale of gossip and many an unkind scandal. . . ." [13]

But how should the new sociality appear and, above all, how could a woman begin to practice their new ways? The answer to this was; With herself in her home circle:

"Let her revise her visiting list and ask to her next "evening" only those who she feels sure will prove their cultivation and refinement by their manner and conversation. Her gathering will be small in numbers doubtless, but will it not make amends in quality? If education, a knowledge of the amenities that render life delightful, and a regard for the etiquette which forms the basis of social science, be maintained as an absolute requirement to admission in this select number, we would soon see a marked improvement in those who are without it pale. Having a goal to reach, having something to attain by individual effort, the best would naturally separate themselves from those of coarser minds. Ere long they would rise to, and would be gladly welcomed within that higher circle, which, at first small, would by these additions soon be swelled to such proportions as to make its influence felt throughout the width of American Jewish life." [14]

Confidence flows from these words, and there is no doubt that dynamic forces were soon to be at work in this access-to-Society question to make, from indifferent people, seekers after the new Society. The conviction that such renewal of Society could be undertaken from the home circle as the starting point if only women would decide to form home circles in accord with the new selective principles is quite remarkable. There was a compensation in view for them, as a reward for their sustaind optimism: conversation as an art did spring from the home circle and was bound to it forever. This art of conversation definitely set aside all hitherto existing drawbacks of any kind, and the result was to be to the lasting advantage of the generation of young women:

The best field for the practice of conversational art is the home circle, . . . merrily chatting at the table, giving the *on dits* of the day—whether social or literary; or yet again, around the fire at night, where a recitation of a favorite poem, an anecdote just learned of some great man, or discussion, a criticism, are all in order and give exercise to a faculty or an accomplishment, which adds a charm to its possessor. . . . At a ball there are never wallflowers; even if they do not dance, there is always a little group of the *best men* about them, for the male dancer of society seldom represents its intellect.[15]

It is also considered a worthwhile effort to seek the same result, cultivation of Society, by forming organizations with the special goal of developing female refinement:

> How many reading and debating clubs, literary circles or art societies, have we heard of among the Jewish ladies? Yet could anything be pleasanter or more improving? I have been told that it was an impossibility to form such associations, that the material did not exist. That is a fallacy; the supply will grow to the demand. . . .[16]

Finally, the full scope of this pioneering into new ways is considered: The world of man will also look different if a new cultivated feminine sphere develops. By the resulting assimilation into American Society, the dignity of the Jew of America will rise in the eyes of the gentiles, and, in the end, there will also remain room for the specific values of the American Jewess:

> Upon the cultivation of our women depends the wisdom of our men. So then to our women let the first step be assigned, with all the *onus* and honor resulting therefrom. Who shall be the first to gather around her the few of both sexes she may know to be possessed of mind and culture, and cause it to be said that admittance to her parlor is better than a patent of nobility? At whose fireside will thoughts be lighted that shall illumine the present page of our history in the United States? Whose magic touch will cause the font of eloquence to flow—bursting forth in magnificent vindication of a despised race? Let an American Jewess act as "the nurse of genius" at the cradle of American Jewish literature![17]

c) The Summer Resort

The end of the season brought a remission from the normal urban forms of social intercourse for a time, and created an extraordinary situation in the Jewish feminine world. Having been transferred to summer resorts, the women are faced with an important restriction: Only the female part of the family goes to resorts, the men merely play a visitor's role. And insofar as social intercourse comes about in the resort, it is transferred outdoors and to public localities. For the Jewess the resort is in no respect an extension of her home. Accepted societal rules in the city caused embarrassment in the resort because there was no room for them there. Jewish sociality in America, like that of many gentiles as well, was for a long time carried out indoors as a kind of parlor entertainment, having no similarity to the garden-oriented societal life as it existed, for instance, in England.[18]

As for sports, there was little interest shown in any sport in Jewish circles—especially among Jewish women. Thus, there was nothing in Jewish urban life that could be applied to the summer resort to create an atmosphere of appropriate societal life. It was, rather, shapeless and mirrored various features of the city, often in snobbish exaggeration, not only causing specifically proper criticism by understanding observers, but also calling forth direct warnings. What could be seen going on in the resort, they said, is fit to damage the reputation of the Jews in the eyes of the gentiles:

The Jewess at Summer Resorts

. . . During this cursory association let them continually bear in mind that it is their bounden duty to so comport themselves in public, as to give the lie to those aspersions cast upon the entire race by a number of hostlery keepers, because of the forward, vulgar and pompous demeanour of a few individuals, whose counterparts in obnoxiousness can be readily found in every average American assembly. The Jewess represents a race, the Christian an individual.[19]

Separated from the eternal questions of manners, subject to discussion in city and resort likewise, the absence of men in the resorts was held to be responsible for the "improper" behavior of the women. The

few men who came to the resort for a short time appear to have been occupied with the women even if they were not marriageable bachelors.
In its satiric emphasis, the following picture is given from the point of
view of the men who justified their own behavior by laying the blame on
the forwardness of the girls at the resort:

The rambler

. . . It was my good fortune last year to spend a week at a favorite summer resort, where I noticed with disdain the bold and in-
siduous way with which a bevy of young women threw themselves
upon the solitary young man of sixteen who passed a week with his
grandmother in that resort. They were constantly meeting him.
They exchanged words with him on the slightest pretext. They
promenaded in front of the ice cream saloon without the least
agitation. They frequented the soda water counter without any
embarrassment. In the evening they would waylay him in the ob-
scurest corner of the porch, or escort him up and down the cliff,
quoting poetry all the time. . . . Young women need not be so
frivolous even in summer. They surely can exist without the sight of
a young man for a few weeks. . . . There are other and more useful
occupations in the summer months. They might review their Latin
and philosophy, botanize in the wild woods, read, paint, sketch or
embroider in the open air. A thousand pursuits and pastimes are
theirs—which are nobler than developing the self-consciousness of
an incipient dude and lowering their own self-respect.[20]

Many Jewish women were now confronted, for the first time, with
the realities of restricted accommodations, having, unlike their husbands,
spent their lives, to a great extent, exclusively among Jews in the city:

Jews and Summer Hotels

. . . to his amazement he has lately learned that his dollar, even
with the imprint of the United States Government upon it, is not
wanted.

It is time that the Jew realize the delusion of the dollar. While Americans are as fond of wealth than other worshippers of Mammon, they prize certain things immaterial, above the possession of money, and especially above its vulgar display.[21]

The renewal cry for refinement of summer mores is the inescapable answer to this criticism, in the expectation that such refinement would eliminate the restrictions on the part of the gentiles. "That Jewess about whom everybody talks," should no longer be seen.[22]

The Jews were able to gain some self-knowledge through observation of the sociological occurrences about them, and thoughts about their effects on social mores intruded on them. The failure of individuals in this respect is seen to be the consequence of surprisingly rapid economical success: "The Jews have moved too fast, they have become rich too quickly." [23]

Such self-recognition was apt to clarify for them the criticism of the gentiles directed at the behavior of some of the nouveaux riches and make it more understandable. Some descriptions of this behavior were also given in the Jewish press where deviations from the traditional Jewish way in the summer resorts counted heavily:

> The [card] game of *rouge et noir* can be studied with much success on the faces of the fair sex at every watering place. . . . Last Sabbath was not observed in any watering-place by the faintest semblance of public divine service.[24]

Profounder minds, seeing these doings at the summer resorts as a complete straying from the nature of Judaism, brooded over the seasonal mutation of Jewish society. They diagnosed as its cause the absence of any care for the spiritual side of Jewish life. This analysis went hand in hand with their demand to restore this spiritual life to the summer season:

Summer Judaism

> . . . could he [the observer] see our summer Judaism, could he witness what becomes of the Jewish sentiment in mountain resorts

and seaside watering places, he well might be prompted to ask,
What is it? . . . on all sides, nothing but keen, almost greedy pursuit of pleasure and pleasuring, coupled with that forgetfulness
of anything pertaining to or mindful of Judaism or any other de-
cent ism. Sabbath desecrated, openly, flagrantly, defiantly; weekly
public worship undreamed of . . . Where is the fashionable water-
ing-place where Jews and Jewesses do congregate, that has a place
of Jewish worship?. . .[25]

This was the situation, and the close of the summer resort season, co-
inciding with the approaching High Holy Days, was apt to emphasize
these thoughts and even to preserve them, at least in the paper, for the
coming summers in the subsequent years.

CHAPTER SIX

Style, Fashion,[1] and Etiquette

a) Style and Fashion

There were some matters in which the Jewish woman simply submitted to the social rules from the outside, and others in which she reacted to the conditions in the New World with opinions of her own, formulation of new rules and—last but not least—with self-criticism. The criticism leveled by men was answered either by understanding consideration or countercriticism. Comparisons were also made with the feminine gentile world. America was still considered to be only an infant in the world of etiquette, entertaining, and other Society arts. The infant was considered not only capable of living, but also of impetuous strength.[2] The American women's press worked laboriously to create a self-confident, dignified feminine image; individual questions of behavior were treated regularly in detail, including the subject of chaperones, visiting, and frequenting public places.[3] Attention given to the same matters in the Jewish press often appears merely to reflect the same problems in the lives of gentile women. There are occasions when male criticism in the Jewish press, however, has no counterpart in the general American press. Jewish family tradition here gave the critics an opportunity of taking a unified stand. In certain things opinions are unanimous: "Ladies who paint their faces," are warned: " . . . your vanity is in vain, for you deceive no one but yourself."[4]

Occasionally we find an attack in the gentile press on the cheap-dress habits of Jewish women "conspicuous chiefly for their inordinate fondness for cheap jewelry."[5] These are the same women "who habitually ask and expect a dealer to come down a few cents on the stated price of every article they purchase" and gentile women are warned not to appear like "Women Jews" in this respect.[6]

In their criticism and their self-criticism, dress habits take first place for the Jewish woman. In their extreme sensitivity on this point may be recognized a concern for the opinions of non-Jews and a reaction to situations common to both Jewish and gentile women.

On the positive side, dressing well is considered a precondition of "good manners":

> Yet in this very essential of "good manners" our Jewess is often deficient, and under that head may be classed most of her errors in society. She is too much given to dress and fashion-valuing her attire by its cost rather than by its appropriateness to her style on the occasion.[7]

There is great elaboration on this theme of poor taste in dressing and mothers and daughters, husbands and fathers are the objects of criticism in this respect as is also a Society assessing the standard of a family according to the amount of money expended on a woman's wardrobe:

". . . foolishly fancying that a certain amount of display will stamp them as being worth a certain amount of money, and that that supposed money gives them position: the grossest of all errors—if their hearts and minds have not made ladies of them and ensured their standing in society, contemptible indeed must their position be, bought by a show of silk, laces and diamonds! It is time that the barbaric love of bright colors and flashing stones be eradicated from among the peculiarities of our race. . . . Lee C. Harby . . ."[8]

Poor taste in clothes at the summer resort are noted: "if a banker's wife dresses so outrageously as to excite the sneers of the ladies and the leers of the men,"[9] and satirized, as she is ironically advised:

> The more richly you dress, the more rightfully you can claim to be refined. Hang out a diamond from every finger. Nothing is daintier than to see diamonds flashing amid griddle cakes and syrup.[10]

On the other hand, where modesty in dressing is asserted, results are attributed to it which should better have been ascribed to general social conditions, for instance, the omission of restriction at resort hotels. Thus, at a watering place in Wisconsin, nicknamed the "Western Saratoga," which was opposed to applying the restrictions dominant at resorts in the Atlantic states, it was said:

At Waukesha

. . . The "Fountain House" could not very well adopt the Hilton principle of excluding the Jews. Many are there, and the social intercourse between Gentile and Jews is unusually unrestrained. Perhaps this pleasant circumstance is due to the fact that the Jewish ladies in Waukesha entirely abstain from unnecessary pomp, and happily avoid loudness of speech and manner. Their diamonds are not large enough to challenge envy, their toilettes simple, and above all, their children well behaved and thoroughly Americanized. The children of Waukesha really deserve credit for propriety and good behaviour; no better praise can I bestow upon them than by declaring that they are hardly seen or heard. . . .[11]

As to the dictates of fashion in clothing, they were as well-recognized by the Jewish woman as by others. The more so because the America of the nineteenth century represented a cultural province of established European fashion empires, and was their overseas market. Thus, all American women, including the Jewish women, fell in step with the fashions in clothing initiated in Europe. The attitude of Jewish men to the new styles in women's dress is mirrored in much of the bitterness with which they castigated what was to them the inconceivable in fashion by verbal irony and caricature. Especially where official affairs were concerned, as the charity balls of Jewish organizations, the voices of men could sound harsh:

Some of the noticeably dressed ladies at the Purim Ball, in their excitement at leaving their homes, had forgotten their sleeves, and many a male dancer blushed at the juxtaposition of his black coat with the undraped arm of his partner, and gently ventured to remark whether it would not be a good idea for him to go or send

to the lady's house to recover the missing portion of her dress. As
a rule, these sleeveless dresse[r]s were not at all of the classic outline
or creamy complexion that would have excused their unhappy
condition—the good arms were generally covered more or less.
But fashion which, on second thought, is responsible for some of
the vagaries of feminine attire, seems to dictate that the more a
lady approaches "full dress" the less dress she is respected to
wear.[12]

On the other hand, the flaunting of articles of fashion are also be-
moaned, as in an announcement of the Purim Association: ". . . no
ladies will be allowed to walk on the floor in their cloaks and hats as
they did on Hanukah." [13]

A perennial theme for attack was the luxurious attire of women at
the synagogue, especially during holidays. This description awakens
memories of the situation in olden times when women were censured
for immodesty at holy places:

It seems to be about time that our rabbis and wise men should
devise some uniform bonnet and dress for Jewesses on Yom Kip-
pur. Seated in my vicinity were ladies in blue and black feathers,
in white and red hats, in green and brown silk, in all the colors of
the rainbow; how incongruous seemed the confessions of the liturgy
from their fair lips!

I remember the time—ah, not so long ago, when my grandmother wore her real white lace cap in the synagogue on the holy
days, and how sweet and placid was her dear face, and how we
little ones then felt devout and good in her presence! And her
dress—nothing could have been simpler than her plain black silk.
Ah, times have changed: We must have rustling trains at service,
colors bright and radiant. Are we more devout? Are we more respected? Do our children show more religious feeling? A little less
style, and a little more sincerity, is what is sorely needed to day.

What example do these gaily-dressed penitents show their daughters? What holy influences are likely to be diffused from their extravagant surroundings even in the house of God? . . .[14]

A London journal notes with dismay the outward show of luxury in dress on the High Holy Days that spilled over into the streets from the synagogue as far as Fifth Avenue in New York: "Zion's women have developed luxury there such as has never before been seen on public streets. Individual ladies appeared in silk, laces, and jewels valued at thousands of dollars." [15]

The theme of dress and style played the same role in the conversations of women in America as it did among women elsewhere; Jewish women were no exceptions. Surely, it was only the bias of the men who expressed their concern in writing, and their lack of understanding that led to their denouncing American Jewish women and asserted that America was worse off, asserting that they were more culpable than their counterparts in the Jewish world of Western Europe. The attempt to interpret their interest in fashion as a sign of the superficiality of the Jewish woman in America, was properly rejected by their contemporaries.

An entirely different matter was the social significance of dressing as a status symbol. Distinctions made, or at least attempted, by higher expenditures on attire, an act often shared with the men, could express social distance even within the same class. Reproaches for her snobbishness were often heard: "She desires thus to outshine her neighbours with this evidence of greater means; and as she ranks herself according to the costliness of her garments, her respect for them is based upon the depth of their purses. . . ." [16]

An explanation for such extravagant display in dress, may be found in the modest circumstances of the newly emigrated women in their adopted homeland. For the new family on this new soil, dress went hand in hand with their success story whose external expression that everyone could see was in their attire. There was a psychological need for this display, heightened by its accompanying circumstances. The people in the old homeland most concerned with the success of their children overseas, lived too far away to see it with their own eyes. But there were enough people in the new world, indeed, all hailing from the same area and holding old memories dear, to make inescapable comparisons between the dress of certain people in previous times and, at the present.

Rude critics never tired of reminding everyone of the poor origins of these women:

> . . . the upstart, the woman who never had a square meal in her father's house and to whom even a pair of wooden shoes was a luxury at the time she carried the *shaalet* of a Saturday, through the market-place. . . .[17]

However, this criticism could only strike at the personal behavior of the newly arrived and not at the general love for clothing as symbols of well-being.

Actually, it is an attribute of all nouveaux riches, of any sex or religion or country, to use dress as an outward sign of their hard-won prosperity. The joy of the woman at the sight of the long-yearned for dress signified only that in this way she was able to share the affluence of her husband. The loud checked suiting and watch-chains and rings of the men were often caricatured in literature and the press. Finally, critics acknowledged the universal urge for beautiful plumage, but insisted that it was the extraordinary display of jewels that made Jewish women so conspicuous:

> In the fashion of wearing highly colored garments our ladies are only obeying the prevalent custom, for I have seen most ladies in Chicago wear patterns that wound the aesthetic eye, and would excite ridicule in the southern country. But as for this unhappy fondness for jewelry—have they forgotten, that a Jewish mother's most magnificent jewels are her children, and that her greatest ornament is a peaceful well-kept home? I make bold to say that nowhere have I seen such a display of diamonds and jewelry as in the Lake City. . . .[18]

Immediately after the Civil War, in the height of New York's prosperity, the critic sees the same picture on Broadway:

> How often I've seen . . . Jewesses-the old and fat ones especially, offending more grossly than the young and pretty ones in this par-

ticular—sweeping the dirty Broadway pavements with the long trains of most expensive dresses; their hair dressed in the most ridiculous styles, because in the greatest extreme of the prevailing fashions; their fingers covered with clumsy rings; their ears elongated by the weight of heavy ornaments; big brooches fastening their ermine comforters, heavy braceletts on their wrists; and the gold watch chain thrust prominently outside the ermine? And what a spectacle does this afford! . . .[19]

He remarks with pompous self-satisfaction that in his own circle of acquaintances such low standards were rejected and that it is in just this reserve that the true lady shows her hand: "There are many Jewish ladies whom your wife regards as intimates and even as friends; do they paint their faces or make jeweler's show cases of themselves? No, sir. Because they are ladies; . . ." [20] Nevertheless, the realization finally came that taste is independent of so many things which otherwise separate or join social groups. The only consolation remaining was that all these Jewesses different in matters of taste, belong to the community of Israel and that the sincerity of their religious belonging could never be doubted despite all this. "Yet I will not say that those who find pleasure in wearing loud colors cannot be devout; their offered prayers to the Almighty are as readily accepted by Him as others'; but do not our "progressive Jewesses" give to the world the opinion that they dress for worldly admiration? Whether in civilized America or in barbaric Africa, freedom or despotism has no influence upon our taste. . . ."[21] The observer continued to hammer away at his obsession: "Why, then, should our Jewesses glitter and glimmer at the Temples, at service? Is our Temple, the sacred edifice, the *place* for the gathering of gaudy styles? Should Fashion have its bazaar there? No!" [22] And at last relenting, he admitted that times change, and fashion with the times. Comparing the garments used in the past for swimming, he finds that the principal change is in the bathing suits of women. Any serious protest in this case, where function defines the dress, no longer seemed possible:

The bathing-suit is another proof of progress. Compare the old-fashioned, ready-made, square, clumsy garment, in all its severe dignity and flannel, with the latest aspiration—soft, clinging folds, dainty trimmings, neat and artistic in every feature, approaching positive elegance, and almost too tasteful and costly for its purpose. What sights we used to be twenty years ago—with huge straw hats and baggy garments, which gave us the grace of porpoises: whereas now the naiads have come to life again.[23]

So at least in this latest development an accord was reached, satisfying male and female alike.

b) Etiquette and the Social Life

Any set of social rules may excercise its power on the individual. Nevertheless, a certain choice remains to the individual person as to which rule he will submit to, especially if certain social situations lack meaning for him. It is quite different, however, with "Society" people. Whoever takes in "Society" as a whole, adopts its entire codex of behavior. He sees as the main purpose of his submission to its rules the fact that they regulate everything and for everyone. For natures of this kind, the rituals also possess the attraction of a rationale, by which they are enabled to explain the individual demands of etiquette as the idea of his "Society." In the first page of volume 1 of 1892/1893 of *Vogue* magazine it is stated quite clearly that "The ceremonial side of life attracts the sage as well as the debutante, men of affairs as well as the belle. It may be a dinner or it may be a ball, but whatever the function the magnetic, welding force is the social idea." [24]

However, that following the rules of etiquette should not be too hard on the individual, his insufficiency in complicated matters of the forms of decorum and breeding is inculcated into him. Excepted from this insufficiency are only the few who received nature's gift of leading others in the matter of social ceremonial. The "led" may be satisfied with the fact that they were spared the grave headache:

> The power of doing and saying the correct thing at the right moment, is a gift vouchsafed to but few. . . . Very good advice these enquirers get on all points of conduct, from the proper use

of the fingerbowl to the wisest thing to do in the crises of their love-affairs.[25]

Nevertheless, etiquette doesn't remain the simple problem of gifted leaders who force themselves on unsophisticated followers. Aside from the feeling of inferiority, the right enthusiasm also has to exist in the masses of "Society" to accept what is laid upon them. In the end, this preparedness is decisive, and actually appears only in the feminine world, having produced etiquette and being the ones to carry it further. That a man was occasionally recruited as arbiter elegantiarum in high society doesn't change the situation. He served there then more as a shield for the devices of the feminine world and his personal standing in the society of men was not founded on it. In the world of men the racing stable and the club presidency decided one's status, and even, sometimes, a literary or half-literary yardstick was applied. McAllister, the master of ceremonies for the four hundred, was finally described in this way: "Yet what has he brought away with him from these feasts? Apparently not one clever story, not one bright bit of dialogue, not one lively gem of repartee. . . ." [26]

As so often when the Jewish world is concerned, the meaningless things of gentile society appeared there as a caricature. Jewish clamor for leadership in a Society depicted as Jewish was derided as an open imitation showing its worthlessness: "Mr. Greenway declared there were only four-hundred persons in San Francisco who were fit to go into good society. . . ." [27]

The ways of the Jewish would-be Society leader were derided as arbitrary Jewish commandments:

> . . . I believe that he is about to hand down from the clock tower of the Parvenu Advertising Agency a new set of commandments to take the place of the old reliable ten that Moses broke.
>
> Some fine morning the new rules for the government of the morals of Parvenucracy will appear in all the papers controlled by Mr. Huntington, and I imagine they will be something like this:
> The commandments of E. Moses Greenway.[28]

The Jew is derided in his totality, not only as in the case of the imitation McAllister, in regard to his fruitless Society doings: ". . . whenever
San Francisco papers feel inclined to ridicule a reputable citizen and call
him all the ridiculous names in the dictionary, they have only to refer
to him as "Mr. Greenway's rival." [29]

Showing Greenway in a typical caricature of a Jew as talking with
his hands,[30] a special appeal to women is nevertheless ascribed to him.
In a further caricature "The Prodigal Son up to Date" he is shown
as being received by two enthusiastic Jewish women at the railway station and we read the lines: "A notable event in Hebrew society circles
last week was the return of Mr. Greenway, the San Francisco society
"leader," on a visit to his people.—Baltimore Society News, 1899." [31]

For the Jewish woman, American etiquette, so enthusiastically pur-
sued by gentile women, appeared less than perfect. She was, in particular, unimpressed by the British model so revered by her American
sisters. The consciousness of the existence of other yardsticks and models
than those of English origin was strong in Jewish women of European
heritage. What was said once of New York generally may just as well
be stated of the Jewish feminine sphere there: ". . . In New York we
have combined much that is agreeable, convenient and worthy of following in the manners and social observances of several of the older nations." [32]

In the end, masculine resistance against etiquette could easier be
handled if those Central European elements were woven into it which
were still known to Jewish men from the old homeland. Thus, in all
details of this complicated wardrobe—from dancing gowns to dress for
outings, from the debut of young girls to their weddings and the Society
page, we still find the European elements as the area of the least masculine resistance.

Not that the Jewish man living in accord with Jewish tradition had
rejected the provisions of etiquette of strange origin as a matter of principle. The old adage that the customs of the country prevail held good
even further. He only reserved for himself the right to choose the best
and combine it with what he already had: "In our present situation
before the world, it is the bounden duty of every Jew and Jewess to

respect the proper rules of the best society as well as to obey the laws of God and man." [33]

New ways should be judged in accord with this principle in general and etiquette was no exception.

c) Promenades and Public Places

The European institution of regular promenades on a particular day of the week, at set places, and customary hours of the day by those whose aim was to be seen, was also established in America. Especially in New York there were Saturday afternoon promenades on Fifth Avenue frequented by the Jewish public. The same locality saw a general promenade of New Yorkers on Sunday morning. Participation in these promenades for the purpose of meeting old and making new acquaintances was seen as an innocent pleasure of young girls, and figured as being among the pastimes a well-advised father could allow his daughters:

"Let her dance . . . let her sing and play, and walk along Fifth Avenue on Sunday mornings and Saturday afternoons, with an I-want-to-meet-someone expression on her face. Let her go to the theatre, and the concert, and the Purim Ball—not in mask." [34]

Critics pointed out that the Sabbath promenade could lead to a transgression of religious observance if it should happen that the young woman was invited to take a buggyride on this day of rest. It was only snobbism, they maintained, that was at the bottom of this breaking of the Sabbath, and Jewish women were the moving spirits of this abominable deed:

> . . . we think there are some offenders against the Sabbath who have no business calls—who bear the honored name of Jewish matrons. These attend Synagogue or Temple in the morning, and drive in the Avenue or through the Park in the afternoon. For these, there is no excuse or palliation. It is a vulgar offence to parade their wealth so ostentatiously and so unbecomingly. Let them devote themselves to their true work, the training of their children in the fear of the Lord. . . . [35]

In contrast with the rigid customs of Europe, American streets were more readily frequented by women, dresses were more often paraded on the streets, and women walking on the streets even on nonpromenade days was widespread. European observers were scandalized that Jewish women participated with other women. A visitor from Chicago related his views in these words:

> . . . There is a large Jewish population in this Western city, it can be noticed at first sight. . . . Well then, almost the very first fact I noticed in this city was a large number of Jewesses perambulating the thoroughfares of the business quarter in the sweltering heat of the day. This might be accounted for by the fact that Chicago tradespeople engage a great many saleswomen, but the ladies whom I have met were dressed in the latest fashion and were bejeweled—I hate to record it—in most extravagant fashion. I have been told, it is one of the customs of western life that ladies walk in the business streets for pastime. The sooner our own ladies commit a breach of this questionable "etiquette," the better for them. I am thinking now how strenuously we have protested against the assertion that we are loud, extravagant and fond of display. And yet have we not to be silent, when some *Judenfeind* would point at the streets of Chicago?[36]

Still, Jewish ladies in the business streets were close to the stores of their husbands who, in the same streets, sold this beautiful apparel and fine jewelry and were therefore not as out of place as it appeared to this observer. Shopping in the business center was equally important for women of all circles and took time, and that was when the ladies were seen. Although remarks like this by Jewish men at the sight of Jewish women on the streets were heard,[37] it couldn't change the fact that all America did the same thing and that adequate dresses for these walks were chosen with the same diligence as for appearances in Society. Whenever a new fashion arose in street dresses, they were shown and described in detail in women's magazines. Rigorous moralists, however, took offence both at what they considered to be the purposelessness of many of these walks and the display of dresses as well:

Floating facts

Some young ladies pass the afternoon by walking up and down a limited distance on Broadway a dozen time or more. As this is all they can do it must be confessed that they do it to perfection. An automaton walking doll might act as well; but then there would be the bother of winding it up; although, for that matter, it is as much bother to dress up as a belle.[38]

In public localities, especially at night, Jewesses still did not move outside freely, nevertheless the old reserve in this respect was partly broken, at least in New York. An observer there reported the rather uninhibited behavior of ladies in public localities:

Young ladies of New York ought to find better places than lager beer and oyster saloons wherein to spend their evenings. It is common talk among men of a certain class that if they want to see Miss This or Miss That, daughter of respectable citizens, dwelling in comfortable houses, they can find them any evening between nine o'clock and midnight at neighboring saloons. Beer is an innocuous drink, if taken in moderation, but it does not add to a lady's grace or reserve. Unmarried ladies can live happily without beer, especially lager beer; and as for oysters, if their spiritual advisers or their own inclinations lead them to indulge in bivalves, they need not patronize public places where reserved and quiet manners are in the minority.[39]

On the other hand, the ice cream parlor on afternoons was considered an innocent pastime for women undisturbed by the presence of men and a "Kaffeeklatsch" was conceded to them there.

d) Dancing and Debuts

Dancing was a sanctioned method of bringing together young men and women of the new generation and was, at the same time, a traditional entertainment within the frame of organized sociality. It was one of the opportunities for the family, after careful preparation, chaperon included, to go out officially. Dancing also had its great special moments if it was combined with festive occurrences, like a wedding, where to bring joy to the bridal couple was considered even a religious duty, or to introduce the debutante into Society. In time, however, official balls of the organized Jewish community of a charitable character prevailed. In Europe, the Simchat Tora ball was an old custom of the German Jews and served the whole local community. This tradition was joyfully transplanted to the new continent and Simchat Tora balls were arranged in America even in small communities: "Eufaula, Ala. . . . We have here fifteen Jewish families, which are all well-to-do, and outside of them about a dozen Jewish single men of all ages between twenty and forty-five . . . Simchat Tora . . . ball . . . a goodly number of "drummers," all nice young men and good dancers greatly increased the demand for partners. . . ." [40]

As a vehicle of sociality and as a backbone of philanthropical endeavor in the community the charity ball achieved great importance. It was a great event with preparations of ad hoc formed committees accompanied with an announcement of the event and publication of the names of the persons in charge, and also of certain rules set up for the occasion. Where the Jewish community was still young, as in California in 1854, the advertisement for the charity ball gives a lively picture of the social situation in the community:

> First Hebrew Benevolent Society. Second Anniversary Ball. Musical Hall, Tuesday March 14, 1854, in aid of its charity funds. . . . Tickets . . . are not transferable and will not be sold at the door on the evening of the Ball.
> The Committee will issue Ladies' Invitations to any gentleman possessing a ticket.
> Ladies are respectfully requested to bring the invitation Cards with them. [41]

Certain ceremonials developed at these balls of which the "ring cake" with its hidden diamond significantly originated in the Golden West. The following description of the San Francisco Charity Ball combines

At the fancy dress ball *(Puck,* Vol. 14, 1883/84, p. 391).

---

all the elements of Society, exhibition, decorum, and gastronomy exercised by the six hundred guests:

The Hebrew Benevolent Ball

. . . Notwithstanding the unpleasant state of the weather, upwards of six hundred guests assembled to join in the "many festivities of the dance," which they kept up with life, animation, and gayety, until a late hour in the morning. Youth and beauty were there, and happy old age buoyant with hope—each striving to excel the other in the pleasant enjoyments of the night, while rich strains of music "awoke the atmosphere with its song." The decorations of the room were neat and tastefully arranged—nothing gaudy, but all in proper keeping, and reflected great credit upon those who had that part of the arrangement in charge. After the supper—which we think, was decidedly the best of the kind we have yet seen upon an occasion like this in California—came the cutting of the "ring cake," a pleasant event in this social gathering. It was attended with some ceremony, which gave *eclat* to the occasion. After the cutting—which was done in the center of the ball room— each gallant marched up his lady to the table, took a slice, and searched among its sweets for the hidden jewel. Many were doomed to be disappointed, for the diamond could fall to but one, and that was in the person of Mrs. Phillip Lewis, who accepted it with a becoming grace. . . .[42]

Dancing parties for charity purposes were arranged everywhere. Occasionally complaints appeared in the Jewish press that due to the lack of enough ladies—a frequent occurrence in small pioneer communities—arranging of balls was not possible. In one of these cases the newspaper humoristically promised assistance: ". . . Too bad you can not get up a ball for want of ladies. Come down here, Mr. Selicho, and bring all the young men in Lynchburg and the vicinity, and we can furnish partners for balls, or for life, if desired."[43]

Purim was hailed by masked balls, like the one in Sacramento, in 1872:

"The balmasque, given at the Turner Hall, by the ladies of the Purim Ball Club . . ." with seventy-five masks participating.[44]

Masked visiting parties to houses changed to dancing groups once they had entered the open house. The following description of such a party in New York (1883) tells the story, describing the masks in details and giving the visitor's list on which appears also "Mr. Theodore Roosevelt":

"Merry Purim" was celebrated in the evening [Saturday, March 24, 1883] by crowds of masqueraders, who drove from house to house in omnibuses and carriages. At the door of a house one of the maskers was requested to disclose his identity and vouch for the rest of the party. The party then entered, and after dancing and jesting with the company drove to another house. Among the houses which were open were those of Mr. and Mrs. Herrman, No. 59 West Fifty-sixth Street, Mr. and Mrs. Herts of West Forty-fourth Street, . . ." [45]

Dancing remained the big vogue of Jewish society in America—in the beginning of the communities an important means to consolidate this society and finance the community-institutions. In part, the balls were arranged by women's organizations. In the period of scarcity of women in the West, a special attraction was added to the balls. Later, however, in the growing Jewish communities with their surplus of Jewish girls introduced to balls, an entirely new ballroom problem arose that, in its deeper sense, can be understood only by a realization that the relationship between the sexes had changed with a consequent lack of male dancers. Although dancing as recreation was revived later among the new Russian Jewish immigrants, most of whom only learned to dance in America,[46] the crisis in dancing among the native youth continued until the end of the nineteenth century, and hailed, above all, from the fact that the marriage market had been largely urbanized by the plentiful supply of women; thus, matrimony for money was available to men, especially in the larger cities. Customary forms of courting that found their sentimental expression in the ballroom, were no longer seen by men as necessary, not even desirable, as marriage initiation. More rational treatment of marriage intent appeared adequate. Moreover, at that time, men's club life, entirely segregated from female influence, opened an independent "Society" for them in which many found a full life. The few club affairs to which women were admitted paid lip service to be sure, to dancing in their programs, but the earnest intent of the men to dance was not present any more. Complaints were heard about the lack of interest in dancing among young men, and about the formation of male islands in the ballroom and catastrophic vistas invisioned for established Society affairs. To a certain degree, however, even some good was discovered in this abandonment of social dancing by young men:

A class of society men

Those who are privileged to attend society entertainments, club receptions, and parties of any pretensions to refinement and style, cannot fail to notice the number of young men who persistently assemble around the doorways and in the lobbies, and pass the evening in absolute contentment, even if their swallow-tails get whitened by too close proximity to the wall. That this class of young men is increasing year by year, is a fact which cannot be denied. That its influence, if unchecked, cannot fail to be disastrous in social circles, produce a dead-lock in the matrimonial market, and make the dancing master shoot himself in despair, is roundly asserted by many people. . . .

But in reality their preference does credit to their taste and intellect. They scorn the frivolous waltz, they despise the lanciers, they hate the shallow gossip of the promenade; and after they have seen their little sisters, if they have any, provided with partners, they hastily leave the ball room and retire to some favored nook, where they can indulge in profound philosophic meditation, or sprightly literary discussion.[47]

Finally the issue became so serious that it had to be dealt with in connection with the opening of the next season:

Dancing, which grows less and less popular among young men over twenty-five, will be seriously retarded this season, unless the friendly services of boys of fifteen and sixteen are enlisted. Such lads are to be preferred who have had one season's experience in croquet. The small talk incidental to that pastime will admirably qualify them to act as partners. How to attract young men of mature age, is a serious problem. Possibly cheques of one hundred dollars and more, as German favors, might not be without their fascination. It is understood that to prevent young men thronging the halls and corridors, instead of boldly facing the music in the parlor and assembly room, barbed wire will be employed in all directions, and such a stout fence will doubtless prove effective.[48]

In such a deteriorating situation where so much was spoken and written to justify the defection of the men, some defense of the dancers was bound to appear:

The number of dancing young men is becoming deplorably small. At a recent entertainment, male partners could not be secured even for the lanciers, and one set was composed entirely of young women. They must have enjoyed themselves immensely. Under these circumstances it is natural that the dancing man becomes eagerly sought after, and is truly appreciated. Non-dancers may sneer at his gyrations, as they gather around the staircase or hug the door in perfect self-abandonment, but the dancer is not to be despised. The mere fact that a man dances, by no means proves him destitute of solid qualities. There is a moral obligation incumbent on the young man of the period to dance—or shun parties. The dance is the first commandment of society.[49]

However, as against these remarks, the same authority presented the actual hard facts: "Club life was never so popular among the men than just at present." [50]

Because of the organic changes within Society as it was expressed by the new attitude toward dancing, an uncertainty developed about the new season. For those active participants to whom the work fell of preparing for the coming social events, this state of affairs presented previously unknown problems. The great mas of participants in the Society play, however, sat in quiet expectation of unforseen occurrences, full of intellectual curiosity about how the new problems would be solved. For one group, however, the very group for which the new season should have brought the fulfillment of their highest expectations—the debutantes—the matter was much more serious. This age group of newcomers to Society was an unchangeable factor in Society management. Society's great obligation was to these young women about to be initiated into its ranks. The Society leaders could only fulfill this duty at adequate social affairs. About the nature of this obligation no doubt existed. The young girls' attainment to marriageable age had to be signalized: "It has been stated that society exists only as a matrimonial bureau, organized and conducted solely for the benefits of the *débutante,* who lives a brief, butterfly existence in a shower of compliments and flowers before she marries and retires from view. This is an overstatement, but not so egregious a one as might be wished." [51]

Patient observers had time waiting for new social revelations, slightly amused about the whole situation:

The Coming Season

Nothing is yet known as to what the coming season will have in store for society people. The air of mystery and uncertainty has its charm for some, and delightful are the anticipations indulged in by young and unsophisticated persons who propose to make their *debut.* Society is rigid—conservative. It indulges in no fancy handbills in advance or glowing prospectus of winter gaiety. So we must wait until the season has fairly begun, fully to learn its programme. [52]

The problems of debutantes was greeted with complete understanding in the Jewish press. Moreover, the commentaries made by the press about the situation are, in themselves, another mirror of the details of the social codex which were still problematic for the young debutante:

Social debuts

Just at the time of the year when the atmosphere is suggestive of falling snow flakes, society is preparing to receive numberless rosebuds just ripening into bloom. These have exchanged the school for the ball room, their college tasks for the calls and burdens of society, their innocent amusements for others far more harassing, their peaceful thoughts for reflections of an entirely different hue. In one word, they are supposed to be "out," these fair debutantes, out at sea amid the breakers of fashionable life.

Of course, the event is one of the most profound importance to the young lady in question. Hers is a double perplexity. It is not only the subject of dress which gives her anxiety, but that of behavior as well. The latter is perhaps the cause of far more earnest thought, because she may safely confide the matter of dress to the *modiste*. She knows that she will be scrutinized for her manner as well as attire; and how to appear unconscious of the fact that this is her debut, and how to assume the easy grace of the experienced belle, are questions which make her little heart sorely palpitate. Then, if she be fair, how to control telltale blushes? And if she be dark, how to relieve the deathly-pallor? What shall she talk about? Should she consult the encyclopedia just before the carriage is announced, and cram for the evening as an intellectual young woman? How is she to judge of the behavior of the men? If one dances with her more than twice, is she to infer that he is in love, particularly if he sighs? . . .[53]

A special detail in the first steps of the debutante in Society was the matter of a suitable chaperon. The problem existed also for the other girls and was discussed often enough in women's magazines and even in the general press. The chaperon was of old European origin and was, at the end of the century, rejected in America as superfluous: "As a social institution the chaperon may be said not to exist in America. There seems to be throughout the land, except among certain families in the older cities, an inherent prejudice against the idea that American girls are to be watched or looked after once they are considered old enough to leave the school-room and step out into the world. . . ."[54]

Jewish mothers, however, raised their daughters according to European tradition and found support in the columns of the Jewish press. No outcry against the institution of the chaperon could be read there.

For special undertakings of young Jewish girls as, for instance, trips to distant places, the company of a chaperon was a requirement, as we may learn from the advertisement in a Jewish women's magazine:

A trip to the Bermudas

A lady of assured social position has been requested to chaperone a party of ladies to the Bermudas in September. Ladies desirous of joining the excursion will please make application . . . care of the American Jewess. . . . [55]

e) The Society Page

The Jewish press, a constant companion of all events in the world of Jewish women and self-styled critic and caretaker of all interests in Jewish community life, finally took the decisive step—and introduced a society page. With this, the press shows us once more the world of women as it appeared in their own eyes thereby escaping the odium of male arrogance. This step, marking the last, high phase of German Jewish sociality, has a long history behind it.

The need for publicity, advertising events in Society, was recognized early in the Jewish community of America insofar as public affairs or membership meetings were concerned. Under these categories fell innumerable undertakings, at which women played the main role: balls, matinées, concerts, and theatre performances—usually for charitable purposes—were very often conducted directly by circles and auxiliaries of Jewish women's organizations. To satisfy this publicity need, the local general press was used. Numerous reports on Jewish social undertakings were dispersed early through the files of the local press, from the Atlantic to the Pacific. The Jewish press later added its own news on these matters; however, due to its regional character, the growing need for local publicity could be filled only partially. Many Jewish enterprises recorded in the local general press do not show up in the Jewish press.

For a long time a barrier existed against reporting purely private news of society, insofar as it was not of public interest. This holds true for the general press as well as for the Jewish press; only weddings were an exception to this habit of newspapers, and grew in time. The English model of a society page registering the smallest details of family news was not imitated in America for a long time. In the Jewish press a position against such a society page was occasionally taken:

A London Jewish Weekly

An American cannot help being occasionally amused and interested by the peculiarities of English Jewish journalism, just as our brethren abroad have at times expressed themselves as amazed at the length to which cis-Atlantic newspapers go. Glancing at the column of "Births," we are told that the wife of Judah Moses has a girl (Eveline)—why the name has any interest so early in that girl's life only the parents understand; that Mr. Isaacs, at 7 P.M. at such a place, in such a square, has a "boy stillborn, prematurely," and a third notice says: "At Sidney, Mrs. Samuel Levy, of twins (by telegraph)"—an astonishing fact to those who may not remember that the Sidney father has telegraphed the news to the London journal. The marriage notices are always full of family statistics . . . American and Foreign Papers please copy . . ." the innocent advertisers, of course expecting that every newspaper in America reads the announcements in the *Chronicle* and *World*, and is eager to publish the item for its hungry readers.[56]

To this it may be added that the German Jewish press which had formerly influenced the literary taste of the Jewish emigrants, was also without such a news section.

However, new things were already on the march in America. An unrestrained use of newspaper pages for private curiosity stories was taking place. Later, when the soicety page was established, it didn't follow the family character of the English pages, but was dedicated instead to news which exhibited society in its leading figures, leading taste, and interesting pastimes. The personal news concerned the private undertakings of these leading personalities for their own circles, thus creating the local "society." Jewish women often did the same things, recording them in the same way as others in the local press, not to speak of the as yet nonexistent society page of the Jewish press:

> Mrs. Julius Janowitz has returned to her town house 221 East 79th street, and has resumed her informal Sunday evening receptions. They are very enjoyable, and in her drawing room one is always sure to meet people of literary, musical and artistic importance.[57]

Even lists of guests and artists at home receptions are given.[58]

In time, the mass of such society material in the American Jewish newspapers, especially at the Pacific Coast, became overwhelming. Together with legitimate news of public social events, they formed a quantity for which even a whole newspaper page was insufficient. Individual newspapers, especially in California, seemed to exist only for this purpose. They were different from the gentile models of mere society-papers in that they lacked the stuff of real feminine interest like fashions, home, and kitchen. At the same time, they functioned as a community newspaper with their news of public Jewish interest and created a hybrid that is easily to be found elsewhere. Opposition to this character of the society page arose even in the Jewish press itself by its serious correspondents, occasionally in a bitter ironic way:

Drop it

> Is it not about time that our Hebrew papers change their Jenkinsisms and stop filling their columns with the names of the Sprinzes, the Guendels and Zurelis who have gone either to the Springs or to the seashore? What do we care whether Miss Feide or Mrs. Gretel is on a visit to Shloime Shlabber in Indianapolis, or that Mr. Shapse Sheigetz has gone to Cleveland, ostensibly to recuperate, but really to drum up customers? Column after column is devoted weekly, in our Jewish papers, to just such nonsense as this, and I am getting unwell of the nasty stuff. If Chayeh Zureh leaves town you may just bet a big American dollar that every one of

her relatives and friends know it, and strangers certainly take no stock in the movements of either men and women whom they do not know. Hence I would remind our Jewish papers who have not much space to spare to eschew that sort of small paragraphing, as it is neither healthy nor interesting to the general reader.[59]

CHAPTER SEVEN

Family Problems, Marriage, and Divorce

a) The Western Frontier

Pioneer life and the continuous mobility of the Jewish family on the frontier presented the Jewish woman with a situation unknown to her in Europe—that of living in substitute homes with all the temporary expedients of homelife. This circumstance was considered by thoughtful observers to be an anomaly in American life because, it was stated, a real family atmosphere could not exist when so many young families lived in hotels and boarding houses. The situation was referred to as the "vice of boarding," [1] and the number of hotel children was considered to be ever growing. The problem reached a special urgency in the Westward movement: "This singular moveable manner of life becomes more pronounced as one travels westward." [2] Such words were well in accord with another idea becoming more and more widespread, that a new eccentric mode of life originated in the West, and that everything new that surfaced, came predominantly from the outlandish ideas of "Western" women. The women's magazines occasionally mention this matter speaking up in defense of women:

The Western Idea

. . . If a woman does everything out of the common or usual custom, and she happens to live in the East, we say "Strange woman, Isn't she odd?" Or we class her among the "eccentrics." But let the same thing be done by a woman residing in the West, and we immediately say: "That's Western; that's the Western way of doing things." [3]

This disadvantageous state of hotel and boardinghouse life for the Jewish family was described minutely in the Jewish press, especially in Chicago. The description also included the depiction of other innovations in dress, promenading on business streets, and so on. An especially intensifying irritation is that in hotel and boardinghouse life, Jewish dietary laws are much less often observed:

> Another fact which came under my immediate observation is that many Jewish families prefer the excitement of the hotel and boarding house to the quietude of the home circle. . . . The civilizing flood which inundated this country has washed away the beauties of Jewish family life, and for the former pride of home has been substituted a decided aversion to a quiet repose by the fireside. In the hotel under the roof of which I slept, I counted at least two dozen Jewish families registered as regular boarders, and, undoubtedly, all other hotels or "inns" in the Lake City contain a proportionate number, for, I assure you, *kosher* board is no object in this cosmopolitan city. In how far the paterfamilias is accountable for this decidedly unJewish proceeding, or in how far his fair lady encourages it out of love of idleness and a sickly fancy that the boarding is fashionable, I repeat, I have been unable to ascertain. But it is necessary that attention should be called to this new phase of Jewish life, which seems to inaugurate an assimilation to an American practice which is thoroughly detestable.[4]

Even if it sounds exaggerated seen from a distance of time, to state that a new phase of Jewish life in America began with living in hotels, combined with other innovations it served, without a doubt, to loosen Jewish family life. With stable living in their own houses the Jewish community in the West was gradually strengthened in later years.

b) Mistress of the House

To guide the household was the Jewish woman's unchallenged privilege. While bringing up the children fell entirely to her, she had no visible help from her daughters in her household tasks. Moreover, their

GREAT EXPECTATIONS.

IKEY GOLDSTEIN.— Papa, I vos eighdt years oldt to-day.
MOSES GOLDSTEIN.— So you vos, mine leedle poy; so you vos.
IKEY.— Gif me a bresent, Papa?
MOSES.— Vait until it schnows, Ikey, and your papa vill make
you some nice, beeg, roundt, vite, coldt schnow-palls!

Great expectations (*Puck*, Vol. 32, 1892/93, p. 269).

interests led them away from household duties to independent lives and decisions, watched, however, by a vigilant mother: "While she guards her daughters with a watchful eye, they are like other American girls— totally independent of her in social matters. . . . it is not uncommon for a Jewish maiden to surprise her parents with the announcement of her engagement." [5]

It is of deep psychological meaning that household worries weigh so heavily upon the Jewess that she exhibits them so often and in detail in public. Deserted by her daughters in her drab duties, she had to depend on strangers to help her manage a household that represented the state of well being of her husband and the marriageable condition of her daughters. To the extent that the wealth of the Jewish merchant class made the employment of female domestics possible, it is upon this class of persons that the mistress transferred her general uneasiness, the servants became an ongoing subject for complaint:

The woman who talks

. . . And the cry of the distressed mistress is once more heard in the land. Her burden is greater than she can bear.

Oh, those inefficient servants! She cannot get a cook that is a cook, or a housemaid that is a housemaid, as for washing—a universal groan ascends. Various remedies have been suggested for this lamentable state of affairs. The press has opened wide its columns to numerous suggestions and plans for training servants in the way they should work. And when these schools are in full swing let us fervently trust they will start similar ones for the training of mistresses. [6]

The situation with domestics as it existed in the Jewish household is mirrored in the Jewish press in respect to any group that filled the position at various times, be it German, Irish, Negro, or Chinese. Beyond this, when the mass immigration of Russian Jews began, a special appeal to their female youth to take household employment with Jewish families, was heard:

If there are any girls among the Russian Jews who are willing
to work as either chambermaids or cooks, let them come to San
Francisco . . . A girl gets twenty-five dollars a month here, a good
cook from thirty to forty dollars, and there are any numbers of
ladies here, who, though brought up as cooks do not want to be
seen in the kitchen. . . .[7]

The lack of success of this advice with the young Jewish immigrant
woman could have been foreseen. Later on (1887), the shunning of
household service in favor of industrial employment was no longer a
characteristic feature of the Jewess alone, but already a general trend
with all immigrant peoples: "The thought of going into domestic service, moreover, does not occur to them." [8]

However, the fact is that the daughters of the Jewish middle class
owed their intellectual rise to having been relieved of household duties.
It was the same also with the lucky daughters of the gentiles who also
and for the same reason owed the domestics their lifelong gratitude:

The daughters of the house, too, set free from domestic duties,
had time for books and music and general cultivation, and a wave
of culture has swept over the land in the path of these Irish [ser-
vant] girls that leaves us owing them an unpayable debt. . . .[9]

Only in the Jewish household was it just as often German girls and
other servants of other new immigrant nationalities to whom the debt
was owed. There was even a time when best-situated Jewish homes were
able to hire such rarities among cooks as a special Chinese cook for their
kitchen, and the remembrance of such help was precious for the mistress of her big house. As for the Jewish cook:

A Jewish Cook

In spite of the bondage to which she is forced on account of her
poverty, she preserves a certain independence of her own; and
although she remains in friendship with the Christian housemaid,
she strikes the latter with awe, partly through her mastery of the

cooking art, and partly through the firm sway which she holds over house and inmates. . . . She is indeed an important personage in such a house. . . . the personified conscience of the kitchen. . . . On Sabbath the kitchen has a rest . . . one may see her, dressed in her best, arm in arm with a lady friend, in lively colloquy on the promenade. A young sprucely clad man, whose crooked shoulder suggest the pedlar, plays the agreeable to them, and is, so we were told, to have the cook's hand in marriage. Lucky fellow! . . .[10]

c) Man and Wife

In the German Jewish period, the marital relationship between man and wife had no public aspect. All the problems of later times, discussed then under exploit of beginning social sciences were still dormant. *Marital* fidelity ranked highest of her virtues when discussing the Jewess as the rock of the Jewish family. Her freedoms didn't count for anything compared with this picture of absolute marital fidelity and dedication to her family:

> . . . there are no women in the world less suave to strangers of the opposite sex than Jewish women. Extraordinary beauty with them does not seem to imply its usual accompaniment, extraordinary vanity—which is generally the basis of that sort of character in woman which renders her agreeable to strangers and indifferent to her own. They love home better than company, husband and children better than the admiration of the crowd. Even their taste for bright colors and sparkling ornaments is not a manifestation of vanity, but springs from an inherited and innate love of the brilliant and picturesque; it is not a thing to catch the eye of the passer—it is for the gratification of those whom they *love*. And profound as is the capacity of loving in the breast of the Hebrew girl, it seldom or never becomes the means of leading her astray. . . . The Jewess seems to defy the evil to which it points, and to possess the power of loving wisely, however well.
>
> It is here that we must look, I am convinced, for the foundation-stone of Jewish national unity.[11]

With such a foundation, the purpose of marriage shone up clearly and without discord; marital bliss resulting in an unlimited number of children and a harmonious life of the parents. These ideals dominated the life of the German Jews without any inroads made by such modern ideas as free love, already heard aloud in the other America, or of aesthetic individualistic protests against marriage bonds. Also for a long time marriage for money and the complications of matchmaking based on it did not play a big role.

Deviations from the norm in these respects did not, as yet, reach the stage of actual chroniques scandaleuses, the more so since the society page was kept free of reports of such cases that were only recorded as extraordinary doings arousing the curiosity of its readers and ending with the refrain "Thank God we are not such people."

d) Exceptions to the Rule

That in some cases Jewish immigrants did desert their wives in the old homeland, we learn from reports of rabbinical decisions in divorce case proceedings between Germany and America and also from resolutions and proceedings of rabbinical conferences.[12] However, these relatively uncommon cases didn't attract too much attention. There were, of course, rare cases of Jewish children born out of wedlock, and this unusual news did not fail to be reported in the Jewish and in the general press. For instance in 1867 we read in the *Jewish Messenger*:

> A Foundling.—On Monday, July 22nd, a female child was left in the Passenger office of the Harlem R.R. Co., having appended to it a letter, written in German, of which officer Joseph Strauss, attached to Police Headquarters as interpreter, has made the following translation:
>
> "I am a Jewess, my name is Ida Cohn, my father is in the South and my poor mother has not means to support me, for these reasons I beg you from the bottom of my heart, to be taken care of by Jews. I will be grateful to you. Should I die among Christians, see that I be entered in a Jewish grave yard. I am a Jewess and wish to remain one."

The child is but one month old, and Mr. Strauss has generously consented to maintain it until such a time as he can hear of any Jewish family who would be willing to adopt it. Mr. Strauss can be seen at Central Police Office, 300 Mulberry.[13]

The non-Jewish press also kept an eye open for news of this kind and the consequences of an illicit love story in Salt Lake City are described:

Rather Romantic.—A woman, said to be a Jewess, and who has been living with her young child, in a house opposite the Walker house, East Temple Street, attempted to commit suicide on Saturday night.[14]

The cause célèbre of a murder by Pessach Rubinstein involved a pregnant Jewish girl and was widely commented on in the press, in a Chicago radical German paper, even in the light of criticism of the social order of the time.[15] There were also reported cases of tragedy in marriage as, for example, a woman's suicide in Norfolk street in New York. The *Jewish Times* gives the case with the following introduction: "The Jewish community rarely furnishes material for scandal or sensation, nor are many of its members found on the criminal records; yet some event, like the late suicide in Norfolk street, does remind us that we all are human, Jew and Gentile, civilized and uncivilized." [16]

Prostitution of German Jewish women was actually unknown in the German Jewish period.[17] All in all, however, in full view of anomalies in the relationship of the sexes, it may be said that the Jewess applied reason to the choice she made and thereby avoided greater mischief. This is how an outsider also saw it: 'The Jewess is not of a confiding disposition; she is not to be deceived by a smooth tongue, or brazen-faced assurance, and thinks twice before she acts once. . . . This art seems to have been almost totally lost to the American woman of the nineteenth century. . . ." [18]

e) Divorce

Divorce as a significant factor in the social life of the Jews in America shows up comparatively late, actually, only toward the end of the German Jewish mass emigration of the nineteenth century and, therefore, so much later than with other Americans. This fact, in itself a theme of research and discussion among non-Jews as well, leads us to search for an explanation in the structure of the Jewish family and the manner of its founding. We would not be going far amiss if we conclude that the frequency of divorce among Jews was lower than among other religious groups of that time—although detailed statistics of other religious denominations are not easily available—perhaps due to the historical circumstances of their beginnings.

From the start, we only learn in America of the dissolution of a number of marriages that were concluded in Europe and that effected their main legal consequences there, since, in some cases, the stream of emigration had carried with it also the stranded partners of a broken marriage. For them, the dissolution of the matrimonial bond with a spouse remaining in Europe was a precondition of their going to the new continent. All in all, such cases were not so numerous, to be sure, as might appear according to their detailed treatment in Jewish literature and, especially, in rabbinic responsa. One must not forget that due .to the complicated circumstances that the partners to the divorce dwelt in different parts of the world, difficult legal questions of drawing up and delivering the documents of the *get* (a religious divorce) required the involvement of rabbinical decisions. Furthermore, the case of the deserted woman—which was the most frequent occurrence—was made all the more conspicuous because the husband had removed himself from any of the social pressure normal under native conditions to bring his married life to a formal end. The endeavours to subject him to rabbinic authority in the New World, together with the fact that there were no recognized rabbinical courts in America and that the questions in doubt were relegated to rabbinic authorities in Europe, gave the whole question the appearance of great importance in responsa literature which was not justified by the actual facts. Moreover, the fact that the rabbinical decisions were published in detail, not only in the American Jewish press, but also in the German Jewish papers, gave the divorce an appearance of great public importance. In early times, this was underlined even more by the fact that the competence of the persons executing the *get* in America had to be publicly discussed, at least for the time that rabbinical authority was not yet firmly established. The *agunah* situation in Europe of a woman whose husband's death was not proven or provable, although always a problem, didn't produce the same proportion of rabbinical responsa as did the situation in America where many new problems were coming to the fore. The civil problems of divorce lying outside the sphere of Jewish law in cases of emigration to America hurt the spouse remaining in Europe so much because, according to international law, all questions of marital status had to be dealt with by the courts of their native countries in accord with the laws there.[19] Moreover, the laws in Europe relating to the subject of the Jewish religious communities' execution of a religious divorce, went hand in hand with laws on the civil dissolution of the marriage. In this way further complications were created, for the rabbinical court of the native place and, in due course, for rabbinical law procedure and for all participating rabbis in America. All these circumstances were discussed as well in the German Jewish as in the American Jewish press, whereby all the facts and all the viewpoints of the participants were given in detail.

A case of this kind (in 1855) has been made known to us by the following circumstances: A married man, having deserted his wife, came to America in the spring of 1848 and sent a *get* written by Dr. Lilienthal in New York to a certain person in his native place empowering this person to deliver the *get*. First the problem of legality arises: Can a *get* be sent by mail? Can it be delivered by a person who is without knowledge as to its contents? And even if this technicality, as an accommodation to modern times, is conceded instead of the older rabbinical concept, the remaining problems of secular law binding for the rabbinate are not solved easily. These problems as formulated by the newspaper are the following:

1) Can a religiously lawful divorce be enacted before the civil divorce is given by the secular court?

2) In America, where marriage is only a matter of civil law, can a citizen remarry lawfully if only a religious divorce has been enacted, without committing the crime of bigamy? [20]

Rabbinical opinion, supported by the newspaper, considered the first question irrelevant in America since only in the native European community could there be a conflict of competence between authorities—

governmental or government-recognized religious authorities. For America the religious divorce had no relevance at all to the civil status of the citizen before the law and could not be considered in any way by an American court or administrative authority.

As to the second question, the point presented was actually also without any relevance. The fact of bigamy could be assumed in any case only where in Europe a marriage had been concluded that was valid according to the laws of the state whose matrimonial bonds had not yet been dissolved according to this law. Due to existing regulations, however, no rabbi in Germany would have been willing to pronounce a divorce without, at the same time, also having been enabled to pronounce the dissolution of the marriage according to the law of the state. For this reason, there could be no case of bigamy in America that would not also be bigamy in Germany. However, this didn't preclude that in America, where the personal circumstances of the emigrant in his homeland were not followed up, some unlawful things took place but were never discovered. Since these illegalities were in contrast to the Jewish mentality that demanded order in matters of family relationships as the basis of stable Jewish social conditions in the communities, when such occurrences were discovered they were also discussed publicly. From the newly consolidating rabbinate in America, a special endeavor was expected to clear all the circumstances meaningful for Jewish marriage in America. This concerned, first of all, the issue of divorce in *agunah* cases that pended between Europe and America. Therefore in the case in question the Rabbinate was asked to speak up publicly.[21]

Vis-à-vis the impression given by the literature and the press that liquidations of marriages concluded in the European homeland stand prominently in the foreground of marriage problems of the new Jewish community in America, an entirely different reality did, in fact, arise. It was the consolidation of the European immigrant marriages by bringing over parts of the family that had still remained in Europe, and conclusion of new marriages in connection with persons in the old homeland that formed the greatest personal endeavors of the new immigrants since their problems in finding the right spouse could generally be solved only in connection with their native towns. When, therefore, brides were not already brought over with the immigrant or arrived afterwards the old homeland nevertheless remained the great reservoir from which candidates for marriage could procure brides.

Aside from the marriages that were bound to the old country, there were a number of mixed marriages—of Jewish immigrants out of the Jewish fold—mostly men. In part, such marriages were a result of the dearth of Jewish women at the remote places of American civilization and as such pioneer marriages they survived, permanent beyond all the stormy events of life. The results of mixed marriages in Europe, where fewer offspring were produced than in marriages between Jews, did not at that time pertain to life in America and the firmness of the matrimonial bond of such marriages was still strengthened by the blessings of children. Confirmation that such marriages continued harmoniously is presented also from the Jewish point of view at an early time: "The marriages are very often mixed but there is the greatest accord in most cases, and, where the mother is a Jewess, the children will be educated in her faith and often even if this is not the case. . . ." [22] In this respect American mixed marriages were in contrast with European marriages of this kind, at least on the average.

The stability of Jewish married life in America was looked upon by friend and foe as an essential cause of the economic rise of the Jew in the new world as demonstrated by the image of the Jewish married man as the patient, tireless, provider for his spouse and children, making his way in just then opened territories as a peddler during his days of merchant pioneering. Recognition of this kind is expressed in numerous products of descriptive and fictionized literature.[23] This has a special meaning also for mixed marriages, because the choice of Jewish husbands by gentile women is attributed to this image of the Jewish man as a good family provider.[24]

All in all, family life of the Jews in America was viewed as exemplary, and created the same good name for itself as European family life had in Europe. Even American popular humor, so often viewing it as a weakness of the Jews that they don't share the weaknesses of the American gentile socially, comes to a halt when the relationship of the Jew to his wife and children is concerned. Moreover, remarks on this question sometimes end with a salute to Jewish family life.[25]

In the same way, American Jewish marriages were also deemed excellent according to the yardstick of the European Jewish community. We find early testimony of this also in the European Jewish press of which the following is of importance because it also includes California. There were generally only distorted notions of the West and California among European Jews, and the sins of America seemed more generally to be happening "in the wild West." There, everything seemed possible— official polygamy in a whole territory and general laxity of marriage and morals and, in consequence, many divorces. Especially California, with a population composed of adventurers from different parts of the Union having come thither because of the gold rush, was of ill fame:

> Social conditions of our coreligionists are, all in all, satisfactory. As in the old world, the marriages of the Jews excel also in the new, and Jewish divorce belongs to that greatest of rarities also in California, where generally very loose morals at home and divorces among other religious communities are daily events. A Jewish newspaper in San Francisco [*the Voice of Israel*] had in pointing out these facts also alleged that the Jews take seriously the word "Those whom God has joined together, let no man put asunder." [26]

Nevertheless, there was at that time a difference in the frequency of divorce cases of Jews in San Francisco and in New York, however minimal the total number may appear according to later concepts. We get a hint of this from the angry remonstration of a New York editor about the revelations of a California Jewish newspaper (this was in 1858): "San Francisco, Cal. On referring to the *Gleaner* of September 29th, we find in the Rev. Dr. Eckman's Jeremiad—that of nine divorces which he had dispensed within four years, his services had only been remunerated in two cases, the other seven had forgotten to pay, thus discharging their wives and their debts by the same process.—California is a great State, producing more gold than happiness. Nine divorces in four years! We have only heard of one in this City in twenty years. We have united hundreds but we have never been asked to *dispense* a divorce. Dr. Eckman, we advise you hereafter to be paid in advance, or seriously speaking, do not officiate on such occasions. It is only the worthless that wish to be divorced from their marriage contracts; let them join the Mormons!" [27]

It was not until the second half of the nineteenth century, that divorces in America became a significant social factor. The necessity arose for individual religious denominations to make inquiries into detailed questions connected with it and to regulate them. At the same time the mirroring of divorce in fictional literature and drama became more and more frequent; the first sociological treatises concerning divorce appeared in the magazines in the forms of essays, and the first divorce figures for the whole of America became available. A little later, demands by citizens for changes in and a unification of all divorce laws in the states began to be heard.

The first usable figures report 9,937 divorces in America for the year 1867. In proportion to the whole population, a computation is made for 1870 amounting to a divorce quota of 0.29% (less than a third of one percent) per thousand persons.[28]

However, it was not the numbers that created the prevalent opinion about the occurrence of divorce, but actual experiences of life in the various regions of the country, especially in the West, and with different groups of the population. For instance, the West offered a variety of events and legal problems, the likes of which were not to be found in other parts of the country. No wonder that in the West divorce problems were discussed in louder tones in the newspapers than elsewhere! Observations of the attitude of certain groups to divorce were reported earlier there than elsewhere, and the general opinion that Jews were less frequently the subjects of divorce actions was essentially built on observations made in the West. In California, for instance, In 1854: . . . " 'Cosmopolite,' a writer in one of the daily papers, cites, as a remarkable fact, the fewness of divorces among the people of the Jewish nation, in which he is substantially correct." [29]

Even so, many years later (1880) the Middle West witnessed the same spectacle of the extreme rarity of Jewish divorces:

> Plenty of divorce cases before the courts of Hamilton County, as usual, and no Jewish name among them. We have watched for years the law reports of St. Louis, Louisville, Chicago and Cincinnati on this special point and found no Jews in the crowd. Judge

Storer, of this city, several years ago, had such a case before him.
On the day of trial the husband failed to appear and the Judge
adjourned the case, because, as he said, there appeared to be
something wrong about it. In his long practice he never had heard
of a case of divorce among Jews.[30]

Even in the much more densely populated East, and at the time that
the mass immigration of Eastern European Jews was already taking
place, a judge (a Judge), reporting on divorce happenings, remarked:

> Foreign born applicants for divorce would rank, in point of
> numbers, thus: Germans, including Austrians, Prussians, and all
> others speaking German, Bohemians, Poles, Scandinavians, Eng-
> lish, Scotch. To these may be added a few Irish and a few Jews,
> generally persons upon whom religious restraints have ceased to
> be operative.[31]

Even the crooked mirror of hostile wit was forced to reckon with this
fact:

A Business Proposition

> Why is it that there are so few divorces among the Jews? The
> chief reason is because the Jew looks upon marriage, like all of the
> other acts of this life, as a business proposition. It doesn't pay to
> marry any one with whom we may not be able to get along. . . .[32]

f) New Times

In the stable marriage relations of the formative period of the Jewish
community in America comprising essentially the adjustment of a whole
immigrant generation up to 1880, we learn only little of the inner pre-
conditions of divorce. Occasionally, a case described in more detail was
of news value by the fact that divorce among the Jews was so rare that
they could even be ignorant about its legal prerequisites, especially about
the lack of legal authority given to the divorce letter (*get*):

"Judge Otterbourg's decision [was] . . . that the divorce gained by the plaintiff against the sued husband by a divorce letter [*get*] has no legal validity in America, and that the couple is therefore to be considered as still married. According to the law quoted, Jews and Quakers are at liberty to marry according to the precepts of their religion but not to dissolve the matrimonial bond without permission of the court. Judge Otterbourg then inquired in detail into the occupational circumstances of both parties and finally obligated the husband to pay the plaintiff a weekly alimony of three and a half dollars. Don Juan Elias, however, decided to return to his wife because due to the crisis on the Exchange it is not possible for him, in addition to his bachelor household, to support a second household wth three and a half dollars a week." [33]

From the Jewish point of view, divorce was placed in the same category as that other anomaly, mixed marriage. For instance we are informed of a speech given by Simon Wolf in 1874: "He said intermarriage with Christians would produce unhappyness and misery, if not crime. . . . Two-thirds of our American divorces owe their origin to religious differences. . . ." [34] Divorce laws were not uniform from state to state in the United States, each having its own and sometimes quite different requirements, with the result that it was easy to obtain a divorce in some states and difficult in various degrees in others. The divorce rate was and probably still is higher in the western than in the eastern states: Illinois and Indiana were considered to have very high divorce rates, but California outstripped both.

Liberal divorce laws have always been symptomatic of a more liberal and progressive attitude toward women, since the privilege of getting a divorce was once, except in rare cases, the prerogative of husbands. The position of women in the Western states was legally and socially in advance of that of their sisters in the East. If we are to believe the male contemporary local observers, the Jewish wife, who shared her husband's early struggles and his financial success was unwilling to stay by him under less opulent circumstances. When the great fortunes built up by speculation were lost again through a change of fortune, the wife, not infrequently, was not of a mind any longer to remain a partner in social decline, whereas a mere thirty years earlier, the strength of the matrimonial bond in California, even under frontier conditions, had been acclaimed clamorously. An amateur statistician, who was by his own evaluation also a social critic, reported to a Jewish newspaper, in 1882, the result of his amateur enumeration of Jewish divorces in San Francisco during 1881. Among the twenty-nine persons seeking divorce, he wrote, there were "Jewesses who were anxious to rid themselves of the ties which bound them to men for whom they had no further use when their money was gone." [35] In saying this the reporter presupposes his classification of divorce cases to be generally known in the city and therefore so indisputable that no one could dare to deny it, and adds, furthermore, that he has taken the facts directly from the records of the court, and in addition, that in that year alone, a hundred eighty divorces took place in the city. He was, he claimed, absolutely certain that his fellow Jews in the community were strictly in accord with him as were all the readers of his report in the newspapers, that this proportion of Jewish divorce seekers in his city must be deemed a high one considering the accompanying circumstances. That these figures were a bad omen for the future was predicted gloomily: "I tell you we are marching on; and if a husband has not the necessary fixings for proper parties, he might as well turn over his establishment to the next best man and that is the truth of the affair." [36]

At this point, social criticism unerringly adhering to its analysis of the unwillingness of the woman to share her husband's decline, enters a new field, the question of mobility for a partner who has been disappointed in his intimate personal life, a mobility that became possible only in cases where an economic cut-off point had been reached by new living conditions. How far it was from here to such a development in a society layer where wealth and a comfortable life was general, is not yet apparent. But greater personal expectations of a partner in marriage were always apt to call out a justification for executing a divorce if the disappointment was final. The end was not yet predictable, at least at this stage of Jewish society life and especially not in respect to public opinion that was provoked by these events of mobility and, in the end, also shaped them. But it could not be very long before these new developments as consequence of new conditions took place, if we consider that not much later there were already prominent Jews among the voices pleading publicly for a new concept of divorce. Among them, for instance, in 1890, was Rabbi Solomon Schindler who demanded in a magazine article a consideration of divorce from the viewpoint of the new living conditions which had, in his opinion, essentially changed the basis of family life.[37] The big cities offered many an opportunity to loosen matrimonial bonds, and the Jewish wife no longer participated in the economic struggle of her husband as she did when his business was just beginning. Despite their slow multiplication, increasing cases of divorce fortified the inner consciousness of an awakening self-criticism, according to which one of the most prominent bulwarks of Jewish life against gentile standards was torn down. The assimilation effected by this, so the critics said, only proved that the Jew is the victim of the same social tendencies as the gentile.

g) Spinsterhood

In the mind of the traditional Jew, spinsterhood didn't exist as a social category formed by innate social forces of society. Where it was the religious duty of everyone to marry, no such category of unwed adults was left. When an American women's magazine published a discussion on sworn celibates, the Jewish attitude was described: "The Talmud is an outspoken opponent of celibacy, and regards marriage as a duty incumbent upon all. . . ." [38]

As to the specific American Jewish situation, it may be said, too, that nowhere was spinsterhood a precondition of the adjustment of the Jewish individual to the new country; the Westward movement of the immigrant, especially, was not dependent on spinsters to take care of the old folk home, as was often the case with non-Jews. Social forces worked on the founding of families among Jews in the West, and marriage was a natural prerequisite, in time involving unmarried males too. In later years, when there were already many marriageable females in the big cities, Jewish mobile merchants, most of all itinerant peddlers, went there to find mates. The Jewish women's press gives us illuminating reports on this search for wives that usually took place on the High Holy Days when the peddler came to town.[39]

However, the trend to industrialization in America worked against a balance of the number of marriageable persons among Jews, too; in the big cities it was women who were in surplus. At the end of the century the unwed woman had become a publicly discussed social category and was, to a certain extent, conspicuous in Jewish life, too. It was a sheer literary curiosity that a newly founded American fashion magazine gave the image of spinsterhood in the words of Israel Zangwill's "The Old Maid's Club": "Marriages are made in heaven, but old maids go there." [40] The economic independence of the unmarried woman who was now able to enter the professions and, in any case, to be self-supporting, made her less anxious to marry just any available candidate in order to have a home of her own and economic security. The *American Jewess* remarks: "Nowadays a woman who doesn't marry is not such an unenviable creature after all." [41]

h) Social Aspects of Intermarriage for the Jewish Woman

As a social factor within the Jewish community, intermarriage arose late in America, and became recognizable only when thorough urbanization of American Jewry had taken place with its majority in big cities. But the dangers for the existence and growth of the Jewish community were foreseen and reacted to even when mixed marriages were rare occurrences:

> Some there may be who have been lured by personal attractions, by fascinating manners, or by the glitter of wealth, to unite themselves with the stranger; and parents there may be, who, after a short estrangement, have clasped them again to their bosoms; and some there are, who have professed to live as Jews with Christian wives, but these cases are rare; and though friends and family have not in all cases looked upon them with the cold eye of disapproval, yet some considered that if child or friend through wilful and selfish act, chose to separate themselves from their kindred they were perfectly justified, and felt it to be their duty to keep within the barrier that the erring one had placed between them: and that the ties of affection thus rudely severed, could never be re-united.[42]

Such private information to a Jewish newspaper in England is confirmed there editorially a short time later by a notice there:

American News

We find from the *Occident,* that intermarriages of Jews with Gentiles have taken place in America, to an extent deserving of loud remonstrance.[43]

In social intercourse developed in the course of time, precautionary measures were taken by parents with marriageable daughters:

> . . . The cause is rather to be found in the fear, which is quite common among even the most intelligent of our people, that the free, social intercourse of Jews and Christians would lead to intermarriages. This feeling is so prevalent, particularly among the Germans, that few Jewish fathers or brothers, no matter how lax in their religious observances, would think of introducing a Christian gentleman to their daughters or sisters.[44]

First, and most obvious, was the fact that, in most cases, it was the Jewish man who was involved. This usual case, normally under the conditions of life in the big cities, represents the economic rise of the gentile partner through the Jewish husband as family provider: "It is conceded on all sides, and no one knows it better than the Christian girls who have married Jews, that the best husbands and providers are those of the Semitic race." [45] On the other hand, it is asserted that a gentile husband is "improvident and will not go out and peddle, and tear and wear and climb steep mountains in Indian territories in order to keep his wife and children comfortable." [46] Such statements rest only on economic observations; but other claims were made that rested simply and solely on the observed attitude of Jewish women to gentile men: ". . . while one hundred Jews will be taken in by the blandishments of an American girl, not one percent of our Jewish girls will care to ally themselves to a Christian." [47]

In time, this situation created a kind of imbalance, especially in bigger cities, leaving a certain percentage of Jewish girls without a choice of marriageable Jewish males. This circumstance, together with the breakdown of other social barriers and the example of intermarrying Jewish brothers and relatives before her own eyes, affected the Jewish woman, too. Elopement and marriage of a Jewish girl to a non-Jewish man was not so rare any more.[48] A much discussed case was the elopement and marriage of Isaac Mayer Wise's daughter to James Malony, a lawyer and the son of an Episcopalian minister. However, more often, the inter-marriage represented an economic and social step down for the woman. As to figures, there were, for example, in San Francisco, in 1883, one hundred sixty-three gentile women married to Jewish men, and only thirty-nine Jewesses to gentile men.[49] In many cases, Jewish women who intermarried raised their children in the Jewish faith.

The rising importance of marriage for money contributed to the rise of intermarriage of Jewish girls. Where not enough money as dowry was forthcoming to drive a Jewish man to propose, the girl risked a social step down:

"Kisses go by favor—marriages by the endowment plan. Who am I and what is my life?" asks the marriageable girl of sense, "unless I have the wherewithal to give a husband a start? And hence it is that another girl in Oakland has given herself away in marriage this week—Miss Jaffee to Mr. Murphy—because our Jewish boys want coin no matter about the hunchback or previous condition. Love is synonymous with a certified check." [50]

The Jewish girl went through a whole chain of difficult experiences connected with these problems, that were not helped by the social criticism of the Jewish community.[51] Only later, when the professional independence of Jewish girls became a reality, was a more favorable position for them created on the marriage market as well.

i) Matchmaking

The period when the dearth of women on the Western frontier ensured that any young woman would be snatched up in marriage became a thing of the past. Only in some remote places of the Far West did it survive, sometimes to the end of the century. Thus, we read in the *American Israelite* a dispatch from Helena, Montana, in 1873:

> . . . twelve Jewish families and a large number of young men of our faith. But I am sorry to say that there is not one young Jewish lady

Deborah.

52508

Ein Beiblatt zum „Israelite," gewidmet den Töchtern Israels.

Herausgegeben von
Bloch & Co.,
No. 43 Dritte Straße, Ecke der Sycamore.

„Es werde Licht."

Redigirt von
Isaac M. Wise,
Redacteur des „Israelite."

No. 1. | **Cincinnati, den 24. August, 1855.** | **Erster Jahrgang.**

Die Deborah.

Endlich, endlich ist sie da, die liebenswürdige Deborah mit ihrem blendend weißen Gewande und rabenschwarzen Augen und kommt traulich gegangen ins Haus eines jeden Freundes, und spendet Belehrung und bietet Vergnügen mit lächelndem Munde.

Endlich ist es da das Weib der feurigen Begeisterung für Israel und seine Lehre. Wie einst Deborah, die Heldentochter Israels, die muthigen Schaaren ihres Volkes führte in die Heldenschlacht am Kischon, zu züchtigen den übermüthigen Feind, und siegend heimkehrte an der Spitze ihrer jubelnden Getreuen, heim mit Sang und Klang, heim zur Gerechtigkeit und Volksbeglückung, heim zu Israels Glauben und seiner Mission; so soll diese Namenstochter stehen kampfgerüstet stets gegen alle Feinde des Judenthums, von Innen und von Außen, und das heilige Feuer aufopfernder Begeisterung im Herzen, gerüstet mit der Macht des Wortes, soll sie kämpfen und siegen, und heimkehren und richten und lehren mit Vernunft und Gottesfurcht.

Endlich ist sie da, die Deborah, die Biene, die ewig thätige, immer sammelnde, Honig spendende. Und sammeln soll sie die Blüthen von Jeschuruns Gefilden, in den Balsamgärten jüdischer Geister, und spenden den süßen Honig in reichem Maße.

Endlich ist sie da, die langverheißene Deborah, jubelt der „Israelite", der klagte gar rührend: „Es ist nicht gut für den Menschen, allein zu sein, und so machten wir ihm eine Gehülfin, die wie ihn sei, und mit ihm durchwandre die weiten Ländereien unseres neuen Vaterlandes, und helfend und treu ihm zur Seite stehe. Wenn der „Israelite" mit Ernst und Würde spricht zu dem Manne, und lehrt und mahnt und erzählt, so soll die Deborah sprechen die lieblichen Klänge der Mutter, in der Deine Kindheit lallte, mit Sanftmuth und Zartheit sprechen zu den Töchtern Israels, lehren, erzählen und unterhalten in anmuthiger Weise.

Deutsche Israeliten! Es geschieht in unserm Lande so wenig für die Belehrung und geistige Unterhaltung der Damen, daß wir glauben, die Deborah müsse jedem willkommen sein, und Niemand wird sie seiner Frau, seinen Töchtern oder Schwestern entziehen. Wir wollten eben sagen, wir werfen uns in die Arme der Frauen, aber das geht nicht an, und da müssen wir sagen, wir wenden uns vertrauensvoll an die verehrten Damen mit der Bitte, dieses Unternehmen gehörig zu unterstützen. Das Blatt ist so billig, daß es nur durch zahlreiche Unterstützung bestehen kann, und darauf rechnen wir.

Schicket die Deborah recht zahlreich nach Deutschland, damit unsere Freunde im alten Vaterlande überzeugt werden, daß wir noch erglühen für den Glauben unserer Väter, und mit aller Kraft dafür arbeiten.

Werfet das Blatt nicht weg; wenn der erste Band vollendet ist, giebt's ein schönes Buch für's Haus. Zeigt es Euren Nachbarn, damit sie das Blatt bestellen. Schicket uns gute Aufsätze und Neuigkeiten, was auch immer in jüdischen Kreisen vorfallen möge. Es wird die Deborah das verbindende Glied bilden in der Kette des Judenthums zwischen Amerika und Deutschland; sie wird Jenen wichtige Dienste leisten, die nicht englisch lesen, und jedem willkommen sein, der das Judenthum verehrt, und seine Muttersprache liebt.

Und so schicken wir hinaus diese Tochter Israels, und empfehlen sie dem verehrten Publikum zur geneigten Aufnahme.

Das israelitische Weib.

Griechen und Römer widmeten den Frauen die schönsten und herrlichsten Erzeugnisse ihrer Muse, und die schönsten und duftigsten Blumen und Blüthen ihrer Dichtung, und nimmer griffen sie stärker und stärker in die Saiten ihrer Lyra, als wenn sie sangen von ihrer Größe, ihrer Aufopferungsfähigkeit ihrer Liebe. Sie waren nicht mehr irdische Wesen, sondern Göttinnen, welche das Leben erhöhten, veredelten und versüßten, und alle großen, schönen und erhabenen Thaten des Mannes, und alle Heldengestalten Roms und Griechenlandes, und alle Größe und alle Hoheit, und alle Majestät und alle Macht, was sie schön nannten, und edel und erhaben, es war nichts anders als der begeisterte Ausfluß ihrer Huldinnen. Das Weib war ihre Göttin im Hause — das Weib war ihre Göttin im Kriege — das Weib war ihnen Alles in Allem — und selbst ein Weib mußte aus dem Haupte ihres Gottes Jupiter entstehen. So besangen sie ihre größten Dichter Homer, Virgil und Andere, deren Töne noch heute, nach Jahrtausenden wiederklingen, denn ihr Stoff ist allerdings dem Erhabensten der Schöpfung, dem Weibe, geweiht.

Ist aber blos das römische und griechische Weib es werth, daß die schönsten nie verwelkenden Blüthen und Blumen der Poesie sie begrünzen? Hat Israel nicht auch seine Töchter Jeschuruns, erhaben und groß in allen Beziehungen des Lebens? Hat es nicht auch seine Ideale, höher und größer als alle Völker des Alterthums? Leuchten sie nicht ebenfalls hervor als nie verlöschende Sterne in Geschichte und Poesie und Leben? Und so mögen denn die Erstlinge dieser Blätter Israels Frauen und Jungfrauen gewidmet, ihrem Andenken geweihet sein. Wir übergehen die ersten sinnigen und in-

First page of the first issue of *Deborah*. (*Die Deborah*, v. 1, August 24, 1855, p. 1).

in our midst. There were three in the city, and they were engaged to be married within a few months of their appearance among us, and all did very well. To those young ladies who are anxious to marry and want good husbands I would suggest that they take the advice of the late-lamented Horace Greeley and "go West." [52]

To make this kind of a decision was not easy for "many a Northern girl," whose blood chilled at the prospect of leaving the civilization of urban life for the unknown wilderness. "The very word Texas seems to vibrate with a sort of horrible sound when whispered in the confiding ears of a girl from Cincinnati or St. Louis. . . ." Still, it is significant that even the need for women did not prevent the men of the Butte, Montana, mining camp from recognizing that among the men of the German Jewish old immigration marrying for money was a completely accepted fact of life, and from feeling that even in Butte a dowry might rightfully be expected:

> · . . . we have no weddings because of the scarcity of Jewish ladies. I believe that a *shadkhen* would prosper here, but he would have to bring along a supply of goodlooking and rich girls because our young men are shrewd business people and do not buy a cat in a bag. . . .

The surplus of marriageable girls in cities created a situation of brisk competition on the marriage market where marriage for money took on ever greater importance. In times like these, the matchmaker came into his own, his function taking on new dimensions and directions. The problem of a disproportionate number of women to men was most severe in the cities of the Atlantic Coast—in particular in New York—where immigrants early on made use of the services of professional *shadkhens*. The Jewish women's newspaper, *Deborah*, gives a semi-humorous description of their activities:

> . . . Every schadkhen always had six to twelve girls on hand and picked the young men eager to marry, who, being peddlers, were without acquaintances in New York. He ordered his man on the

holidays in the White Garden. "Look there at the blue one" . . .
meaning, to be sure, the color of her dress. . . . In this way, often
two to three hundred girls came together there. . . . The schadkhen
introduced the man to his client . . . the marriage subsequently
worked in most cases just as well as those which are effected nowadays in the big parlors of the upper classes.[53]

The critical point in mating was reached when the second generation
of German Jewish immigrants grew into the marriage market. The character of all marriage factors, valid up to that time, was changed by the
upcoming urbanization. At that time it was already decided that the
overwhelming majority of American Jews were destined to live in big
cities. The social picture in the big communities rapidly became uniform, and one of its most prominent aspects was the changed marriage-
market. Marriage for money came more and more to the fore and took
on a specific American color. Both the young man and the young woman, looked for future sustenance, and the standard for security in
marriage was defined by the economic developments in the country. The
big cities in the West, different because of their economic conditions,
formed regional marriage markets. Thus, girls living at home with their
parents in smaller cities were at a disadvantage, since the marriageable
men could go to the larger city for a wife. Their aging fathers had bigger businesses and marriageable daughters too, and their sons-in-law
could be established for life by a junior partnership in their businesses.
In the following cry of a Milwaukee woman we find a realistic description of the mutual influence of three Western marriage markets, Milwaukee losing out, Chicago winning, and Cincinnati, the "Queen of
the West" pronounced the victor in advance:

Milwaukee, Wis. . . . What shall we do with our girls?
Upon this question I desire to say a few words knowing that it is
a topic very dear to the heart of many a good mother in Milwaukee. Now, dear reader, allow me to introduce you to my subject by
imparting the valuable information if a young man that we have
to-day, in our midst, in round numbers, at least seventy-five Jewish

young ladies of all styles, sizes and complexions, varying in age from seventeen to thirty years, consequently marriageable. Ay, there's the rub. Not that our young ladies are less attractive, less educated or less worthy of the best of husbands that the world nowadays produces. No, but there appears to be a scarcity of this much-sought-for commodity in this part of the country, and if perchance, an opportunity does appear to be dawning for a good-looking, intelligent and highly respected girl to throw herself away upon a second-class "commercial tourist," at least; whereby she hopes finally to rid herself of the everlasting sympathy that is expressed for her by her uncles and aunts, and the fears and heartaches of her parents lest she is destined to remain an old maid; yes, when this poor girl has lavished many of her most precious hours at club parties and picnics and other entertainments, and she has even condescended at times to pay him undeserved compliments as to his wisdom, good manners, etc., all at once this Knight of the "Big Trunk" becomes imbued with the knowledge of his greatness and a desire to travel in search of a wife. The immensity of Chicago business houses, owned by old fathers with many daughters, loom up before him in all their grandeur, inspiring him with the ambition to follow the throng of young men on that great highway to wealth, fame and opulence; and should his manifold virtues not be fully appreciated at this great market of the West, he beholds another vision. Cincinnati, with her alluring golden smiles, beckons to him, signifying her delight to receive him with open arms. Ah, what chances are there for a modest, unpretentious, fortuneless Milwaukee girl against such competition? We give it up, and will allow the young ladies themselves, or some one else so inclined, to offer the proper solution to this important problem. Of course there are some few happy exceptions on the marriage question occasionally here. . . .[54]

The Milwaukee girl stood up here for all her sisters in her accusation of Jewish society. No wonder, therefore, that in the answer given to her all kinds of social questions connected with the marriage problem were

discussed—including the education of young women. Some of what was said appears to have been justified by later developments, other advisers were fine in diagnosis, but quacks in respect to therapy:

What should we do with our girls?

Our Milwaukee correspondent asks, What should we do with our girls? Do precisely as we do with our boys. A wise somebody says he who brings up his son without a trade, profession or occupation, makes a highwayman of him. Train your girls for some special work, no matter if it be housework, some congenial life work. You owe it to them the same as to your boys. Those young ladies of the middle class who are brought up too genteel to do anything except watch and wait for a husband, are in my eyes pitiable. Oftentimes it is the good mother, whose daughters happiness lies so near her own heart, who is responsible for this. Any effort on the daughter's part to put her talents, if she possesses any, to use, is strenuously opposed, on the ground that she must assist in domestic duties. 'Tis better, the house mother thinks, to learn to mix up puddings, than to mix up gases, and it certainly is a part of woman's education to know how to cook, especially for those young ladies who were born a generation too soon, before all avenues of employment were opened to women, or colleges admitted both sexes, and women of ability were debarred from receiving that higher education which fits for intellectual achievements. One can't blame young men for not marrying until they can support a wife or if they do, for marrying one rich enough to keep them. To look upon marriage as an easy means of maintenance, is not only to lower the dignity of womanhood, but to degrade the holy state of matrimony. There is a sphere of usefulness for the single, and work laid out for them as well as the married. We know that old-fashioned educators of female youth taught the doctrine of lovely dependence and charming weakness, but that day and hour is past. We have not all got protectors who protect, nor is it right or in accordance with nineteenth-century ideas, to burden a young brother with the care of unmarried sisters who would have been mentally and physically as able as he to take care of themselves had they been taught that self-support was not only proper, but necessary since, as Lillian rightly says, there is a scarcity of husband supply. Show me a girl who has some healthy pursuit, and you show me one to whom marriage will come as it does to man, not as the end and aim of existence, but as a by-play. In the natural selection which Darwin talks about, it is not romance, but reality, that guides our young men.[55]

However, marriageable girls could certainly not wait until the issue was decided by society. Under these circumstances, criticism uttered aloud could do no more than act as a stimulus to keep an awareness of the problem.

But what could be seen even with closed eyes was that matrimony for money entrenched itself ever more and more, and that the first signs of modern tendencies like women's professional education didn't change the marriage market to any rapid degree. Parents were again seen re-enacting in their old, European roles now in America:

". . . it is a purely mercantile transaction, entered into between two business men, who barter away the happiness of their children for so much coin. . . . We rarely hear among the Jews, that wealthy young man has taken unto himself a worthy poor young lady as his wife. . . . In other words, the girl without coin, no matter how well educated, how nicely behaved or how richly endowed by nature, has to take a back seat, while the graceless butterfly, with nothing than her father's large store and big feet to recommend her, takes the pie." [56]

Slowly, there also arose a kind of youthful protest against what was conceived of as a parental scheme, marriage for money without considering the daughter's feelings. News of elopements set the relationship of parents with daughters in the limelight. This at once brought to the surface social criticism of the entire issue with the purpose of rehabilitating daughters and leading parents to the right path:

Daughters

In what we are about to say, we wish to disavow at once the intention to refer to any one of the recent elopements which have startled the reflecting and amused the thoughtless. These cases have followed one upon another with such hurried frequency that some consideration should be given to the operating causes.

. . . When the ripening years bring the daughter near to a "marketable age," then plots, schemes and careful calculations disturb parental breasts. Busy eyes spy out each friend she makes, lest peradventure some bold, presuming man may cross their purposes. The bond-slave to be trafficked with must be well watched. Her affections disregarded: her feelings ignored. Like horses at the country fair, she is to be "trotted out" in public places for general inspection, and in the privacy of the parlor, before the silent circle of prospective purchasers, her "accomplishments" are to be duly exhibited. Rumors rend the air of the large "bonus" which the anxious father will endow him who takes his daughter off his hands. Should she by some mishap, notwithstanding all the careful surveillance, have given her affection to one who does not meet the financial ideas of her parents, then the floodgates of reproaches, curses, vituperation, threats and coarse insults be heaped upon her head.

. . . It is time for fathers to realize that the "cruel parent" business is antiquated and only survives as a but for burlesque. They must recognize the facts of life, and treat their daughters as human beings, with hands to work, with brains free to think, and hearts subject to generous and noble and pure emotions.[57]

All that the older generation could do once its conscience was aroused, was to wait for the results of its endeavors along beaten paths, such as the arranging of fairs where boys and girls could meet. The comparison of these results with those of earlier years were not wanting:

It is surprising that so few matrimonial engagements can be attributed to the late Fair at the Brunswick. We have waited patiently for six weeks and more and have yet to learn of many such interesting "results." We have ever regarded engagements and fairs as effect and cause as closely as a healthy rainfall and the wholesale visit of the Quaker brotherhood. It cannot be that this last was an exception. Some cynical youth may suggest that, being managed exclusively by ladies, the fair may not have had the usual positive quality that was conducive to matrimony in former years; but this suggestion is clearly crude. The management is not at fault and the lady attendants were certainly as charming as their elder sisters who in past years presided at similar entertainments. Explanations are in order and will be gladly received.[58]

Naturally, such explanations differed according to who gave them, men or women. Men, as usual, complained about women's lack of understanding and inability to recognize that the pressures of business limited their cultivation of dancing and other social pastimes.

The marriage outlook

Owing to various causes, the summer season which has just closed has not been remarkable for engagements. Of course, a few are announced, but the number is so limited as to excite surprise. There have been the usual moonlight nights, walks on the cliff, strolls along quiet country roads, hops, dimly lit verandas, drives, rows on the lake, hill-climbing, convenient showers, scheming Mammas, docile girls, etc., etc., but unaccountably little powder seems to have caught fire, and few men have been brought down.

It is useless to trace this abnormal state of affairs to the dearth of young men out of town. In the most crowded resorts, where at least for one or two days weekly there is a phalanx of eligible gentlemen, the same peculiarity was observable, a certain dampness in the atmosphere which made matches fail to strike. Nor would it be just to blame fond mammas, who the entire season have been indefatigable, often frantic, in their exertions to secure the coveted result, and who are utterly at a loss to account for their wretched failure. Whatever other causes are to be held responsible, it is clear

that one important factor is not to be omitted—the growing inclination of young people to be philosophical on the subject of marriage. Of course when philosophy enters the brain, romance flies out
of the heart.

The views which many eligible young people hold in reference
to love and marriage would scandalize their grandparents. They
regard marriage as a lottery with few prizes and countless blanks.
They dread the uncertainties of married life, the thousand social
entanglements, the slavery to somebody's whims. . . . If they are
wealthy, they fear, that their wealth is the magnet that attracts;
if they are poor, their poverty which repels. Reflecting on the fortunes of their married friends, they begin to doubt whether marriage necessarily ensures happiness. They are sharp in their
remarks on engaged people, and deplore the condition of those who
marry to secure cooks or bankers. .   [59]

How great were the worries, not only of the mothers, but also of
fathers, we may see in a number of social parental situations connected
with these concerns:

The Orphan Bride

. . . The fact that this was the first wedding in the Asylum was
duly commented upon; and as one gentleman remarked quietly,
"Now that one girl is married, there will be little trouble in marrying the rest," the gentleman evidently a family man, who appreciated the parental anxiety in obtaining a match for the first daughter, but felt uneasiness as to the fate of the others.[60]

In spite of all the headaches of individuals and communities on the
problems of marriage, the objective situation was that a brisk welling
up of the marriage market occurred in good times, as, for instance, in
New York, "From the most authentic sources at our command, we find
there are about four hundred marriages among the Israelites in this city
yearly, while in the kingdom of Great Britain, including Scotland,
Ireland and Wales, there are about two hundred and fifty solemnized"[61]

Mrs. I. N. Spiegelberg president of The Ladies Sewing Society of the Hebrew Orphan Asylum. (Official *Souvenir Book of the Fair in Aid of the Educational Alliance and the Hebrew Orphan Asylum, New York,* 1895, p. 57).

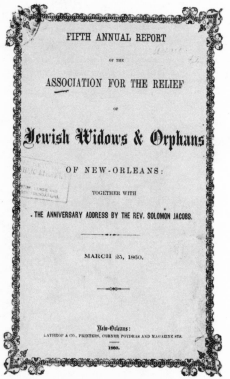

FIFTH ANNUAL REPORT

OF THE

ASSOCIATION FOR THE RELIEF

OF

Jewish Widows & Orphans

OF NEW-ORLEANS:

TOGETHER WITH

. THE ANNIVERSARY ADDRESS BY THE REV. SOLOMON JACOBS.

MARCH 25, 1860.

New-Orleans:
LATHROP & CO., PRINTERS, CORNER POYDRAS AND MAGAZINE STS.
1860.

Cover of the Fifth Annual Report of the Association for the Relief of Jewish Widows and Orphans of New Orleans.

—to a quick letdown of the marriage market upon a reversal of the economy:

> Marriages affected by the recent Panic
>
> We state facts, in asserting that in the marriage line, as well as in commercial circles, there has been suspicion as well as extension. The *chazonim* [cantors] have suffered considerably from the decrease of marriage fees. Births appear to go on as much as usual. We earnestly hope that times will improve, and that engagements, on a sound basis, will soon be the order of the day.[62]

This tendency did not, of course, affect only Jews. Seeking a match by advertising in newspapers was practiced early by Jews in Germany in a more or less dignified manner. The appearance of this usage in the American Jewish press was only the application of an already proven procedure in other countries. For the student exploring it, there can be no doubt about the seriousness of the Jewish marriage advertisement. Nevertheless, by placing and repeating certain types of advertsisements, the impression is created that no immediate search from partner to partner is at issue, but only the professional endeavors of *shadkhens,* who were analyzing the marriage market in the same way as any other producer tested the market for his product.

A good example of a Jewish paterfamilias worrying about his unmarried daughter and finally deciding to try the new method of advertising, was a characteristic sample of this kind of endeavor among Jews. Reprinted in the Jewish press in England, it reads:

> "Matrimonial." We clip the following from a Californian Jewish paper: "The advertiser, a gentleman of the Jewish faith, of the most respectable social standing and in good circumstances, but living somewhat retired and quiet, conscious of the purity of his motives, and the high integrity of his acts, has no hesitation in adopting this mode of announcing his desire to have introduced to him some respectable and honorable man of the same faith as himself, to whom he can give his daughter in marriage. Riches of

course acceptable, but any honorable man with a start in life will not be objectionable. The advertiser thinks it as well to state that his child is not a perfect beauty; very good looking, young, well educated, of domestic habits and brought up to walk in the right path. Communications will be received and attended to with all the sacred honour which the subject is entitled to. . . ." [63]

In time, serious thought emerged as to the ethical basis of such marriages. An evaluation of all the elements of marriage for money or that were believed to be only motivated by money, occasionally calls forth a voice which at least find some vindication for the marriage partners if not for the scheming parents. In this, the dignity of the girl is upheld first, but the young man is also not considered to be a person without feeling. Thus the ideal basis of marriage is held intact despite all the temptations of money for the rich girl. [64]

CHAPTER EIGHT

The Education of German Jewish Women

a) Problems and Institutions

The peculiar educational problems of girls did not arise during the years of early childhood. Until the public school emerged, private instruction of small children was given in homes or in elementary schools of Jewish communities.[1] With this age group's general schooling later taken over by the public school, there remained only religious instruction to take care of. Jewish communities fulfilled this duty by providing religious schools for both sexes. In large measure, Sunday schools were conducted by partly voluntary instructors who were women, and later they became an overwhelming majority in girls' as well as boys' classes.[2]

Material for instruction in these schools was created early by women. Isaac Leeser introduces one such textbook of 1845 with the following words:

> This time it is a lady who has drawn her first breath in America, and who is, despite the absence of a European education, imbued with high thought and deep reflection. All she desires is to be admitted to the ranks of those who defend and expound the immutable principles on which Judaism is founded, . . . the American Jewess wishes to remain unknown and do good without having the public gaze directed to herself. . . .[3]

The author herself pleads for tolerance as a Jewish woman and as a writer: "This little book . . . the mere fact of its having been composed by a Jewess for the instruction of Jewish children will not cause it, if otherwise approved, to be rejected by the Christian community . . ."[4] As the years went by, an ever greater part of instruction material was composed by women. Furthermore, as long as general elementary instruction was given in Jewish community schools, their staff also had a number of female teachers, especially for English.

Public awareness and discussion of adequate instruction for girls therefore only concerned post-elementary schooling. Here, the whole concept of the position of the Jewish woman in the family and in the community as well as her personal views on life are mirrored. Traditional ideas appear side by side with new general demands for girls' education as sponsored in gentile circles. The existing educational institutions mired in old ways, and the new desired paths of women were in the limelight of public discussion.

The predominant school type, in accord with an old concept whose models were admired in England and Germany, was the "academy," "höhere Töchterschule," or finishing school—where a girl received a kind of educational veneer in languages, literature and music, and that for Jewish girls was embroidered with religious instruction and a smattering of Hebrew. This is what the future parents had seen in Germany and preserved as an ideal in their memories. Such schools, often combined with a boarding school, sprang up in America and we find them advertised in the files of Jewish newspapers throughout these years. Boarding out was not accepted without certain doubts, writes Leeser in the *Occident* (1843):

> Now, in the abstract, we disapprove of boarding schools, deeming, as we do, domestic education to be of paramount importance. But as people will support such establishments, and as circumstances may occur when it is absolutely requisite to find a home for the scholar under the teacher's roof, we are pleased. . . . The course of instruction includes writing, arithmetic, geography, astronomy, grammar, composition, philosophy, history, mythology, with all the branches of an English education.
>
> Instruction will also be given in Hebrew, the modern languages, music, singing, drawing, etc." [5]

Boarding at a school at that time could very well represent a status symbol where only parents of considerable means could afford to send

Cover of the Eleventh Annual
Report of the Jewish Training
School of Chicago.

✤ELEVENTH ANNUAL REPORT

OF THE

Jewish Training School

OF CHICAGO.

FOR

1899-1900.

Girls Social Room. (Official *Souvenir Book of the Fair in Aid of the Educational Alliance*, 1895, p. 17).

their children. Blessed with many children, only parents of the upper middle class could afford this luxury. Boarding schools, therefore, also provided day-classes.[6]

In exceptional cases wealthy parents even sent their daughters to boarding schools (*Pensionate*) in Germany and occasionally advertisements of such schools appeared in the American Jewish press.

As status symbols the gentile "academies" surmounted anything the Jewish girls' boarding school could offer. A considerable number of Jewish parents were willing to trust their children to these boarding schools, but not all the schools were ready to receive Jewish girls. In the eyes of many gentile parents the presence of Jewish girls at their girls' school would mean a weakening of its status. In any case we know that when a school resolved to become interdenominational, it had to count on diminishing numbers of pupils:

> In private schools the repugnance is more manifest, and is on the part of the parents rather than of children. Jewish parents do not object to the coeducation of their progeny with that of non-Jews. Many professed Christians oppose it. An able and experienced woman teacher, author of an esteemed volume on the education of girls and the proprietor of a private school, suffered a reduction in the number of her pupils, among whom was the daughter of a cosmopolitan Christian editor, from a hundred ten to sixty or seventy, because she admitted Jewesses. Where reasons for the withdrawal of patronage were assigned, it was evident, that the caste spirit, as well as alleged peculiarities in the Semitic damsels, did much to formulate them. Private Hebrew seminaries are not open to the same objection, perhaps because admission into even the best of them is not generally desired.[7]

In part, the unwillingness of gentile parents to share private educational institutions with Jews were misgivings about the higher grades that Jewish girls achieved at such schools: "Still, notwithstanding these drawbacks, it is an admitted fact, that Jewesses head their classes at school." [8]

There were also many parents that did not scruple to entrust their daughters to convent schools, which was especially the case in small western communities. Occasionally, a refusal to receive them could happen for religious reasons which was accepted as reasonable by the Jewish press:

Jewesses in Convents

Some indignation is expressed in the press at the exclusion of Jewesses from the Sacred Heart Convent School at Omaha. . . . We see no reason for censoring the Mother Superior for requesting the Jewish girls to leave for "not accepting the doctrines of worship of the convent." The request seems reasonable enough. . . . In brief, the Jewish girl in a Christian institution is in a false position.[9]

The offensive remark "she is only a Jew girl" was occasionally heard in places of instruction and reported in a Jewish youth magazine.[10]

The educational results of all these private academies, boarding and convent schools were hard hit by criticism at the same time as the demands arose for a new education:

Most of the female academies or colleges are founded by religious societies and stand under the direct influence of their ministers. . . . pupils, those of the Jewish faith not excepted, were required to attend the chapel every morning. . . . we should have a female academy, where the daughters of Israel would be offered an opportunity to finish their education, and have the benefit of a thorough and enlightened religious instruction. . . .[11]

However, where parents had undertaken to avoid such institutions and base the education of their daughters on private instruction only, the results were, in respect to religious affiliation, even more disastrous:

They procure her a finishing music teacher, a finishing singing teacher, a drawing master, a *gouvernante* to keep up her French, teach her to sew, knit etc., and a Hebrew instructor to impart to her the alphabet. . . . With this last teacher, she becomes first disgusted, finds Hebrew too tedious, too difficult, cries over her lessons and her too indulgent parents . . . dismiss the master, whom they should have engaged first and sent away last, which course, through their want of proper religious feelings, they reversed, engaging him last and dismissing him first.[12]

It was *Deborah,* the only German-language Jewish women's newspaper in America, that in 1855 combined its criticism of raising "parlor" ladies in academies with the proposal for a new type of girls' school, no doubt partly influenced by the experiments with Jewish schools in Germany:

> A girls' school connected with an industrial school is the essential thing, and should be the next school to be established. . . . Rich people can afford to send their daughters to distant and famous girls' schools; the middle class is deprived of all means of giving them an adequate education.[13]

Such advocates of a new education were, however, at that time still gravely handicapped. The girl of German Jewish descent, although already native-born, stood only at the threshold of the kind of modern women's education which could have given her a dignified profession. It was the conviction of her parents that the only goal of education should be to make her marriageable. Under such a system, her intellectual inclinations could only lessen her chances to marry: "But what if a young Jewess has her own ideas about a woman's destiny? Why, she is put down as "strongminded." She is spoken of as a girl "out of her sphere." . . ."[14]

That all her thoughts were marriage-oriented because the sole idea of marriage was inculcated in her mind so that she was unfit to do anything else, remained the criticism of girls' education through many years. The discussion of this theme was endlessly carried on through the columns of the Jewish press and finally spilled over into non-Jewish women's journals.[15] The attitude of the *Jewish Messenger* toward the complaints of the *Israelite* in this respect, is defensive: "The *Jewish Messenger* which has taken a good position on the education of women, speaks sensibly for the girls who have left school, because no provision is made for growing girls to improve themselves in any respect after leaving school."

b) German Education in America

In the background of the problem of the Jewish family concerning the German language, affecting the Jewish woman much more than her husband, stood the problem of the German synagogue and its future in America. To preserve it with German sermons and religious instruction of the children in German appeared to be a goal worthy of the greatest effort of men who were disciples of German Enlightenment and had been active participants in the German revolution—or, at least, her silent admirers who formed a periphery around that movement. A policy of strengthening the German synagogue in the Jewish community seemed to be possible, especially when viewed from the standpoint that with such a policy, an inclination toward the cultural institutions of the Germans in America and their support for a German milieu outside the synagogue could be found.

But in due course even enthusiastic adherence to the ideal of a German synagogue confronted the stark reality that a native-born Jewish generation was lost for such a cause. This was true even among persons who were emotionally strongly bound to the German language and culture.[16] Stalwarts on the side of German were even to be found later on, but could do no more than give testimony of their good will, enabling us to gain an insight into their hopes:

> The *Leader* has been earnest in its defence of Germanism, because we have recognized the advantages to be derived therefrom, and we hope soon to witness a movement from the Pacific to the Atlantic that will establish the German language in its true position in the Jewish community. To our German Israelites its introduction and permanence is a sacred duty. . . .[17]

Thus the German synagogue lived on a little longer in a twilight between those opting for its future in English, and the efforts of dedicated men to create a link to cultural institutions of the Germans in America by teaching German literature and history there.[18] For the German Jewish young women, a door to instruction in the German language was left open in a type of *Töchterschule,* with German Jewesses as directors.[19]

The transition to English from German in the synagogue, so painful for the lovers of German, called forth recriminations against fellow German Jews deemed wavering in their loyalty to the old home synagogue and to German in the education of their children. Their point of no return was seen when they joined a Sephardic synagogue without even a sermon in German:

> The Portuguese congregations stand and endure by the support of these German Jews with delusions of aristocracy who would rather not be Germans and more and more by the youth who have escaped totally from their German heritage.[20]

German was taught as a foreign language in many of the existing private schools and also in a number of public schools at that time. Although we have no statistics as to the number of pupils who attended, we do know that German language was taught, to the satisfaction of many parents. The German Jewish mother, however, who tried to maintain a feeling at home for this language as the mother tongue, met up with new problems peculiar to America. At the same time, situations reappeared that had tortured German Jews in the old homeland, but with different language elements. The *Deborah* recapitulates all the difficulties of a bilingual education from the viewpoint of the home as well as from the effect of this education in public life:

> "My children have to speak German at home," mothers say with special self-satisfaction. It sounds beautiful, not because the children learn German, because the two or three hundred words of the homey vernacular are only an infinitesimal part of the language, but because the heart of the German woman beats faster when she hears these sounds of her homeland, and because the German mother wants to be loved by her children in German. The disadvantage of this, however, lies in the fact, that the poor English of

the children is not heard in the house and therefore not corrected. Every child who is educated in this way is recognizable by his distortion of the simplest expressions of the daily vernacular and by his germanizing or circumscribing them in a ridiculous way.[21]

This is the case not only with the children of uneducated parents but also of educated ones who are required to speak good German and study grammar. In this way, the paper concludes, the children speak a jargon, and in the German schools poor English is spoken.

In connection with this, a situation is recalled that evoked great criticism when the same Jews lived in Germany: The old Jewish folk tongue, lingering on in the midst of the modern German language acquired by the German Jews, had left its traces in their new mode of speaking, and this had been considered "jargon" too, with unfavorable consequences for the Jews.

The well-meaning summary of bilingual facts by the paper however missed the point: The German Jewish mother was in no case fit to impress good English on her children, or even keep up with their linguistic development in the new English milieu. The English language therefore had to be taught in any case outside of the family.

However, any further comparison of the English-German jargon with criticism of Yiddish in Germany would be a mistake. The fight of the German Jews against the refusal of Yiddish to disappear drew its strength from the forces of the Enlightenment, in the belief that Enlightenment was superior to Jewish traditions. The German Jews in America, however, were not pursuing any new idea in connection with English language assimilation. German rabbis at the helm of Jewish intellectuals together with all Germans in America and also with many Anglo Saxons believed that German education and culture was superior to anything contemporary America had to offer. The belief that the woman of German descent was superior to other women in America was widespread. The traveler Benjamin makes a great point of this and doesn't seem to expect any opposition to this assertion.[22] In surrendering the German language, the German Jew felt that he was relinquishing something spiritually superior to English confessing to himself that it was for purposes of convenience only.

Thus, and with some vengeance, there came back to him the situation in which the traditional Jew in Germany had felt the passing of Yiddish in his time.

The standardbearers of Enlightenment had made the fight against Yiddish a rallying cry in the execution of their program. No trace of it should remain in the speech of the Jews, and school administrations were especially warned against it.[23] Nevertheless, it was hard going and the more experienced teachers saw with complete clarity that this process would take the lifetime of a whole generation:

"Only the few better schools of some bigger cities and the free intercourse and public school attendance have partly effected that the *German language* became the mother tongue also of the Jews on this side" [of Germany].[24]

A German-speaking female element also came to America from the eastern end of the German-language empire, from Posen province after its incorporation into Prussia, where public education of both boys and girls in schools with German as the language of instruction had been introduced already in 1833.[25] But the German-language culture had entered Jewish communities in Posen well before, as Maskilim (the "enlightened ones") prepared the ground for it. In Lissa, for instance, German was the primary language of instruction in the Jewish community when it still belonged to Poland. In 1833 two women were already teachers there. In the city of Posen, the first Jewish private school whose classes were conducted in German existed in 1816; in 1831 forty girls received instruction in private German schools; in 1833 there was a Jewish girls' school there for eight girls. As in the Jewish schools of the other Germanies, "Jüdisch Schreiben" was still taught there for the same reason as elsewhere in Germany.[26]

Popular Jewish writers of the nineteenth century recognized the immense spiritual value of the Yiddish as Jewish folk language. To arouse the feelings of their readers, they use words of this language in the speech of their characters in specific situations that were bound to Jewish experience.

The painful feelings of American Jewish parents at giving up their mother tongue, was even strengthened by the fact that their children, addressed by them in German, answered only in English.[26] It is no

wonder, therefore, that experiments with teaching German proceeded
more smoothly where no family problems were aroused by it. For instance, in 1866, the "Öffentliche Prüfung der Zöglinge des hiesigen
[N. Y.] Waisenhauses" (Public examination of the inmates of the
[N. Y.] orphan asylum) took place in German. Only 'the translation
from Hebrew was done in German as well as in English." [27]

The struggle of the native-born American-bred girl of German Jewish
extraction for higher education became articulated only in the last two
decades of the nineteenth century. Even a small number of college
women, Gentile and Jewish, were concerned with such professions as
lawyer or physician.[28] However, the teaching profession became, more
and more, a green pasture for women and great numbers of students
frequented normal schools for teacher training.[30]

c) In the German American School System

To all the parents who wanted to incorporate German-language instruction into an otherwise rudimentary Jewish education, there are to
be added others who wanted to entrust their children to secular schools
with German as the language of instruction similar to those that existed
in the school system founded by the Germans in America. Jewish radi-
cals had been active in the process of founding these schools since, for
them, a Jewish religious school was considered incompatible with German secular [day] schools, although radical Jews in other sectors of
German organizational life did not hold to this view. Both groups, however,belonged to them, a situation which sometimes brought up delicate
questions when, for instance, individuals were officers of congregations
and members of freethinker's organizations at the same time.

In the world of Jewish women, the situation in the German American
schools meant a split because there a considerable number of German
Jewesses were employed as teachers. At the same time, the endeavor of
Jewish religious schools were directed toward gaining more and more
women teachers for religious instruction. Between these two groups of
women, the teachers in the religious schools and the secular German
Jews, existed no contact whatsoever. On the other hand, a number of
noted Jewish male personalities were without scruples, members of the

German American *Lehrerbund,* on the side of secular Germans, as for instance, Dr. Samuel Wolfenstein in Cleveland, Dr. Sonneschein, St. Louis, Dr. L. Kleeberg, Louisville, and Dr. Chronik, Chicago.[31]

However, there was at least one German Jewess with convictions of her own and with enough prestige to utter in public her opinion of the compatibility of Jewish religious education with frequenting the German secular school in America. Significantly this pronouncement came about in the organ of the German American teachers' organization.[32] Her name was Minna Kleeberg, she was the wife of a rabbi and, at the same time, a representative of German revolutionary poetry outside the Fatherland; she was recognized as such by the Germans in America.[33] In her eyes only the Temple [Reform] and religious schools had a right to exist; she rejected any other kind of Jewish organizations, especially social clubs. She even had scruples about justifying an independent Jewish press.

Minna Kleeberg defended the German Jew against attacks in a typical way of claiming for Jews the honor of being more patriotic Germans than the Germans:

> The immediate approach of the educated German community of this country directed to German American Jews are the words: you don't love your German Fatherland! Does the educated German Jew really not love his homeland? I wish to assert that his love is the purest and most sacred a German might feel for his Fatherland. . . . And shares the emigrated German Jew the longing for home of German emigrants?

Lastly, she pointed out Heinrich Heine as typical of this longing.[34]

Her answer to the question above reflects her positive attitude to German cultural institutions in America and her participation in the most important of them, the German school. At the same time, she was a fierce adherent of the Jewish Reform movement, hoping that Reform Judaism and German culture would find a way of proceeding hand-in-hand, as noted German Reform rabbis in America would have liked.[35] At that time, when the day schools of the Jewish communities were already on the eclipse because Jews were already sending their children to elementary public schools, a special appeal for German American day schools was made by a religiously conscious Jewess. Minna Kleeberg deemed it especially necessary to condemn Jewish "Sektenschulen" unfortunately blind to the developments in her adopted country which in time would mean that German secular education would descend to the status of a foreign sect—which, it was even at its height.

Also, if she found German secular schools justifiable, why then should the "French schools" meet with her reproach? She named them together with the objectionable Jewish "Sektenschulen."

The Jewish day schools in the communities had women teachers, too, especially in English. Unfortunately neither they nor the other schools raised Jewish religious women teachers: "It is strange that primary classes are not taught by young ladies. . . . An ulterior and important object would also be effected by encouraging young ladies to become teachers in the Hebrew as well in the religious classes." [36]

From its beginnings, the number of Jewesses in the teaching profession was considerable in the German American school system and it continued to grow. A comparison of the membership list of the *Lehrerbund* at the time of the first and second *Lehrertag* in 1870 and 1871 with later *Lehrertage* and finally, with the teachers list of 1897, of 600 persons, reveals that there was an increase in the amount of Jewish names. [37]

CHAPTER NINE

In the Public Eye

a) Synagogue

At the traditional services of the synagogue there is no such thing as the duties of women. Whatever extended synagogue activities were left to women was of an auxiliary nature, conditioned by new circumstances in America. Changes in the direct participation of women in prayer meetings came only as the result of synagogue reforms, more or less willingly conceded by more or less traditional congregations and really purposefully instituted only in Reform synagogues. Outside the common prayer meetings, the feminine sphere of congregational life developed fast however, particularly the new activities that accrued to the congregations; philanthropy and the early religious training of children. This field of child education was created by women and, in time, entirely managed and directed by them. For instance, the signers of the constitution of the Hebrew Sunday school in Philadelphia in 1858 were mostly women and their twelve managers for 1859 to 1870 were women only.[1] The textbooks of the Sunday schools were, as soon as their women teachers had gained some experiences, nearly exclusively produced by women. As the years went by, the Sunday schools became the mainstay of synagogal life in many Reform congregations that had abandoned the more thorough Jewish education of congregational afternoon schools.

The Sunday school was only one case of applying models from gentile life in this country to synagogue activities executed by women. Others followed which dealt directly with the prayer meeting, such as adding female voices to the choir, seating men and women together, abolishing the women's gallery, and introducing the family pew. Finally, woman's vote in the congregational meeting constituted the first female duties

121

there in respect to matters resolved in meetings and binding on all members of the congregation. All these developments were felt so much as being in the direction of womens' rights in this country generally that it is only natural that their growth should be followed by the general women's press.

To these changes in more formal matters was added a slow but irresistible transformation in the milieu of the synagogue effected soley by women, dealing mainly with the style of religious family celebrations, above all, weddings. It is hard to find the gentile model for such novelties as in any specific case, and surely many of them hailed from the imaginary power wielded by Jewish women only, but all in all the feeling prevailed that they were only an imitation of features in the gentile world. Naturally, the greatest attention were given the cases of the greatest luxury, but this does not prove the fact that the urge to imitate was less virulent where the expense was not so high.

While the discussion of whether the singing of women in the synagogue was permissible, on rabbinical grounds, was still going on in America,[2] rabbis were organizing mixed choirs in youthful congregations. Thus they lay a firm foundation for an acceptance of this innovation in Judaism. The prior organization of these choirs made it easier to introduce this German Protestant custom of hymn singing into the synagogal services. Of the hymns sung, a large number were written by female poets. Although hymns were also sung in Germany's temples, women writers of religious poems were extremely rare there. The different situation in American synagogues was partly due to the influence of the example of the hymn singing of church choirs. Printed Jewish hymn books not only included many creations of Jewish writers but also some gentile ones if the spirit of the hymn was close to Judaism.

With no deviation at all in the function of the hymns, even their place in the service is unchanged compared with the Reform service in Germany.[3] Reform temples in Germany, in which the Hamburg temple took the lead, had produced bulky hymn books in systematic order suitable for all intended uses of hymns. A thorough check of American Jewish hymn books proves unmistakably that only a few of the hymns of German Jewry entered these books. The hymn writers are American Jews and—even more—American Jewesses, who create both in English and in German, the vernaculars of the service. It is as if they were saying that dependence on Europe should never be conceded in the true expression of religious fervor, for which purpose congenial men and women were not wanting in American Jewry. Foremost, the women's zeal in this was expanded by their station in the synagogue—most conspicuous in the Reform temple at first, but followed by a short distance by most of the other congregations.

The Jewish male in general was unpoetical in America and the laurels of religious poetry fell on two Jewish women at that time, one rhyming in German and one in English. Minna Kleeberg's fame was accepted even by German-American versifiers; Penina Moise's literary creations were recognized representative expressions of the traditional Jewish spirit. The pride of American Jewry in their two poetesses, in view of the lack of poets, was boundless; there was no one comparable to them in the Fatherland, and certainly not among the creators of hymns for the Jewish congregations in Germany. No wonder, therefore, that the hymn book of the congregation of Charleston, published in 1842, is filled to overflowing with Penina Moise's poems, as is Isaac Mayer Wise's edition of a book of hymns in 1866 with those of Minna Kleeberg. The two books together represent the most effort that American Jewry spent in early times on a genuine part of the service in the vernacular.

Only by the most minute assembling of data of congregational life could the extent of the actual use of these printed hymns be established beyond any doubt, but they were, in any case, authentically all the synagogue had to offer in the vernacular, and it was eager to parade it before the world of the gentiles as the Jewish religious expression of the time.

The so-called women's taste obtained an upper hand in the style and arrangement of weddings in the synagogue to the degree that they were handled by a greater public like any other society event:

A Jewish wedding is an event in New Orleans; the curiosity to behold it arising both from its infrequency and its secularity. It is the topic of conversation for a week previous to its celebration; when the fated day itself arrives, the interest is equal to that excited by a ball. To obtain a good seat in the synagogue, you must enter a couple of hours earlier than the appointed time.[4]

In time, synagogue services seemed an excellent opportunity for women at least to be seen in attendance by young men there. Slowness to appear at the synagogue on the part of the men therefore proved to be a great disappointment to the ladies as noted by an anonymous "observer":

> He would see there every Sabbath, the gallery filled with members of my sex, while there is a very poor showing in the place where "an Observer" would be likely to sit. If my new bonnet had not been held back by the odious milliner, I should have been in my seat myself. As it was, I hear that the ladies were there in good numbers. . . .
>
> A Lady[5]

This could, in the end, cause the ladies, too, to be rather weak on the issue of participating in services:

> I do say—much as I dislike to confess it—and how few will there be who will have enough honesty to acknowledge it, that were the young men to attend Synagogue regularly each and every one of them, the young ladies would also be found there, two where there is now but one. Now why is this?—simply one of those wonderful laws of nature which we cannot understand. . . .
>
> Enfant Terrible[6]

And the pervasive feeling hung on that a good deal of showiness appeared to be reason for attendance with quite a lot of people, male and female:

> Now, young ladies, and gentlemen too, why is it that it is only on Holy Days and fine Sabbath that you come to Shul? Do you think the good God listens to our prayers more attentively, because we have our new bonnets on? . . .[7]

Nevertheless, many young women felt at home in the synagogue, experiencing fully their religious responses to prayer in communion and were deeply impressed by the rabbi's sermon. In the youthful memories of creative women this point plays its role, as in Edna Ferber's case, that led her to visit Rabbi E. G. Hirsch's sermons and religious lectures regularly.[8]

In rare cases, a woman achieved a speaking voice at synagogue services.[9] Finally, the Reform Movement in Judaism produced a woman rabbi, arousing great curiosity in the gentile world: "To Miss Ray Frank, of California, is recorded the distinction of becoming the first woman rabbi in the world. She is the first woman student in the Hebrew College in Cincinnati and has been urged by Rabbi Moses, the most celebrated Jewish divine in Chicago, to accept a congregation as he says women are needed in the pulpit." [10]

b) Women's Organizations: From the "Frauenverein" to the National Council of Jewish Women

The traditional sector of Jewish community functions which was partly left to independent women's organizations, was philanthropy. In Germany, in the nineteenth century, the Female Benevolent Society was firmly installed in most communities. Its common name, *"Der Israelitische Frauenverein,"* was transplanted to America to designate institutions of the same kind, and even shows up in city directories.[11] Its function in the American community was much broader in scope than it was in Germany because young communities with new activities were involved whereas in Germany it was only an addition to an otherwise well-organized community organization. Due to continuous immigraton, westward movement, and general mobility from community to community, the Hebrew Ladies Benevolent Society became an important instrument of organized Jewish life in America. In small communities it was sometimes the only Hebrew society, next to the congregation which was for worship. A women's society as the philanthropic arm of the community existed widely throughout the West in various locales, as for instance, in Salt Lake City,[12] and in communities of the Middle West as well.

In Los Angeles, a Hebrew Ladies' Benevolent Society, "was established as early as 1870, and was the first women's philanthropy organization of any kind in this city." [13] In Akron, Ohio, the Hebrew Ladies'

Society was the first among any of the German-speaking organizations.[14]

In a number of small communities urgent help for the needy was given partly by the congregation, but the further field of philanthropy was left to the ladies' organizations. Thus, there is no record of the existence of a Hebrew Benevolent Society of the men. This was, for instance, true of Madison, Wisconsin, where the ladies' organization officially represented any philanthropy dispensed by the Jewish community:

Hebrew Benevolent Association

We organized, in the Year 1862, a Ladies Hebrew Benevolent Association numbering twelve members, for the purpose and object of assisting and relieving those needy and in distress, particularly our object has been to aid widows and orphans, though by no means do we make it a point of exclusively assisting those of our faith. . . .[15]

In comparison with this, in Madison, Indiana, during the same year, in a Jewish community of sixty-nine souls, a ladies' society also existed in addition to the Hebrew Benevolent Society of the men, and a congregation.[16]

It was more usual, however, especially in the larger communities, for corresponding men's and women's benevolent societies to exist in addition to congregations, starting in northern Atlantic communities and moving down to the communities of the South, as, for example, Atlanta.[17]

Wherever new Jewish organizations, especially the B'nai B'rith lodges, were being established, they met up with an already existing women's society. Thus, a women's benevolent society was founded in Stockton in 1863, whereas B'nai B'rith dates from 1869.[18]

Groups originating inside of the Jewish community also appear to have joined with each other in philanthropic societies. Sometimes, when a German Jewish *Frauenverein* was founded, there already existed another organization of women, carried on in the English language.[19] The German ladies, like the men, founded their societies to retain their milieu and the common German language:

As regards the Ladies Benevolent Societies the simple reason of some of the German ladies for refusing to join the one first started, is, that not being fully competent to express themselves in the English language—most of them being but a short time in America—they thought it best to form an association, in which their mother tongue, which they can all understand and speak, should be predominant.[20]

In most cases help was given in money, a rational way to give it, especially in the West where stranded wanderers were a frequent problem. For the purpose of being able to give quick money support, western ladies' as well as men's Hebrew Benevolent Societies (often at the same place) had ample means ready.[21] In the big cities direct necessities were also offered—such as coal and clothing. A ladies' society in the West was often an annex to a congregation.[22] To furnish clothing, Ladies' Sewing Circles were established.[23] At a few of the larger places that received direct immigration, women's organizations could start even as self-help societies.[24] Even permanent institutions like homes for orphans and widows, showed traces of such beginnings in their regulations.[25]

The local ladies' societies were not united under one roof either regionally or by state or nationally. The way to collect money was, in most cases, by arranging affairs, a ball or a Fair.[26]

With the years, even in these Benevolent Societies the meetings took on, more and more, the character of socials in an informal circle.[27]

The Civil War, the greatest emergency in American history, brought out the best in these societies, Northern and Southern, in tending the sick soldiers and helping their families. The same instruments, the money campaigns, socials, and balls, continued, wherever possible, during the war.[28]

In addition to benevolent societies, women's circles were also formed with social programs, including local philanthropy; more often it was common literary or even musical interests that drew them together; and then there were the social women's clubs that existed side by side with the benevolent societies, whose ladies were members of both organizations.[29]

The first regular Jewish women's club was the Pioneers in St. Louis, founded on January 25, 1879, by Rose Sonneschein, wife of the rabbi there.[30] It claimed to be "the first Literary Society of Jewish Women in America," whose purpose was 'promoting literary taste and cultivating general knowledge. There were fifteen original members . . . attendance was compulsory, and lateness was subjected to fine. No men were admitted to regular meetings. . . ." Among other motives, this was an attempt on the women's part to create their own clubs on a par with the Jewish men's clubs which only admitted visiting women to its premises on extraordinary occasions.[31]

When the first Jewish fraternal order, the B'nai B'rith, originated in America, the secret element in this form, in imitation of non-Jewish organizations, inspired women to found a sororal order of their own.[32] However, this trend didn't go too far since, at a later date, the men's order instituted women's auxiliaries.[33] The fight for female membership in B'nai B'rith started in 1859. Motions to this end were tabled for a time or ruled out of order. This was followed (1890) by a referendum on this question with negative result and more than two-thirds of the lodges voting nay. The first auxiliary lodge was finally established on August 8, 1897, in San Francisco.[34]

The direction of women's organizations also tended to become a part of the synagogue and the activities that constituted the legitimate social work of the synagogue in the latter part of the century. Remarkable results were often achieved in this field which found recognition in the gentile world:

> The Emanu-El Sisterhood of Personal Service is an active, incorporated society of Jewish women, which was organized in New York, March 3, 1889, with forty members. Its purpose is to render direct personal aid to those who are in need of it. No dues are required of the members; they serve and give, according to their time and means, and select their work from one of the four sections into which the society is divided: "Friends of Children," "Friends of Working Girls," "Friends of the Sick and Needy," and "Friends of Working Women." The Sisterhood maintains a home where an industrial school and a day nursery are carried on, and where the

"Friendly Club," which it organized among the Jewish working girls, holds evening meetings. House-to-house visits, relief, employment, classes, entertainments, lectures and a library are features of the work. The Sisterhood is raising a building fund for a larger home to accommodate its growing work, and it published a "Monthly Record." [35]

The businesslike execution of organizational matters through gained administrative knowledge is pointed out even if old-style benevolent societies are concerned.[36] In this respect, political training received by women in the movement for women's rights played a role. This is not to say that things from the outside were not brought to the synagogue by women which were anything but businesslike: the ball-like atmosphere of the socials could occasionally bring a headache to the rabbi who had to perform religious ceremonies in the synagogue. Dr. Emil Hirsch once complained to the women:

> Why do you have that wonderful bridal procession? It is a marionette show, and you have seen it as often as I have. Where did you get the idea of that procession with all the childish fuss that really makes the rabbi feel he is out of place? . . . No wonder they have to have six or seven rehearsals. . . .[37]

From the synagogue, in its search for the broadened activities the times demanded, a cry went out to the ladies for serious co-workers who could help out with the immigrants in fields where men were not competent:

Let the ladies help.

> . . . the work of the Emigrant Aid Society . . . young . . . society . . . novel its work . . . [we] suggest . . . organizing Ladies' Auxiliary Society . . . The care especially of the Russian women and children form a department which no gentleman can undertake . . . why not enroll every lady whose heart may prompt and give all the opportunity of doing similar work?
> Besides, the department suggested, there are others, such as the

clothing, the cooking, the housekeeping generally, which ladies only can effectually and economically perform, and in all of these ladies stand ready and willing to give efficient and valuable help.[38]

Great things usually come about by combining a society-need with an ideal. The need to recruit the Jewish woman for urgent social work was obvious as the century came to its end. To combine it with the idea of renewing American Judaism by women's work in Jewish society was the happy deed of those who founded the National Council of Jewish Women in 1893. At that time Jewish women's organizations had long enough been under the influence of the "Association for the Advancement of Women" [39] to achieve mature judgments in organizational matters.

The participation of Jewish women in the woman's branch of the World's Congress of Religion in that year, where enthusiasm for the idea of such a council was overwhelming, precipitated its establishment. On the performance of the Jewish women there we find a report in the Woman's Journal:

Jewish Women at the World's Fair

On the opening day of the Women's Congress at the World's Fair, Mrs. Minnie D. Louis came first on the programme with a paper on "Woman's Place in Hebrew Thought." Her essay was discussed by Emil Marshall Wadsworth and Mrs. John F. Unger, representative of the Woman's Foreign Missionary Society of the Reformed Church of the United States. Eliza Ann Toyer read an address on "The Light of the East," meaning the Hebrew Woman. The discussion that followed was led by Mrs. Ella Dietz Clymer.

Mrs. July L. Simpson, the New York State Delegate to the woman's branch of the World's Congress of Religions, is a writer from the West, who, before coming to New York to live, did much good work on the Denver and Chicago press. As the head of the Jewish women's branch in New York State, Mrs. Simpson undertook the task of arousing enthusiasm in the principal cities suffi-

ciently to get meetings called and names selected of women who
are competent and willing to prepare and read papers before the
Congress to be held in Chicago in September.

One of the essayists selected for this Congress is Miss Lizzie
Bloomstein, of Nashville, Tenn.[40]

The founding organization, later a section in the Council, had been
in Chicago, the place where the women's congress had assembled. Its
mentor, Dr. Emil Hirsch helped delineate the task of the Council in its
first attempts to organize. It was his task to see to it that the Council
should not lose itself in a vague program of world reforms instead of
stepping forward to achievements in Judaism:

> Representatives from Jewish women's societies assembled in mass
> meeting in Sinai Temple, Chicago, on January twenty-second, to
> establish a local branch of the National Council of Jewish Women,
> an institution which came into existence when the Jewish Congress
> was held in that city. . . .

Dr. Hirsch opposed the motion of women as a society attempting to
"reform" the world. He said that when such men as Rothschild and
others, *men* representing vast capital and influence, had failed to remedy
affairs existing in Russia, it was useless for a new association of women
to try to do anything by "raising a howl." [41]

The Council found its way and became a pillar of American Jewry,
for all times recognized as such in the Jewish world:

Woman's Awakening.

At all events, Chicago was the city where an awakening first made
itself evident, and the demand for something better that went up
from the Jewish Women's Congress there assembled, soon found
immediate responding voices from all sections, so that to-day, East
as well as West, and South as well as the farthest West, unite in
voicing through their most sensitive mouthpieces, women's hearts,
the cry for improvement. . . .[42]

Improvement meant, first of all, Jewish studies, programmed in forty-two groups for 1895/96.[43] Educational work followed and found support everywhere.[44] At the monthly general meeting of its branches, Judaistic lectures were given and purely social meetings were included in the programs.[45] Generally three sectors of activities were formed: Religion, philanthropy and Sabbath school. Each of the branches had taken over an activity in one of these branches already in the first year of existence of the Council.

The growth in members of the Council was not spectacular, nevertheless their number reached four thousand seven hundred eighty-five in 1900.[46] In comparison with it the United Order of True Sisters, which had existed nearly a half century at the time the Council was founded had not more than two thousand members.[47]

c) Jewish Women at the End of the Century

Any new evaluation of the changed position of the Jewish woman at the end of the century had first to consider the changes in the religious life of American Jewry from decade to decade. The traditional piety of the German Jewess, described to us even during the stage of emigration,[48] held on for a certain time as a stable element in community life. Even when the men had early already loosened the traditional bonds with weakened interest, women kept up traditional customs. A letter written in 1845 from America to a Jewish newspaper in England points this out:

> The ladies of America, I must say, are in general less apathetic and more religious than the other sex; and where there exists not a school for inculcating of Jewish principles and knowledge, Sunday schools are formed by them. Thus the majority of our respectable and educated young ladies, devote the Sunday morning to inculcate Jewish knowledge and the beauties of our cherished faith upon the ductible mind of the children of *all classes* of society; nor do they forget that precept is best taught by example, for their regular attendance at the house of prayer might shame their manly relatives; nor are their loud aspirations less fervently expressed, or their silent

prayers less deeply felt, than those of their brethren below, whose voices as they ascend are joined to theirs. . . .[49]

Even higher levels of Jewish learning seemed, hopefully, not closed to some exemplary Jewesses as also the thoughtful knowledge of the phases of Jewish history:

> It may appear presumptuous in a female to enter into comments upon scriptural themes, but the daughters of Israel have always felt that allegiance to Zion was paramount to every other sentiment or patriotism, and above all sinister or secondary considerations.
> None can take this glorious privilege from us, accorded to us throughout every phase of our eventful history.[50]

Kashrut was observed in small communities entirely on account of the women: "Every household . . . strictly kept *Kasher*." [51]

However, the change came, and, as always, first in the big cities. In Chicago, where so many families lived in hotels as regular boarders, it was obvious: ". . . *kosher* board is no object in this cosmopolitan city." [52]

Especially grave was considered the violation of the Sabbath by women, because, with it, any hope for betterment of an already deplorable situation dwindled:

> If Sabbath-breaking were confined to the men alone, there might be a possibility that, in time, the influence of the women would keep them from doing it, but now that the women violate the command as flagrantly as the men, where is the chance of better times? Don't you see that this matinee business destroys the last vestige of the home-life, in which we used to rejoice so much? But again its no wonder. When the men are at the store hunting the almighty dollar, what pleasure has a wife in staying at home? Shall she look at the white table-cloth, that is laid out for a sham, and have no one to speak to? Shall she kindle her lights and make them dumb witnesses of her husband's transgression? Shall she go to the synagogue and rejoyce on the Sabbath and not grieve

over the empty seat beside her—the seat that belongs to her husband, who goes to the store and makes a profit on the day
of rest? . . .[53]

However it may have been with the Sabbath violators, male or female, the case of synagogue visiting stood in favor of the women: "Decades ago, among our fathers in Europe, the women rarely attended service . . . America changes matter. The young Jewess attends service at
the sanctuary, and the young Jew attends service at the counting
house." [54]

While obviously rights for women in congregational matters could
be concluded from such conditions, the actual demand for such rights
came simply from an application of the new principle of the equality of
the sexes as the world outside the synagogue saw it: "Why has the educated American Jewess no voice in the synagogue, while every clerk or
dry goods drummer can record his vote and be eligible to office? . . ." [55]

And to achieve this goal, the same methods of organization and propa-
ganda was to be used as in the outside world: "Let the women speak out
in their churches. Let us vote; let us work; let us influence and organize
until we see a congress of all the Jewish congregations in America in
session. . . ." [56]

In catching up with this situation and incorporating womens' right
into congregational life, the Reform movement was quicker than the
other branches of Judaism. In looking back at these conditions Isaac M.
Wise says:

> The Jewish woman had been treated almost as a stranger in the
> synagogue; she had been kept at a distance, and had been excluded
> from all participation in the life of the congregation, had been rele-
> gated to the gallery, even as was the negro in Southern churches.
> The emancipation of the Jewish woman was begun in Albany, by
> having the Jewish girls sing in the choir, and this beginning was
> reinforced by the introduction of family pews.[57]

The wide circle of persons who did not see in mere synagogue innovations a women's emancipation, as the Reformers did, also made their

own observations, and the result was the recognition that the mere fact of a change in the religious notions of the males also created a new sphere for the woman: "Of late years, the class of Jews known as Reformed has become considerable in this country, and, naturally, where the men change their views, the women under their influence do likewise; but the reformers are a small portion of the sum to total." [58]

In the end, circumstances decided everything, and not men of this or any other branch of Judaism: "The admirable combination of circumstances, and the irresistible onward march of women has placed the American Jewess on a par with American womanhood. . . . The American Jewess is an important element in congregational life. . . . She labors in the sphere of charity. This is her real realm, her scepter and her crown. . . ." [59] In short, she entered the American century of woman, as other women did.

Discussion of all these changes and evaluations of the new position of the Jewish woman fell to the Jewish press,[60] and a better understanding of the general status of the American woman is also illuminated there.[61] Countering the much interpreted purely traditional features of the Jewish woman, her revolutionary impulses are also shown, albeit in a fictional instance:

> . . . woman's rights and connected therewith in a way, a study of the Hebrew of to-day, are the main motives of the book . . . the rebel-queen herself—a rich, beautiful and clever Jewess, who refuses to submit to her husband after the manner of her people, and becomes a champion of the rights of her sex. . . .[62]

The value of the German Jewesses' independent social work for the immigrant masses after 1880 is shown as a decisive factor in their rise to the good life in a not too distant future: "Exiles in a new world, where every man works for himself with unheard-of vigor, persistence and perseverance, there could scarcely be any alternative for them than to fall a prey to the gallows or to die of hunger, were it not for the tireless compassion of women which assures to them bread and creates work for them." [63]

Finally also the new companionship of the sexes is heralded in real terms of their social intercourse in organizations of a literary and highly spiritual character:

> The companionship of intellectual Jewish men is afforded to American Hebrew women through the Young Men's Hebrew Associations . . . they have been equally beneficial to Jewish women in giving the latter many opportunities for valuable interchange of thought with the other sex.[64]

The relationship between the sexes finally also impressed the old timer and caused him to reorient his outlook: "The poor man, who, in olden days, took his surroundings for granted, is now questioning the justice of his position, and beginning to demand a radical change of the conditions of society." [65]

Chapter Ten

The Women's Rights Movement

Social Reform in America of the nineteenth century was the fruit of an active Protestant conscience. As a woman's activity, it manifested itself for the first time in the Christian Temperance Movement, whose goal was the elimination of the saloon through a religious crusade, its theaters were mainly the small cities in the Middle West, where the church represented this conscience. In the big cities, where the immigrant masses were clustered, the good work was not mastered because of the sheer bigness of the city. For instance, a canvass in Philadelphia in 1876 found no less than 8,034 places where intoxicating liquors were sold.[1] To gain contact with the temperance problem was reserved for a much later time, when the social settlements in the slums finally recognized the social function of the saloon and tried to create a substitute for it.[2]

In the Midwest, however, the big war went on in the small cities without interruption and forced all elements in economic life to an orientation from which also the Jews living in these cities could not escape.

In direct collision with the crusading women, the Jew was hurt only in a few cases. Big as the role of the Jew was in distilling the strong drink, wholesaling and selling it over the counter as a saloonkeeper, he was rarely seen. He perceived the movement more as a traveling salesman who served the local stores and came personally in touch with it only where the antisaloon movement tried to persecute the suppliers of liquor as well.[3] Nevertheless, there were also cases where the Jew as a saloonkeeper had to make good when the warlike ladies came to him:

"Granville, Ohio.

There were only four saloons in Granville. One of the dealers, being a Jew, would not on "account of his religion" allow the ladies to come into his saloon to pray. But he spread a carpeting on the sidewalk, and brought out chairs for their accommodation, and they held their prayer-meetings daily in front of his saloons. . . ." [4]

Such a remarkable occurrence is well apt to symbolize the true meeting of the Jew with Christian Temperance, whereas the Jewish woman doesn't enter the picture at all at first. To the Jew the work of Christian Temperance appeared worthy of being honored and, at the same time, it was clear to him that he could not participate in it because of its Christian character. Nevertheless, it stimulated his thinking about the temperance problem in a forceful way and compelled him to clarify his position in regard to it and to express it. It is, therefore, only natural that at least in one case this position was formulated and given to the crusaders in a direct answer. There cannot be any doubt that the writer of this answer expressed what the Jews of America felt without speaking out:

> Among the various responses called forth by my circular letter was one from Mobile, claiming to be written by a Jew, which, for its peculiarity, I feel disposed to copy here:
> ". . . The savages of America knew nothing of poisonous drinks, till Christian civilization planted it among them. Christian efforts . . . are so blinded in one direction, that honest and true believers in Christ overlook the essential teaching of the Savior. Christ lived up to the essence of Moses' laws. His last hours were spent in celebrating the Passover; showing that he was a good Jew. Go to work and teach people to live up to the sanitary teaching of old Moses. You can do it and not sacrifice Christian doctrine. Ask your Jewish neighbors to explain their mode of living and you will learn how to cure drunkenness. As I am a sober person and belong to a sober race, your appeal does not concern me beyond the natural inclination to live in a community, whether Christian or heathen, where morality is the rule instead of the exception. And as I live in a so-called Christian community, where we have drunkards, murderers, thieves etc., I shall glory in your good work. . . ."
> He tells of his good, sensible wife and eight children, all sober

and home-keepers, making a very interesting picture of the Jewish home.[5]

The phenomenon of the Jewish home free of a mania for drinking could not fail to awaken thoughts about the Jewish people also in the crusaders, and then to support them with further personal experience. In her answer the crusader recognized the hygiene of the Mosaic law and confirmed the picture of the Jewish home:

"I am also prepared to give witness that Sarah's daughters are keepers at home, wifely, motherly, virtuous. And in regard to the home enjoyments and keeping, I have in mind now a family, once my next-door neighbors, who were very beautiful exponents of the principle." [6]

As a result the crusader comes to the practical conclusion: 'We can unite at least, for the sake of bettering the community, in which we live. . . ." [7]

Nevertheless, the crusader cannot help but hope for the conversion of the Jews and express this hope.

In following up this theme of abstinence from liquor among Jews, the crusaders also initiated their own research on the state of their drinking habits. The following represents the result of one such an exploration:

> The Jewish people are freer from the vice of intemperance than the Christian communities around them. On this subject I was informed by the chief Rabbis of New York City that among the sixty thousand Jews, their thirteen Rabbis knew not even one of any of their congregations who was habitually intemperate. They supposed such cases might be found outside of their congregations, though they knew of none. When I inquired the cause of this it was ascribed, chiefly, to great care and faithfulness in family training. . . .[8]

In the struggle for women's rights, pros and cons were divided along strict ethnic lines. In the American scene of women's movements, the attitudes of Jews were not only assessed objectively, but also evaluated in comparison with the attitudes of other ethnic groups among whom women's suffrage met with nearly complete hostility, the masses of immigrants having hailed from Europe's peasant milieu where traditionally, all rights belonged to men and from the Irish Catholic tradition. In an article "Jesuitism and Women," directed by a woman against a manual used in the Jesuit's College in Rome the author finds a "profound contempt for Woman . . . these sworn celibates despise, in their hearts, the daughters of Eve . . . those who labor for the elevation of Woman must not look to the disciples of Loyola for help." [9] In an earlier article, "Woman's Suffrage and the Jesuits," exception was taken to the widely spread argument "that it [woman's suffrage] would tend to increase the power of the Jesuits." [10]

In further cool assessments of friend and foe, the curious attitudes of certain opponents of women's suffrage among the intellectuals is noted first: "John Boyle O'Reilly will soon enjoy the distinction of having called women's suffrage more bad names than any other man of his generation. He has referred to it as a "humbug, a hypocrisy, a sentimental disease." [11] In this case the contrast between Jewish and Irish attitudes shows up even on the local Boston scene: O'Reilly's friend, Rabbi Solomon Schindler, was a fierce fighter for women's right to vote.

Mere lip service to women's rights by politicians is compared with the Judas kiss of the woman's press, and no further attention is paid it. Among the Germans, a majority were opponents, together with many lukewarm politicians; only Karl Heinzen was a radical fighter for women's suffrage.[12] On the other hand, most German Jewish intellectuals, gave unmixed vigorous support to women's suffrage and women's equality, as acknowledged in the women's press. Thus, in the medical field which proved to be of such great importance to women in America, Dr. Lilienthal wrote: "The physician who would refuse to consult with a colleague because she is a woman, offends against the code of ethics." Rabbi Felsenthal, also a German Jewish intellectual, aroused admiration in his gentile audience, and inspired the coupling of oppressed Jew and oppressed woman. "Yea, verily, Rabbi Felsenthal was among the chosen," wrote Kate Dogget, "to enlighten these Christian young men . . . for the benefit of those who still consider Jews, like women, as something to look down upon." [13]

The fruitless search for real support among the immigrant groups finally pushed the suffragists into the arms of immigration restrictionists. The immigrants were seen as a political obstacle to the success of women's voting rights. This trend gained an official character by the statement of the leading personality in the National Council of Women in Washington, D.C., Elizabeth Cady Stanton, in a lecture titled, "The Perils of Immigration." The arguments of this lecture are in accord with those of the Restrictionists' movement originated in Massachusetts:

> The fact that all foreigners are opposed to the enfranchisement of women, compels us, in self-defense, to oppose the extention of the suffrage to them. And worse still, our rights are not only at their disposal, but the liquor vote, the Irish vote, the German vote intimidate our politicians; hence it is their policy to keep our question ever in the background. In this way the foreign vote holds the balance of power and in a measure dictates the policy of our government . . . we ask Congress for a sixteenth amendment to the national Constitution, enfranchising all women who can read and write the English language intelligently, and further providing that no native or foreign men shall be allowed to exercise the suffrage except on the same basis. . . .[14]

Jews are not mentioned in this lecture, an omission which is the more remarkable in that there is talk there of "strike-breaking mobs."

Seen from the angle of the direct fight for suffrage, the Jewish woman in America was a latecomer. In the America correspondence of Jewish newspapers abroad we find statements early that Jewish women are not to be found in the suffrage-movement.[15] In spite of the favorable attitude of the Jewish public to women's rights, we find occasional opposition to female candidates to school boards as, for instance, in San Francisco in 1886:

> In the campaign that followed, a peculiarly bitter fight was made against these nominees and they were defeated. An analysis of the vote by wards showed that the German and the Jewish resident district had cast the heaviest vote against them.[16]

Thus it was always only one woman who was seen in this fight, the Jewess from Poland, Ernestine Rose: "Mrs. Rose, at present the most eloquent female advocate of woman's rights and the philosophy of Thomas Paine, is a native of Poland." [17] The distance between the gentile suffragettes educated by Fundamentalism and the Jewish atheist Ernestine Rose comes to the fore ocassionally: "Ernestine Rose . . . could not sit silent and hear Antoinette Brown prove from the Bible that man was wrong in his attitude toward women, since one of her reasons for discarding the Bible was the narrowness of the Christian Church toward women, and Miss Brown could not keep silent when Mrs. Rose was unorthodox."

Against this, however, a leading Jewish philosopher, Felix Adler, was considered in circles of the women's rights movement as active against their interests because of his opposition to divorce.[18]

Utah was seen early by the women's rights movement as a probing ground: "We are told that, in private, Brigham Young expresses the most unqualified opposition to woman's political equality. However this may be, both parties have appealed to the women for help, which is a new proof that "when rogues fall out honest women get their due."

Jewish women took an interest in the polygamy question of Utah and occasionally commented on it.[19] Because Utah was one of the earliest states to introduce women's suffrage, Jewish women were among the first women voters there. A lady correspondent in a Jewish newspaper reports about this in an ironic vein:

> At the last election I presented myself at the poll of our district as a voter, but the Judges of election watching the purity of the Ballot Box, were all old bachelors, and when they saw me, with a ballot in my hands, one of the Judges fainted, the other went into ecstasy, and the third one shrugged his shoulders and remarked: "Miss, your dresses are not long enough, and therefore we are forced to refuse your vote. No woman's-right-men in this district." I told them that I would send "Miss Mary Walker and she would snatch them bald-headed." [20]

The inspiration Christian America drew from the Bible in the shape of Fundamentalism also made encroachments on the old image of woman. The following enunciation of a Free Church organ is a programmatical declaration of the true purposes of the modern woman measured by biblical standards. It is at the same time an assessment of woman's contemporary situation, in which she is found to be far inferior to the biblical models:

The Jewish Women

While reading the story of Judith in the Apocrypha lately, I received a new and vivid impression of the character of Jewish women. It appears to me of a very different type and greatly superior to any that the Gentile world can show, either ancient or modern. The trait I was peculiarly struck with, was their patriotism: and patriotism in a true Jew was something different from what it is among the Gentiles; it was one and the same as loyalty to God, as their King and Husband. I have often thought of the expression, "Every woman that was wise-hearted." It is applied in Exodus to those who wrought in furnishing the sanctuary; and is, I think, particularly descriptive of Jewish women. They appear to have been, from Sara down, marvelously endowed with wisdom and beauty. And here we see their wise-heartedness, and the great distinction between them and their Gentile sisters; instead of perverting these gifts to the ignoble arts of making themselves centers of worship, they, with manly faith and purpose, made them cunning ministers to the advancement and glory of the Theocracy. Esther and Judith are especial examples of this kind of patriotism—Miriam and Deborah, and those daughters of Israel by faith—Rahab and Ruth—the mothers of Samuel and Sampson, Abigail and the Shunamite, are noble specimens of loftiness of soul, heroic faith, and loyalty to God, and utter exemption from the pitiful vanity and narrowmindedness, which a false religion and false education have tolerated and encouraged in modern women. . . .

C.A.M.[21]

As a consequence, the women's rights movement, however much it took over this evaluation of Bible figures, nevertheless rejected any ideas that tried to slight modern woman vis-à-vis the biblical ideal: "The women commemorated in the Bible were political women."[22]

Instances of biblical life give color to the stuff of a woman's newsper:

New York Chivalry

Since that eventful day when Moses acted the gallant to Jethro's daughter, and put to flight the gang of rascally shepherds, chivalrous devotion to women has been often tested and illustrated. We strongly doubt, however, whether New York now offers many examples of this kind of chivalry. The other day, in a street-car, twenty-two men were seated and twelve ladies were standing, holding despairingly to the straps, which were almost beyond the reach of their gloved hands. . . .[23]

However, the awakened sense of modern woman also interpreted other instances from the Bible giving them a contemporary meaning:

Hagar

A domestic scene? The particulars are not given, but the result was that Hagar and her child went forth with only a loaf of bread and a bottle of water. . . . There has been many a domestic episode since the days of Sarah and Hagar. We sincerely pity the Sarahs and deplore the Hagars, but where there is a Hagar there is always an Abraham and we deplore the Abrahams equally with the Hagars! [24]

In further penetrating into the spirit of historic Judaism, the women's press points out the dignified position of woman in the Talmud and in the rabbinical literature.[25] However, the leitmotif of these studies of ancient Jewish women was to apply the findings to modern situations:

"It is remarkable that while all the women of the Bible were what we should call to-day strong-minded, so many persons still insist that both the letter and spirit of the Book are opposed to the political, religious, and social equality of woman." [26]

With such biblical aspects of the Jewish woman for the women's movement of the present there begins a unique interest of the woman's press in the American Jewish community insofar as the Jewesses are involved, and parallels to the gentile world are always made. The basis of this interest has a Fundamentalist undertone as is found in the Christian mission: The potency of Christianity would increase out of all proportion if the historic Jew would come to it. As its secular side, the women's movement, too, was convinced that the Jewess could contribute much more to a heightened position of modern woman than was her share in numbers. This conviction finally became a kind of infatuation with the happenings in the Jewish community. The many cases in which the *Jewish Messenger* is quoted as source and authority in the woman's press, bears witness to this.[27]

As the first object of the vigilance of the women's press appears the position of woman in the synagogue. The interest in it was great because a parallel existed with churches where women sought rights as congregants. There was also a personal interest in church groups where the wives of Protestant ministers were active feminists.

The first suitable point of attack was seen in the traditional seating of the synagogue, where the women were separated from the men. The demand for family pews was the first issue to gain an advocate in the women's press, and in this connection the Reform synagogue had an advantage over the other branches of Judaism, even before its claim could be put up pro foro interno, to have done the most for the Jewess:

> Abandoning an Old Custom.—The San Francisco Bulletin, of the 29th ult., says:—The old Jewish custom has been for many years that in the synagogue the men and women should sit apart. An attempt to do away with this form of the olden time has been made by several members of the sect within the last few weeks, and on Sunday last a meeting was held in the synagogue to decide what course should be taken upon the matter. Some argued that the manner of the ancient Jews should be adhered to, and some that the sect should not be an exception to the general custom of civilized nations at the present time. A vote was taken on the matter, with the result of eighty-eight in favor of the sexes sitting together, and

twenty-four on the other side of the question. Henceforward, therefore, it is decided that the proximity of ladies does not interfere in the least with devotional exercise.[28]

The paper uses this opportunity to give an interesting report on the service in this synagogue, written by a non-Jewish woman:

> I have always coveted the purity of lineage, and the steady persistency (I know there is no other name for it) of the Hebrew race. So to be a "Hebrew of the Hebrews," perchance of David's royal line, seemed to constitute a claim upon the reverence of all embraced in the covenant with Abraham who are not of his blood. . . . Besides I always believed that Saturday was the Sabbath and kept it holy with the children in the fields and forests, whenever I could. . . .
> We went early, and were of a humble mind, consequently were invited to the highest seats. . . . I reached for the "prayer-book," and with the help of a youth seated near me found the place, an English translation of the Hebrew text occupying each alternate page. . . .

In paging through the prayer book the female visitor also discovered the line of thanks to the creator "who has not made me a woman." However, the most peculiar fact of such a Friday night service was, to the gentile observer, the predominance of women and children as its participants and the absence of men out of proportion to their actual numbers. It was not until much later that the Jewess used this fact to support her demand for greater equality in the synagogue.

In New York, where the struggle for the rights of women in the synagogue was long drawn out, the women's press had an opportunity of following all its phases. Its spiritual mentor in it was *"The Jewish Messenger,* a paper ably edited, and always dignified and fair in the presentation of both sides."[29] In connection with this, the women seemed to have little interest in participating in the administration of the synagogue or in electing its officers; and, entirely in contrast to the Protestant denominations which at the turn of the century could count on several hundred

women preachers, they showed no interest in taking over the pulpit.[30]
The *Messenger* approached this question with caution, because the editors knew very well that in the background of all discussion of women's
rights in the synagogue stood the demand for a change in its seating
order:

Woman in the Synagogue

The *Jewish Messenger* states that "as yet, the Woman's Right
movement has not reached the synagogue. No Jewess is, to our
knowledge, emulous of Miss Smiley, the fair Quakeress, or Mrs.
Hanaford, the Universalist, and desires to preach to her brethren.
The preaching propensities may exist among Jewesses, but is con-
fined to the family circle or to some of our ladies' societies, where
such astounding parliamentary rules are at times in order. Even the
important matter of voting at synagogue meetings is a subject of
no concern to our ladies, though they are members and seat-holders,
and legally entitled to vote. None demand the right of suffrage or
the power to determine what shall be the duties of the *chazan*. This
may be an evidence of their degeneracy or of their common sense."
Whereupon the *Christian Register* remarks, "But we advise the
Messenger to beware of premature exultation. When human nature
has had its perfect work among the daughters of Israel some of the
kinswomen of Miriam and Deborah may entirely eclipse the Universalist and Presbyterian prophetesses." [31]

One year later it was reported that a struggle about the seating order
was taking place and the women's press had the opportunity of entering
into the merits of this fight:

Light in the Hebrew Church

The position of women in the Hebrew Church has been, and
still is one of more marked subjection and inferiority than in any
other church, except perhaps the Mormon.
In the Hebrew church women have always set apart in the gal-

lery, old ladies toiling up the stairs, while their vigorous sons sat
with all other men in the body of the house below.

Even in the Hebrew church it is proposed to bring women from
the gallery, and to have "family pews" in the body of the house,
where the mother and daughters may sit with the father and sons.
But a usage so old and time honored is not given up without a
struggle. In the congregation Bnai Jeshurun, in New York City, last
May a resolution was adopted by a plurality vote, at a special meeting, for the introduction of an organ and family pews, whereupon
Israel J. Solomon brought a suit in the New York Court of Common
Pleas, to restrain the congregation from taking such action. . . .

This disturbance in the Jewish Church, caused by a growing
respect for the equal rights of women, is a cheering sign of the
times. . . . So we rejoice at this movement among the Hebrews,
which will help to bring the sisters of Rebecca to places where their
great power, purity and goodness will tell in the welfare of the
world. . . .[32]

The struggle in other synagogues lasted for years and the women's
press followed it up:

The *Jewish Messenger* urges not only to abolish the lattice work
in the women's gallery, and then the gallery itself, so as to allow
the women to sit with their husbands and brothers, but that the
women should be allowed also to vote in ecclesiastical matters and
hold office. "Why," it asks, "has the educated American Jewish
[woman] no voice in the synagogue, while every clerk or dry-goods
drummer can record his vote and be eligible to office?" The *Jewish
Messenger* expects the German Hebrews to meet the proposition
with ridicule; but its proposition is American, if not Teutonic, and
we do not see why a female seat-owner has not the same right of
representation as a male.[33]

In time, the question of full participation in the administration of the
synagogue also became ripe for judgment. Demands and rejections were
carried on in public. Actually, the loosening of the old rules had already

been accomplished by Jewish ministers. Among them, the convinced adherents of women's rights formed a majority:

Women in the Synagogue

Caroline C. Joachinsen, in the *Jewish Reformer,* publishes a spirited defence of the Ministers' Conference, which was criticized by the *Hebrew Standard* for granting to women the right of suffrage in congregational matters. . . .

"I deny the necessity of regulating our lives and actions by those who perished many centuries ago. . . . The American woman . . . is not less an American because she is an Israelite. She has the same inborn sense of liberty, the same capacity for management, the same active working powers. She has latent talents that must force recognition; she has training and culture that enable her to speak intelligently, logically and comprehensively. With what show of reason can you curtail her privileges? . . . As far back as 1881, the *Jewish Messenger* urged that women be allowed the same voting privileges as men . . ." [34]

The further activities of Jewish ministers who prepared for this change by years of work, was later reported in detail:

Women in the Church

At the recent meeting of the Central Conference of Jewish Rabbis in New York City, a resolution was introduced that women shall be eligible to full membership in Jewish congregations, with all the privileges of voting and holding office. The resolution was referred to the executive committee to be reported on at the session to be held in Washington in December. Even if it should not pass, the fact of its introduction shows a decided advance with respect to the position of women in one of the most conservative religious sects. [35]

Interdenominational fraternization was dealt with in the women's press as a theme of general progress. Consequently the performance of women as guest-preachers at services of other denominations as theirs was expected and correspondingly celebrated whenever such an event happened:

Thanksgiving Day in Cleveland

Plain Dealer says: "The new synagogue of Tiffereth Israel Congregation. . . . [has] thrown open . . . its platform [that is] occupied, not only by members of a Gentile religion, but to the women leaders of that religion. . . . Miss Marion Murdoch preached the sermon. . . ." [36]

It cannot be asserted that the Jewish women's organizations that existed before the National Council, directly supported the fighting suffragists. On the other hand, the example of Jewish personalities in and around the Movement was appreciated in the women's press. This is the more understandable since these Jewish women brought to it an intellectually advanced and socially dignified and middle-class element. For instance, in the reports on the movement in Germany, it was again and again pointed out that Mrs. Goldschmidt, wife of a Rabbi Doctor was involved in the struggle for women's equality. [37] In accord with the need to show that the leaders of the movement were women who led a rich family life, fulfilling all its duties, the example of Jewish women of whom this was true, was often given Lina Morgenstern in Berlin, was a pioneer in creating public kitchens for people in need. It is said that she ". . . . is a Jew, and possesses the talent and energy, which is prevalent amongst the descendants of that race. . . . [she has] a husband and five children." [38] Her American counterpart is pointed out as a model housekeeper fulfilling her difficult family duties:

Miss Nina Morais. . . . is the daughter of the Rabbi of the Portuguese Synagogue in Philadelphia, in the Sabbath school of which she is an efficient teacher. She is described as an unassuming girl, with a practical knowledge of what is commonly called a woman's sphere, inasmuch as she is a model housekeeper for her widowed father, and takes excellent care of half a dozen younger sisters. She has contributed for some time past to various journals, without having previously attracted marked attention.[39]

Apart from these newspaper stories, Jewesses also appear in the news as speakers at women's rights rallies, as the German Suffrage Association of New York which was also supported by Jewish men.[40] In particular cases, such support at meetings is especially pointed out: ". . . . Rabbi Gottheil, who has long been an advocate of our cause, has recently addressed some parlor meetings on the subject." [41]

With the founding of the National Council of Jewish Women, a direct way to the Jewish women's organizations was opened and its importance was stressed in the women's press: "One of the most noteworthy of the many confederations of women recently organized throughout the country is the National Council of Jewish Women, started in Chicago during the World's Fair and whose headquarters are in that city. . . ." [42]

Reports on Council activities, subsequent to its having joined the general women's organization of the country, acknowledge that with the creation of the Council the women's movement has been strengthened:

Jewish Women's Council. Editors Woman's Journal

The latest accession to the membership of the National Council of Women of the United States is a valuable one, though it is a very young organization.

The National Council of Jewish Women was indirectly the outgrowth of the great Congress of Representative Women in the Columbian year; but it has already made good progress, and can be said truly of national scope, judging not only by the territory in which it has officers, but by the value of the names upon its long official list. Among them are those already known in both literary and philanthropic work, as well as probably in the work of their own church.

But the National Council of Jewish Women, while it is certainly an organization for the furtherance of its own religious

work, does not confine itself to that in its statement of purpose as
set forth in its own Constitution, Article II. . . . the National Council feels itself strengthened by the accession to its membership of
those earnest Jewish women, with their memories and traditions
reaching back to the time when Miriam sang the song for the de-
liverance of her people, and Deborah prophesied their triumphs,
and herself led them to victory.

Rachel Foster Avery[43]

Two years later it is also clear to the outsider that the Council's real
essence is striving for Jewish religious renewal, and this is described in
detail:

Progressive Jewish women

It is very probable that the majority of Christians do not realize
the deep religious feeling of Jewish women. Perhaps an inkling of
this may be gained when one hears that the foundation of this
National Council is the study of the Jewish faith as found in the
Bible, and also the other literature that pertains to it.

The enthusiasm of the members is unrivaled by any similar
organization, and this may be easily accounted for when one remembers that this is the first time the Jewish women have met
together on a basis of work and study.

. . . the writer was greatly impressed by the conversation of
these Jewish ladies as they gathered in little groups, chatting together, before Miss America addressed them as a body.

They were probably all wealthy women, and their talk showed
them to be well educated. The sociological and philanthropic questions were much the same as one hears among other liberalminded
women, but the discussion of the religious question, the fervor with
which they spoke of the need of greater spirituality amongst those
of the ancient faith, the necessity of training their little ones, not
in the letter of the law alone, but in that true spirit which giveth
life, made an impression on the listener that will not be easily
shaken off.

One cannot help feeling that here is a set of women whose

power for good in the community would be very great, and whose cooperation with their so-called Christian sisters is something to be earnestly desired.

Florence Hunt[44]

A closeness to the life in the Jewish communities, especially in bigger cities, had early produced an interest in events there in the women's press. Especially when matters concerned general progress of any aspect relevant to the women's rights movement were involved. For instance, the exchange of pulpits starting at that time is reported as a progressive sign of the times: "The Chicago *Pulpit* tells of the fraternization of sects brought about by the last fire. A Jewish and a Presbyterian congregation use alternately the Second Presbyterian Church. The Universalists by courtesy of a Jewish congregation, worship in a synagogue." [45]

Contrasting instances of intolerance at the restricted hotel-resort or the humiliation of Negroes in white churches are likewise reported and connected directly with aspects of the women's rights movement: "Have patience, despised Jew, ostracised Negro and disfranchised woman. The end is not yet. . . ." [46] This is true especially of the Hilton-Seligman affair in Saratoga which is illustrated also by other critical voices of the time.[47] Furthermore the legal inequality of the Jews in Rumania is ranked with that of the women in America.[48] Nevertheless, as a consequence of free discussion, there are also occasionally heard unfriendly opinions about the Jews in the women's press: ". . . As a sectarian body they are building fine synagogues and some charitable institutions for their own people. But of what use are they to the country at large? . . ." [49] Recriminations against such an article are rejected with a reference to free speech:

> Our neighbour, the *Jewish Messenger,* complains of a correspondent who gives his opinion as to quality and value of Jewish citizenship in the United States. . . . *The Revolution* is open to free thought and speech, and would rather the right were at times a little abused than that it should be denied or abridged.[50]

Sometimes, unfriendly references to Jewish woman are masked as referring to "many poor and ignorant Jewesses" rather than "educated and intelligent ones like the late Baroness Hirsch." [51]

Finally, a Jewess as the martyr of the times is shown to the reader and honored in the American way:

Madame Dreyfus

> As an expression of their sympathy with Captain Dreyfus, the people of Wichita, Kan., have selected Miss Sadie Joseph, a Jewish girl, as queen of the street carnival to be held next month.[52]

As a contrast to the highly honored Jewess appears the controversial "Sarah Bernhardt—The other side" with her four children out of wedlock in a discussion drawn out over quite a few numbers of the newspaper.[53] Even the gossip of Jewesses was newspaper material, as, for instance, the conversion of a Christian woman in Hartford for the purpose of marrying the Jew Dr. Jordan: "The diamonds given to the new daughter of Israel at the nuptials are valued at $50,000. Thus has Miss Livingstone "passed over (to) Jordan." [54] Social intercourse of Jewish and gentile women was lifted to an entirely different plane by the women's movement. The instrument effecting this change was the American women's clubs in which Jewesses mingled with gentile women of various milieus and classes. With the general rise of club life in the world of men, the leisure world of woman also began to take on organized forms, developing a proper women's life in a club world challenging the men's prerogative. It became more and more important that the women's leisure time coincided with the working hours of the men and the social life of women could therefore bring about a broadening of the interests of the men:

> And the husbands, brothers and sons bear them no grudge. They think it delightful to come home after a day devoted to business, and be told by their womankind all that is going on in the world of leisure; the women skim the reviews, the books, and the news for the benefit of the men.[55]

By the end of the century, the Jewess was already quite at home in the women's club. Thus, a speaker at the Jewish Women's Congress in Chicago, in 1893, pointed with pride and hope for the future at the Jewish woman:

> A potent factor toward the production of one of the finest accomplishments of the age—the fin-de-siècle woman—is the club.
>
> All over the United States, in city and in hamlet, are ethical, philosophical, historical, and political organizations, whose one great aim is the betterment of humanity through the elevation of the sex. The majority of the members of these clubs are Christians, but some are Jews; in the chronicle pertaining to the advancement of Jewish women, the history of the position of the club is therefore still an unwritten chapter. The fact that the honored president and projector of this present congress [Hannah G. Salomon] is an enthusiastic club woman, should be eloquent testimony in favor of the further extension of organization among the women of Israel.
>
> This is called the "Woman's Age," and America is called the "Woman's Paradise." The intellectual and civic liberties more and more recorded to our sex, are open to Jew as well as Christian.[56]

Indeed, the openness of the women's clubs to Jewesses represented a complete contrast to the club-world of men which was generally a "restricted" place for the Jew. There was also entirely different social functions in the two club worlds; for men the club signified an achieved social position justifying their exclusive leisure. For the American woman, however, her club was an instrument of the personal rise of woman as a human being using her free time to gain a better basis for her demands to American society. In this liberating struggle the Jewish woman was a welcome participant from the beginning.

Especially valued was the club-joining of women in small places: "Especially is this so of women in the small cities. To them it is the stepping-stone by which they can reach the advantages of their more fortunately situated sisters."[57]

A certain pioneer pride animated the Jewish members of these clubs

in the first phase of the club movement which could well have slowed
up the formation of women's clubs. But "We are beyond the false pride
of a decade or two ago, when many so-called cultured Jewesses boasted
of their admission to non-Jewish circles, marked by a corresponding re-
tirement from Jewish associations. . . ." [58]

This transition was all the easier since the open club world of women
was such a contrast to restricted men's clubs; the achievement of Jewish
women could therefore be contrasted to the unsuccessful endeavors of
the Jewish men who wanted to achieve admission to clubs. By a subtle
process, often with the help of active persons from gentile circles, the
atmosphere of the general American club world of women was transferred to the Jewish women's clubs. In a rather short time, the club
sphere of the Jewish woman appeared as an arm of the general consciousness of the American woman. Soon this process is seen in historic
retrospect:

> The club movement in this country is about twenty years old.
> At that time women began to feel that they must pass out of their
> narrow individualistic lives into a broader communion; that they
> must prepare themselves to enter new industrial, new social, new
> political conditions. [59]

The transition from the habitual small social circles of the Jewish
woman to wide-open clubs with cultural programs occurred all over.
Its social consequences of broadening the interest of one person in
another is valued as the great novelty of the time: "Not only in the
small country places is the club movement breaking down artificial
barriers, but also in the great cities. The club women are becoming so
sensible that they do not attempt to keep up a formal calling acquaint-
ance with club members. They meet in this informal pleasant way once
a month, twice a month, all discussing subjects of interest. . . . a social
life that is narrow and contracted, bringing together only a few people,
is like a dwarfed flower. . . ." [60]

Hopes for a complete triumph of the new forms of social life over the
habitual old ones, however comfortable they might have been, was announced openly: "The council may take the place of the oldtime Kaf-

feeklatsch, so endeared to many by long association and familiarity." [61]

In giving full weight to the new developments in the women's organizations the ongoing process of changing the life of the synagogue by new forms of social life, highly dependent on a transformed women's life, came to expression in the Jewish women's press: "The Jews of the Western metropolis have inaugurated a new Friday evening feature . . . The balls, fairs and festivals held on Friday evenings are for the benefit of charity or in the interests of congregations, and while the temples are empty, the members flock to the Friday evening festivals with the earthly zest for pleasures." [62]

In surveying the influx of Jewish women into the women's movement it may be said that although it started late, the ferment produced by it was already effective among them. This is especially true of young Jewish women who were forced seriously to survey their possible future way of life, and no longer considered marriage as the only possible alternative. Models from the gentile world of professions achieved by women began to prove their effectiveness, since the general changes in the American woman's life were bound to spill over into Jewish society, too. Jewish women writers, however small their number, carried this conviction to the Jewish press and expressed it in their books.

CHAPTER ELEVEN

The Creative Woman

This chapter tries to evaluate the creativity of Jewish women, native and otherwise, under the general aspects of women's creativity in America of the nineteenth century before it goes into a detailed picture of the creativity of the German Jewish woman's immigrant generation.

The nineteenth century merely indicated the plane on which the rise of the second generation of immigrant women would take place in the future. Even in cases where creative natures had found already their paths in life, the period of their full achievement fell mostly in the coming century.[1]

Nevertheless there were a number of female personalities, some of them even of foreign birth, whose creativity was fulfilled in the century in which they were born.[2] Some of them were performers on the stage. Jewish stars of the theater were, like other performing artists, American residents only for part of their lifetime; the great exception to this was Adah Isaac Menken, the talk of America for a long time and whose way of life was deeply deplored. Thus, Leo Shpall wrote:

> Poor Adah! when she died she left the world a book of poems that reveal an inner life of love for the true, the pure, the beautiful, that none could have imagined possible in the actress, whose public and private life were alike sensual and scandalous. . . . This unfortunate girl, a victim of society, was full of genius and tenderness. . . . under more fortunate circumstances she might have been an honor to her sex.[3]

Of the touring stars, it was the "Jewess," Sarah Bernhardt, who caused a real commotion from the Atlantic to the Pacific. Commentary and caricature secured for the "Jewess" a page in the chroniques scandaleuses, which was new in America.[4]

There were some Jewesses also acting on the American stage.[5] With the flow of Russian Jewish immigration there came about the arrival of whole artists' families and of troups with women members. By this time, the days when, due to the dearth of women, men had to play female roles, was already over.[6]

A different class of creative Jewesses achieved its standing in American literature, although under circumstances different from that of gentile female writers.[7] In public life they were already speakers, organizers, and reformers,[8] some of them, products of the native Sephardic Jewry, Lea Harby, Emma Lazarus, Penina Moise, Ada Menken as writers, Nina Morais and Maud Nathan as fighters for women's rights. The latter had gone among the English suffragists and became their historian.[9]

There was however one outstanding personality that couldn't be ranged among others due to the extraordinary circumstances of her life and mental growth. All that can be said of her in comparison with the others, was that earlier than all other Jewish women in America, she opened the eyes of the world to what could be expected from the Russian Jewess in the future. Ernestine Rose's course of life ended in the nineteenth century, the Russian rabbi's daughter had risen to the position of leading ideologist of the women's rights movement, and so she remained all the days of her life. She was a child of the Enlightenment, but from the sparse data about her life it cannot be deducted that she was at any time influenced by the specific Jewish form of Enlightenment, the Haskalah, since her secular philosophy had no connection with the Jewish community in America; her achievements, however, were fully recognized there.[10] She defended the Jewish community wherever it was wronged.

Hers was a kind of philosophy of law deeply embedded in a conviction that to bring order to the world, only good laws are necessary.[11] She transplanted the basic concept of Jewish law that regulated Jewish life for many generations, to the secular realm, with no reference to Jewish religion. In fact, she denied that rules for the religious life of the individual could be of any help for order in the area of secular life. Only cooperation for practical purposes with religious persons was possible for her.[12]

Nevertheless, if we analyse the conceptual basis of her ideology, we discover that it is essentially Jewish messianism under the cloak of secularity. With her rejection of speculations on the Hereafter, stressing that only this world is given to man and his works, she remains in the midst of the Jewish world of thought.

As the great infidel of the women's movement, her Jewish mainsprings of thought never led back to the source, and always remained cryptic. This hidden nature, however, is also conditioned by the contemporary situation; at the time of her great fight, no organized Jewish social movement of humanism existed. It is therefore conceivable that only a spiritually cryptic Jewess was in the position to be leader and main speaker for the movement of the women of her time. In the same manner, even much later, Jewish men could still lead the social movements of humanism of their time.

Her philosophy was in sharpest contrast to that of the other great woman agitator, who matured in the nineteenth century, Emma Goldman. To her, every evil originated in the law as a matter of principle, and it did not pay to seek good laws; only freedom from law could avoid evil and bring good into the world.[13] The great paradox in Emma Goldman's life was that she did not find any contact with the Jewish social movement of humanism, at that time already advancing strongly. In Europe the combination of Western European ideals with Judaism (cultural Zionism, Martin Buber, André Spire and Bernard Lazare), was already a reality. In Palestine, the Jewish Labor movement, building cooperative settlements and institutions, was applying to the education of children the things she so admired in educational systems like the revolutionary one in Spain. In addition to this, the previously artificial estrangement of the Jewish workers in America from the building process in Palestine caused by their leaders had been set aside. Insofar as there still existed threads to her past, spent in the Jewish workers' milieu, and her present thinking, she might have, but didn't, find the way to the Jewish workers organizations in Palestine.

These two, Ernestine Rose and Emma Goldman, were the Jewesses of whom America spoke when the world of serious thinking was concerned. Aside from them, there were still other voices of female writers who could influence public opinion.

a) Female Writers

In the gentile world, the figure of the female fiction writer was already familiar to readers of the popular magazines as well as other readers of fiction who bought light literature on the book market. In the literature of etiquette, the female writer held a dominant position. What was clear to contemporaries, however, was that fiction writing had become a woman's profession, a number of whom were earning their living by writing. Most of them were spinsters and widows who did not feel that they would go under without a husband to support them, and insofar as their product was salable, they moved freely in the commercial world of publishing, its contracts with writers in the magazines, and had connections with publishers. That there were no such professional Jewish women writers, was seen to be a result of a defect in the education of Jewish girls.[14]

As for the few Jewesses who did undertake literary adventures, only a few succeeded in breaking through to fame—in the twentieth century—where their names became known throughout the world. The others were women from well-to-do families for whom every step outside the family into the public world was taken only with the greatest effort. There could be no question of professional writing for them, connections with popular magazines existing only in extraordinary cases; the door that was open to them was through the Jewish press. In the Jewish newspapers we find the results of their poetic fancy in great numbers of poems, short and longer novels as serials. Much in contrast to fiction written by non-Jewish women, which were on the whole conventional society novels, the Jewish writers worked on Jewish historical themes, into which naive love stories were woven. There were also typical stories of immigrants, where the "green" character maintained his moral concepts from the old world into the new.

Some of them also excercised social criticism in the Jewish press, discussing intimate questions of women's concern such as how to meet members of the other sex, courtship, matchmaking and matrimony, especially marriage for money. All this criticism remained inside the Jewish community; there was no woman writer who would have written these things for the popular magazines of the gentiles.

The only one personality of this group of writers who went outside the Jewish world at the same time was Emma Lazarus, who was of Sephardic descent. She was extraordinary in that her work that belonged completely to the nineteenth century, was accepted as the literary heritage of Judaism and the Jewish people by the gentile world. At the same time she was acknowledged to be the active speaker for her people by the Jewish world and above all for its new immigrants, the Russian Jews, in the American women's press:

> *Miss Lazarus* has reviewed Mme. Ragozin's second-hand arraignment of the Jews point by point. Miss Lazarus speaks not only from her reading, but from conversations with the expatriated Jews in this country and she describes the "hundreds of homeless refugees on Ward's Island, New York harbor, among whom are not a few men of brilliant talents and accomplishments, the graduates of Russian universities, scholars of Greek as well as Hebrew, familiar with all the principal European tongues—engaged in menial drudgery, burning with real zeal in the cause." [15]

Emma Lazarus's sister, Josephine, a gifted essayist, created an image of Madame Dreyfus as the symbol of the martyr Jewess: ". . . especially for us, Women, nineteenth-century, twentieth-century women, the star shines immortal, throwing light upon the path for every one of us, an ideal of true womanhood. . . ." [16]

To her belonged also the distinction of having been the only woman who ever created a religious controversy by a collection of essays: "The spirit of Judaism." [17] Her opponents included men of the orthodox as well as from the new liberal wing of Judaism.[18] Emil Hirsch took exception to her partial identification of Judaism with Unitarianism: "Miss Lazarus has not grasped the principles of Jewish Radicalism . . . the Radical cannot exchange the sound, soul-inspiring 'law' for this sweet sentimental hysteria dignified by the label 'love.' Unitarianism and Judaism are not identical." [19] Some fiction publications outside of the Jewish press group of writers deserve special mention because of the personality of the author, her special theme, or her achievement under special circumstances:

Annie Nathan Meyer, of old Sephardic stock, published a novel in 1893 dealing with the conflict between career and marriage in the life of the modern woman.[20] She was also the editor of *Woman's Work in America*. In her autobiography[21] the strong influence of her Jewish family life are described. She received her education in Columbia University's Collegiate Course for Women which was "a substitute for a college education."[22]

The intermarriage of Jew and gentile was the subject of Emma Wolf's novel *All Other Things Equal* and deserves a place in this group.[23] It is characteristic that, as in later times, this serious theme was treated by a woman in a more serious vein than by men who only described what they saw superficially. Of Emma Wolf, however, could be written: "Through the medium of this strong, pure and artistic romance, the author, herself a young Jewess, treats the question of intermarriage in a novel and peaceful manner."[24]

The exception to the rule was Mary Antin, a Russian Jewish immigrant girl who was an accomplished author in American literature by the nineteenth century.[25] Her autobiography, was written in Yiddish and appeared in English translation.

A full breakthrough to the heights of American literature, beginning in the nineteenth century and reaching full productivity in the twentieth century, is symbolized by three figures: Gertrude Stein, Edna Ferber, and Fanny Hurst, descendants of German Jewish families. Feelings of their Jewish descent are always present and strong in their family memories that comprise impressions of religious education and first thoughts of the values of the Jewish religion, as they remained in the memory of Gertrude Stein,[26] Edna Ferber and Fanny Hurst. The last two, in addition to their Jewish education and self-education, also wrote about their impressions of the Jewish atmosphere of women in the nineteenth century.[27] Of other women authors of the second German Jewish generation the same may be said.

All in all, female Jewish authors in the nineteenth century moved in a modest framework. Nevertheless, due to the advantages of higher education many young Jewesses gained a start in literary artistry. For instance, an article, "The Jewess in San Francisco," was able to mention a number of literary personalities together.[28] Even more hopeful was the prognosis, set up for the Jewess as an author:

> It is not difficult to forecast the future of the Jewess in authorship. She is a partaker in the new education; she enters all the professions; she shares the ripest culture of the time; she responds to every movement that leads to honest, helpful living. The educated Jewess who graduates from Vassar or Bryn Mawr, from Cornell or Barnard, who pursues higher collegiate training at Harvard or Yale, is on the same intellectual level as her non-Jewish chum.[29]

In Yiddish literature in America, only Anna Rappaport published poetry as early as 1893.[30]

The German Jewish immigrant woman took her unique place in the Jewish women's world of America by the fact that a literary activity in her mother tongue—German—was granted to her twofold. First in the natural frame of German American literature and then in the German Jewish press of America. In German American publications, Minna Kleeberg held her unique place as standard-bearer of German poetry until her untimely death.[31] Her thoughts on educational and other matters of public interest were published readily in the main German American educational periodical, the *Erziehungsblätter*.[32] There are also literary contributions of Jewish women teachers in editions of the German teachers' organizations in America.[33]

In the frame of the Jewish press, two women's papers in German existed: the *Die Deborah* and the *Ordens Echo*. *Die Deborah* was founded by Isaac Mayer Wise in 1855, by the side of his *Israelite* in English, which stayed on, under different editors, until 1902. Its main purpose was illumination of the German Jewish woman in the tenets of Judaism through the voices of learned Jewish men, and, next to it, also entertaining through the medium of the light novel.[34]

Entirely different was the *Ordens-Echo,* organ of the first woman's Order, the *Treue Schwestern* (True Sisters), founded in 1846 by Henrietta Bruckman with the declared purpose "to learn and to teach, to observe and to exercise" (zu lernen und zu lehren, zu beobachten und auszuüben). All activities of German Jewish women in the order and in other befriended organizations of German Jewish women, show up there in detailed reports, next to articles on questions especially important for these women.[35] Their artistic creativity is given expression by publication of numerous poems of German Jewesses in America in their mother tongue, German.[36]

Publication of their collected German poems in book form was achieved by Minna Kleeberg and Minna Neuer.[37] Both collections include religious poems next to worldly ones. In the case of Minna Kleeberg her poetical gift of giving Jewish religious thought a classical form was crowned by the inclusion of ten of her poems representing a cycle of the Jewish festivals in the most important book of hymns of the Reform Synagogue, compiled by Isaac M. Wise in 1866.[38]

The anglicization of the German Jewish woman in America is fully reached in the last decade of the nineteenth century and *The American Jewess* is the milestone of this achievement. This women's paper enjoyed the spritual guidance of the rabbis Emil G. Hirsch and Dr. Adolph Moses from its first number of 1895, the year of its appearance. Further on, the paper, edited by Rose Sonneschein, consisted of articles on all questions conceived as important for Jewish women, as written by women.[39]

b) The Jewess in American Folklore and Popular Literature

Certain strains of literary notions of the Jewess spring from concepts of her in real life. In addition, there are also romantic concepts of her which spring from a need to confront the extraordinary, unexplainable in the stature of the Jew and his female counterpart in the history of mankind.

Reduced to its simplest form the romantic concept is used to create a feeling of the extraordinary in a situation by the intercession of a Jewish figure, preferably the Jewess herself. This device was used in European popular literature and spilled over into early American creations of the same kind. If a man was concerned, it might have been the arrival of a Jewish peddler that triggered off a turn toward the extraordinary; if a woman, she filled the literary prescription even more easily. The description given of her did not need to be very original: ". . . a young girl made her appearance, with fine Jewish eyes . . . tall and nobly formed. . . . 'But do you know, fair Jewess?' he demanded quickly." [39a]

The modest device of having the situation turn on her is followed by a much more literary adventure of romanticism: The mental attitude toward the historic Jewish people living under the onus of the crucifixion story is to be changed by this new concept of the Jewess, in which the magic notion of the Jewess's beauty, otherwise just an inexplicable as the historic stature of the Jew, was most instrumental:

Beauty of Jewesses

It is related that Chateaubriand, on returning from his eastern travels, was asked if he could assign a reason that the women of the Jewish race were so much handsomer than the men, when he gave the following one:—"Jewesses," he said, "have escaped the curse which alighted on the fathers, husbands, and sons. Not a Jewess was to be seen amongst the crowd of priests and rabble who insulted the Son of God. . . ." [40]

It is highly significant that the literary-folkloristic concept of her beauty, originating in Europe, traveled so early to America. Actually, in descriptions by travelers to America and their diaries pointing out certain figures and social events, like the Franks, and the famous "Meschianza" would lead us to believe that the reverse was actually true, that the notions flowed from the New to the Old World. This romanticism was, to a great extent, a substitute for the real situation—which was that the American Jewess did not appear in public life—but included a few romantic figures known by hearsay. But through Europe, in returning the literary beauty motif, religious tradition was added that America could build on further: "The women of Judea believed in the Saviour; they loved, they followed him; they assisted him with their substance, they soothed him under affliction," [41] and were rewarded with beauty.

Her beauty is also the bearer of all the hopes left to the Jews: "As every beautiful Hebrew maiden hopes to be the mother of *Him* who, in their estimation, will restore their ancient glories, let us all, at least, wish that their emancipation be near at hand." [42]

The literary beauty motif, moreover, doesn't exclude more prosaic observations in daily American life, attributing beauty where it belongs or, for that matter, even claiming it where this becomes necessary:

Feature of Broadway

"The wonderful influx of well-dressed and handsome young Jews, lately, in Broadway, has astonished the promenading public . . . *Home Journal*." . . . In justice to the daughters of Judah, we must press an amendment, and if the"fashionable editor" will give himself the pleasure of another promenade up Broadway, he will second it—for "handsome Jews" read "neatly attired and beautiful Jewesses." That is the way to put it. . . . [43]

The prerogative of romanticism didn't last too long, as always when poetry tries to live at the expense of prose. The shining Jewess may become the evil-doer as in the old English ballad of ritual murder, transplanted to different regions in variants and finally taken down to Virginia.[44] The story of the converted Jew is matched also by that of the converted Jewess.[45] The usual prosaic stereotypes are also dealt out to her: "She is a plump *little* Jewess" [46]; and just as she is "little," she is also "rich," which circumstance makes her a better person: "It is true she is a Jewess. But she is rich." [47]

Richness with cupidity had to be shown in the great social sensations of the time: "In justice to Mlle. Rachel, it should be said, however, that it is not she so much as her father, a regular Hebrew, who has displayed such indecorous cupidity." [48]

In the end, it was still the stereotype of the stingy Jewess that was victorious: "Now, it must be borne in mind that the veriest Shylock of her race was not more keenly alive to the value of money than Rachel. Paris is full of stories illustrative of this. 'She is not a Jewess—she's a perfect Jew,' said someone who wished to give epigrammatic intensity to the expression of the general sentiment." [49] But the crowning story of her avarice is the "Mosaic mother," a space filler of American humor in general newspapers transported here from England: After her son plunged to his death from the theater gallery, she demanded reimbursement for the ticket he bought.[50] The story also exists in a rhymed version.

Occasionally, prudence was a characteristic attributed to her. Sharing a hatred of pork with the rest of Jewry, she might have used it for a protest against the rude demeanor of some man, and the story ends with gallant words in her favor:

> A well known rake, sitting in Drury Lane Theatre behind a very pretty girl, was very crude to her. The girl, however appeared as if she did not or would not hear him, but as he became more bold and impudent, she at last turned round and said with an angry countenance: "Be pleased to let me alone!" To which the surprised and confounded freebooter could only answer, "Nay, do not eat me!" upon which the girl said was a smile—"be not afraid, *I am a Jewess.*" [51]

The many stories with a Jewess or, at least, a biblical female figure in the title, makes use of this device simply to awaken curiosity and romantic feeling.[52] The overwhelming majority of Americans, at least until 1880, may never have met a Jewess in life.

On a purely folkloristic basis, as a good-luck charm rests the use of "Jewess" in naming a race horse: *"Miss Jewess . . . a beautiful four-year-old filly,"* [53] or even a biblical name like *Vashti.*[54] The compliment to the Jewess by this naming of the horse was the more remarkable because in many other areas of folklore, the mere sight of the Jewish man meant bad luck.

The more visible the Jewess became in American life, the more did the romantic aspects of her image in literature give way to realistic descriptions in humoristic literature, even in caricature. The special events in Jewish family life as conceived in American humor and caricature gave the Jewess a place beside her husband. Engagements and weddings were the favored subjects of the humorists as well as the children tutored by their mother.[55] The wife also shares her husband's fate in the ups and downs of social life. For instance, the caricature "No Jewesses Admitted" showed the Jewess standing before the hotel-keeper as the "one who is not admitted under any circumstances." [56] Although his loyalty to his wife was never doubted, the husband's lack of gallantry to her was derided.[57]

In Germany, a familiar role of the Jewish woman was to be her husband's economic helpmate.

c) The Social Worker

As a connecting link between the two Jewish female immigrant generations, the German and the Russian, the female social worker achieved an importance far beyond her numbers and institutional employment. New life came to the philanthropy of the Ladies' Benevolent Society through the new institutions for working girls. Industrial schools, settlements, girls' clubs and homes demanded older full-time philanthropists as planners of all these institutions and as the persons to realize these plans. This kind of philanthropist accommodating to the new demands of social work, originated in the older generation of German-born Jewish women.[58] Their enthusiasm for this new work was kindled by collaboration with young professional social workers to whom fell the executive roles in the new institutions. The older philanthropists were mostly the same personalities who recognized the whole field of women's activities in the Jewish communities and founded the National Council of Jewish Women that built up social help for the working girl through its local branches. In contrast, the young social worker was wholly the product of her times which had given to the female youth of America their first chance at a higher profession. It is possible to survey their biographical data through their own statements, and to group them according to viewpoints significant for the whole picture of the Jewish social worker. The means to this are the answers to an inquiry of social workers, worked into 327 biographical sketches, of which 89 were women. Although published in 1905, their contents prove that all these social workers were already employed in Jewish institutions in the nineteenth century.[59]

With few exceptions the young female social worker was native-born and American bred.[60] Her schooling reveals the complex picture of the restricted possibilities for the Jewish girl even during the last two decades of the nineteenth century; On the other hand, we learn that new opportunities occurred for her, and were fully exploited. Thus, a not inconsiderable percentage of Jewish female social workers were already graduates of higher schools. Furthermore, there was among them a fresh influx to special courses in universities and colleges—even if all of them did not achieve academic degrees.

Only in a few cases had a social worker received her schooling in a convent school or a French school.[61] It was largely through the higher girls' school that the future social worker got her start. This school, under different names and variants in the curriculum, especially in the selection of languages, included Jewish and other private schools. Only the local historian could evaluate the standing of each.[62] Most often, the girl chose the regular teacher training in a seminary of the state or in a private school recognized by the state as a teachers' seminary, known as normal schools or colleges and the degree granted in them started the only publicly secured career of woman of that time.[62] In a few cases, the girl conquered all obstacles to medical study and achieved an MD.[63] There were special courses as close as they could get to practicing medicine, such as nursing and obstetrics. With the spread of specialties in medicine other auxiliary professions supporting these special fields were available to women.[64] The variety of university courses, taken according to the individual interests of the applicants, was most far-reaching in its influence.[65] Among the courses were such as criminology, sociology and in other fields important to the social worker.[66] Special places of training social workers, like the graduate school of philanthrophy, started about the end of the century.[67]

At the beginning of her studies the girls' future was still uncertain; even a graduate of a business college could finally end up as a social worker.

On Jewish instruction we learn only little from the biographical sketches. In some cases, the Talmud Yelodim in Cincinnati is mentioned.[68]

Notes

Abbreviations: AI: American Israelite, Israelite
JM: Jewish Messenger.

NOTES FOR INTRODUCTION:

1. This was the case especially in the local trade of Jews in small towns: "If one considers that in the whole class of Jews occupied with itinerant trade, second-hand and detail merchandizing, the women very actively participated in the business of their husbands, and, loaded with heavy packs, filled business errands, the proportion of the Christian journeying and the Jewish peddling women comes close to one another." (Dr. Ludwig Philippson. *Wie sich der Statistiker, Staatsrat, etc.* Dr. J. G. Hoffman verrechnet! Leipzig, 1842, p. 12.)

But also in the beginnings of early industrial capitalism of the Jews, female occupations can be proven to have existed in Germany. In 1785, the court Jew, Benjamin Veitel Ephraim, employed seven hundred Jewish female lacemakers in his factories at various places belonging to the Netze district incorporated into Germany in the year 1772. (Heinrich Schnee. *Die Hochfinanz und der moderne Staat,* vol. 1. Berlin: 1953, p. 163.)

2. Max Grünwald. *Die moderne Frauenbewegung und das Judentum.* Wien (Vienna): 1903.

NOTES FOR CHAPTER ONE:

1. Hutchins Hapgood. *The Spirit of the Ghetto. Studies of the Jewish Quarter of New York.* New York: 1902.

2. E. G. Hirsch. *A Tribute to the Memory of Liebman Adler.* Chicago: 1892, p. 11.

However, in 1902 Emil Hirsch wrote: ". . . We must cooperate in greater measure with Russian Jewish societies than we have done hitherto. All brain is not found on the East Side of the Chicago River. The Russianization of Judaism is a bugbear which has frightened us beyond all reasonableness. The Jews in the Ghetto also have hearts and some of them—let it be stated here—bigger hearts than many a professional charity lodge orator." "Emil G. Hirsch," *Reform Advocate,* vol. 23 (1902), p. 37.

3. Of forty-nine women in the "Biographical Sketches of Jewish Communal Workers in the United States" in the *American Jewish Yearbook* 5666(1905/6), pp. 32-118, are eleven born in Germany and five in Central and East Europe. They are:

Amram, Esther, b. Liebenau, Hanover; Baum, Esther, b. Tiefenthal, Germany; Bienstock, Sarah, b. Germany; Feustmann, Rosalia, b. Dürkheim am Haadt, Rhenish Bavaria; Steinem, Pauline, b. Memmingen, Bavaria; Weinschenker, Esther T., b. Mohileff, Russia; Joseph, Annie, b. Germany; Kohut, Rebekka, b. Kaschau, Hungary; Loeb, Johanne M., b. Rendsburg, Schleswig Holstein; Lubitz, Bertha F., b. Grodno, Lithuania; Mandel, Babette, b. Aufhausen, Württemberg; Mandl, Emma B., b. Pilsen, Bohemia; Mearson, Ida Charlotte, b. Jassy, Rumania; Schwab, Flora, b. Germany; Weinhandler, Hattie, b. Germany; Wirth, Sophia, b. Oppenheim, Germany.

4. A good picture of such eventual experiences we are gaining from Emma Goldman's memories of her days as a working girl in Rochester, in Richard Drinnon. *Rebel in Paradise.* Chicago: 1961, pp. 14-15.

5. *The Hebrew Watchword.* Devoted to the Interests of the Hebrew Sunday Schools of Philadelphia, vol. 1 (November, 1896), p. 6. "The Story of the Strike" describes the situation in the strikers' homes; October, 1896, p. 12, contains "Little Itzig, A story of real life," describing the heder and child peddlers.

NOTES FOR CHAPTER TWO:

1. *Allgemeine Zeitung des Judentums,* vol. 3 (July 20, 1839), p. 347.

2. *Der Orient,* vol. 7 (1846), p. 184.

3. A. Taenzer. *Die Geschichte der Juden in Jebenhausen und Göppingen.* Berlin: 1927, pp. 299, 301, 306, 338, 343, 364, 368-371.

4. Adolph Kober, "Jewish Emigration from Württemberg to the United States of America," in *Publications of the American Jewish Historical Society,* vol. 41 (March: 1952), pp. 225-273.

5. National Archives, *Passenger Lists.* 1837-1889.

6. Ibid. 1837-1890.

7. "Ein- und Auswanderung in Bayern während der Jahre 1835-1839," *Deutsche Schnellpost,* no. 41, (May 24, 1843).

8. *Allgemeine Zeitung des Judentums,* vol. 3 (1839), no. 24, p. 210.

Many who had hoped to found a family in Bavaria and missed the emigration, remained bachelors. In small communities it could take a number of years before a wedding was brought off. Simon Krämer, "Zur Geschichte der Juden in Bayern," in *Jewish Times,* vol. 5 (1873/74), p. 622:

"Our dear children and relatives in the thousands have they torn from us to seek true happiness in life in the far-off blessed America. . . ." (Ibid. p. 702.)

9. The most curious of taxes was the continuing of payments for reception and protection (*Aufnahme und Schutz*) to the noblemen who inherited estates, although the owners of these estates no longer retained the right to receive Jews because they had lost their sovereignty. In some places, these payments amounted to ten gulden a year per family. (*Sinai. Erlangen,* vol. II. 1847, p. 61, "Aus Unterfranken."

10. "Bayern," article in the *Encyclopedia Judaica.*

11. *Der Orient,* vol. 7 (1846), p. 184.

Blätter für Israels Gegenwart und Zukunft. . . . von Rev. R. Bellson," Berlin: 1845, pp. 373-374. "Of the German countries, it is mainly Bavaria from which a great contingent of Jewish emigrants wanders to North America every year. . . . Often they are young Jewish men who, in order to marry a beloved girl or bride, have to grasp the wander staff to the New World together with her."

12. *Jüdisches Volksblatt,* vol. 6 (1859), p. 8. The worries of the father of many daughters about securing a dowry for them are mirrored in old German Jewish folklore. Anecdotes prefer the scholar, as the sufferer blessed with four or even eight daughters. Also, *Jüdisches Volksblatt,* vol. 1 (1853), p. 80; vol. 2 (1854), p. 68.

13. *Niles Weekly Register,* vol. 51 (1836/37), p. 37.

14. "Eine jüdische Trauung im Zwischendeck," in *Jüdisches Volksblatt,* vol. 13 (1866), pp. 91-92. This marriage played a role in a much later lawsuit involving an inheritance.

15. L. Maria Child. *Letters from New York.* New York: 1843, p. 30.

16. Taenzer, *Geschichte der Juden,* p. 350.

17. Ibid., p. 369.
18. At first in Breslau in 1801. See, Martin Philippson. *Neueste Geschichte des jüdischen Volkes.* Leipzig: 1907, vol. 1, p. 151.
19. *Israelitische Annalen,* vol. 1. 1839, p. 102.
20. "Frankfurt am Main," *Sulamith.* 1809, vol. 2, p. 346.
21. "Aus Halberstadt . . . Schule . . . Lehrplan," in *Allgemeine Zeitung des Judentums,* vol. 1 (1837), p. 388.
22. "Aus Böhmen," in *Zeitschrift fur die religiösen Interessen des Judentums,* vol. 3 (1846), pp. 68-70, 69.
23. *Israelitische Annalen,* vol. 1 (1839), p. 49.
24. *Israelitische Annalen,* vol. 2 (1840), p. 101.
25. *Zeitschrift für die religiösen Interessen des Judentums,* vol. 3 (1876), p. 71, "Bayern."
26. "Bayern," in *Zeitschrift für die religiösen Interessen des Judentums,* vol. 3 (1846), p. 108.
27. "Über die bairischen Schullehrer," in *Allgemeine Zeitung des Judentums,* vol. 1 (1837), p. 374.
28. *American Jewish Yearbook* 5666 (1905/06), pp. 32-118.
29. Three Goldschmidt's in New York in "Mitgliederliste des Vereines deutscher Lehrerinnen in America, 1902."
30. Herma Clark. *The Elegant Eighties.* Chicago: 1941. For the status of German Jewish women in the *Chicago Woman's Club,* see pp. 58, 59.
31. Kober, *Jewish Emigration,* "Rosenheim Jette, 1400 fl. marriage."
32. Ibid. "Gideon, Lina, Rexingen, 72 fl. 50 fl. from the Jewish community, 22 fl. from private individuals."
In a case which we may assume as typical for families that could not spare money for dowries for growing girls, a father emigrated with his family: "A Jewish teacher, with his wife and three daughters, a dignified man with solid knowledge, experienced in life, full of tact and sound, correct judgment. . . . The Jewish girls . . . prayed on the deck on August 16th, reading piously from their prayerbooks. . . ." See, Leopold Kist. *Amerikanisches.* Mainz: 1871, pp. 95, 119.
33. "We took pains to open a branch of earning for the women and girls by instruction at the sewing machine . . . furthermore, we achieved work with preservation of food whereby $2.50 per week was earned." See, "Hebrew Emigrant Society" der Vereinigten Staaten (Gesellschaft zur Unterstützung israelitischer Emigranten), "Bericht des Präsidenten und Schatzmeisters für das Jahr 1882." New York: 1883, p. 15.

NOTES FOR CHAPTER THREE:

1. *Die Deborah,* vol. 2 (1856), p. 244.
2. *Allgemeine Zeitung des Judentums,* vol. 3 (May 4, 1839), p. 215.
3. *Jüdisches Volksblatt,* vol. 12 (1865), p. 104.
4. Ibid., "Aus Californien," vol. 4 (1857), p. 129.
5. Sonneschein, Rose, "The American Jewess," *The American Jewess,* vol. 6 (February, 1898), pp. 205-209, p. 208.
6. *Facts by a Woman.* Oakland, California: 1881, p. 280.
7. Rev. S. M. Isaacs, "The Reform Agitation," *Occident,* vol. 2 (1844/45), p. 283.
8. *Facts by a Woman.* Oakland, California: 1881, p. 280.
9. *Deseret News,* vol. 9 (1859), p. 48. "While the descendants of Cain, by the decrees of Him who framed the world, are ordained to be servants of servants to their

brethren, it is no part of that righteous decree that their masters shall mingle their seed with that of the negress and sell and mart their own blood for gold, thereby transferring the curse of Cain to their own prosperity. . . ."

10. *Shoe and Leather Reporter,* vol. 3, No. 52 (July 26, 1860), p. 1.

11. William Z. Ripley, "Race factors in labor unions," *Atlantic Monthly,* vol. 93 (1904), pp. 299-308, p. 300.

12. "Simon Krämer," *Die Wahrheit,* Prague, vol. (1872), p. 47.

13. *AI,* vol. 9 (1862), p. 155.

"San Francisco

. . . Many a hundred, yea thousands of humbled hearts in Europe are cheered by the remittances from California. We also have frequently noticed that husbands generously send to the relatives of their wives and wives gladly see the means of the house sent off to relieve the wants of the relatives of their husbands. —Large sums are expended by brothers and sisters to bring out their kin to this country to settle here."

14. *Protokolle der Rabbiner—Conferenz abgehalten zu Philadelphia vom 3. bis 6. November 1869.* New York: 1870, p. 25.

As to the weird problem of polygamy, German rabbis in America never tire of presenting to the German Jewish immigrant the terrible example of the sinister Mormons. See, "Die Geschichtsschreiber der Zukunft in Sachen der Frauen in der Neuen Welt," *Zeichen der Zeit,* Chicago, vol. 1 (1863), p. 28.

15. *AI,* vol. 9 (1862), p. 2. "Berlin." For other cases in which cooperation with rabbis in Europe was forthcoming, see *AI,* vol. 11 (1864/65), p. 357. In all these cases the by far graver situation in this respect in the following New Immigration already threw its shadow ahead.

16. Augusta Levy, "Recollections of a Pioneer Woman of La Crosse," in *Four Episodes in Wisconsin Pioneering.* Wisconsin State Historical Society, Madison, pp. 201-215.

Jacob R. Marcus. *Memoirs of American Jews. 1755-1855.* Philadelphia: 1955, vol. II, pp. 351-375.

For other Jewish pioneers' married life, see, Helen Smith, ed., "Pioneer Jewish Women" in, *With her Own Swings,* Portland, Oregon: 1948, pp. 219-223.

At Pine Lake, Wisconsin, lived the intermarried couple Von Schneidau, the husband a former Swedish officer, who emigrated with his bride, the former Froecken Jacobson, a Swedish Jewess. See, Mabel F. Hansen, "The Swedish Settlement on Pine Lake," in *Wisconsin Magazine of History,* vol. 8 (1924/25), pp. 38-51, p. 41.

17. *JM,* vol. 1 (1881), No. 10, p. 4.

18. Ibid., vol. 53 (1883), No. 2, p. 5. "The Visiting Question."

19. *The Jewish World, London,* vol. 3 (February 26, 1875), p. 3, "American Notes."

20. *Deseret News,* vol. 20 (1871), p. 379.

21. "Immunities of the Jewish Race," in ibid., vol. 18 (1869), p. 436.

22. "Maftir," in *AI,* vol. 34 (1887/88), no. 51, p. 8.

23. *JM,* vol. 50 (1881), no. 8, p. 1.

24. Fanny Hurst, *Anatomy of Me.* Garden City, New York: 1958, pp. 44, 71, 80. Some of these words stuck in the memory of children born in America. Thus Fanny Hurst, third generation of Bavarian Jews, remembers *gensbebla* (little goose), *shlemiel, rishus,* words used in the speech of her parents.

25. "Der Jargon," in *Die Deborah,* vol. 14 (1868/69), p. 190.

26. "Customs in the Jewish Quarter," in *Evening Post,* April 11, 1896, p. 2.

NOTES FOR CHAPTER FOUR:

1. *Nachrichten von der vereinigten Deutschen Evangelisch-Lutherischen Gemeinen in Nord-Amerika, absonderlich in Pennsylvanien.* Dr. Johann Ludwig Schulze. Halle: 1787, vol. 1, p. 417 (Pastor Handschuhs Tagesregister).
"On October 5, a child of an Englishman was baptized in his house in the presence of many other Englishmen and five Jewesses who appeared on this occasion to be quite suitable and devout. Thus, I wouldn't have believed that they are Jewesses if I hadn't been informed of it later."

2. "This was the illustrious celebration known in history under the name of "Mischianza" which was arranged for the departure of the general Howe . . . The queen of this feast was the beautiful, ingenious Jewess, Miss Franks, who was at that opportunity the lady of the British High Commander Sir Henry Clinton. . . ." (Doehla, Johann Konrad, "Amerikanische Feldzüge, 1777-1783," *Deutsch-Amerikanisches Magazine,* vol. 1 (Cincinnati, 1887), p. 398.

3. Doehla, p. 384.

4. Saratoga, the scene of a flagrant case of exclusion against the Jewish financier Seligman (1887) was, in the early national period, the place of the social swingers:

"The vacation

. . . Saratoga was indispensible. . . . Everyone is at home at the springs. People go there for amusement, and either as actors or observers they find it. There is no unnecessary etiquette, . . . the finest grouping in the world. —The "blood of the Howards," and the nouveaux riche, meet at the same table . . . The city belle and the dark-eyed Jewess float together in the dance. . . ." Cherry Valley Gazette, vol. 10 (1827/28), December 4, 1827, p. 4.

5. *The Nation,* vol. 41 (1885), p. 532, "Jews in American Society."

6. *AI,* vol. 28 (1881), p. 282 "San Francisco." The Maftir, at that opportunity makes a comparison with the much more favorable situation of past years in which invitations occurred in San Francisco more frequently.

7. *Young Israel.* An Illustrated Monthly for young people. New York. Vol. 1 (1871), p. 286.

8. "The blackballing of a Jewess in Martha Lodge, Sons of Herrman [sic], has resulted in the lodge being rent asunder, and fifty-four of the hundred and twenty-seven members have withdrawn and will form a new lodge. The Martha Lodge is composed entirely of women. The fact that the would-be member who was blackballed, as well as her sponsor, were Jews, led to the belief that Jews were not wanted in the lodge, and the fifty-four members who were of that belief decided to withdraw. Efforts were made to prevent the secession and patch up the differences.
The grand officers were brought here to effect an amicable settlement, but their visit was futile, and they allowed matters to take their course." "Milwaukee, Wisc.," *Hebrew Standard,* vol. 41 (1900), no. 34, p. 6.

9. In criticizing the Jewish women for hiding the evidence of their faith, the Maftir praises Irish women who displayed their religiosity on their walk to church: "It is refreshing to see the Catholic Irish attending church every morning during Lent. . . . I rejoice to see them as they proudly display their *Key of Heaven,* with the gilt Roman cross upon its covers. . . . There is certainly no use in being ashamed to let the world know what you practice, as is the case with most of our Jews, especially with the female portion thereof. . . ." *AI,* vol. 33 (1886/87), no. 36, p. 9.

10. *The Nation,* vol. 41 (1885), p. 532.

11. *AI,* vol. 14 (1867/68), no. 7, p. 4. See, "In New York,".

A further turn for the worse came in later years when the husband did his card playing at the club, that in many cases removed him from the family table. This situation aroused the critic:

". . . . for a man blessed with a good wife and children to abandon them repeatedly for the attractions of a club can not be excused upon any ground except incompatibility of temper." *JM,* vol. 51 (1883), no. 21, p. 1.

12. *JM,* vol. 50 (1881), no. 15, p. 1.

13. *JM,* vol. 53 (1883), no. 3, p. 1.

14. *JM,* vol. 51 (1882), no. 12, p. 4. "The question of visiting."

15. Ibid.

16. *JM,* vol. 49 (1881), no. 10, p. 1.

17. *JM,* vol. 51 (1882), no. 5, p. 4.

18. Ibid.

19. *JM,* vol. 49 (1881), no. 10, p. 1.

20. Louis Finkelstein. *Jewish Self-Government in the Middle Ages.* New York: 1924, pp. 61, 240.

21. *AI,* vol. 29 (1883), p. 341.

22. *JM,* vol. 57 (1885), no. 2, p. 1.

23. "The question of visiting," in ibid., vol. 51 (1882), no. 12, p. 4.

24. Ibid.

25. Ibid.

26. Ibid., vol. 53 (1883), no. 3, p. 1.

27. "At home," Ibid., vol. 51 (1882), no. 5, p. 4.

28. Ibid.

29. "Our Society," ibid., vol. 51 (1882), no. 5, p. 5.

30. Ibid.

31. Ibid.

32. Ibid., vol. 53 (1883), no. 7, p. 4.

33. "The Coming Saison," vol. 54 (1883), no. 12, p. 4.

34. Ibid., vol. 53 (1883), no. 5, p. 1.

35. Ibid., vol. 53 (1883), no. 15, p. 1.

36. Ibid., vol. 53 (1883), no. 6, p. 1.

37. Ibid., vol. 53 (1883), no. 5, p. 1.

38. Ibid., vol. 53 (1883), no. 6, p. 1.

39. Ibid.

40. "The visiting question," ibid., vol. 53 (1883), no. 2, p. 5.

NOTES FOR CHAPTER FIVE:

1. Arthur M. Schlesinger. Learning How to Behave. A Historical Study of American Etiquette Books. New York: 1947.

2. Gottheil, Dr. Gustav. "The Jewess as she was and is," *Ladies Home Journal,* vol. 15 (December, 1897), p. 21.

3. "San Francisco," *AI,* vol. 28 (1881), p. 282. "The lady, whose husband does a very fair business and is able to give poker parties at least once a month, reached Europe with a plethoric purse and lots of fine dresses and a miniature pawn shop of jewelry. . . . After showing her fine dresses and jewelry to all Schwersenz, and strutting about like a peacock in the highways and byways, without recognizing the women who used to work in the same kitchen with her, she kept her room and courted the Moses. . . ."

4. "The American Jewess. II. In Society," *JM,* vol. 50 (1881), no. 9, p. 1.

5. Ibid.
6. M. E. Sherwood. *The Art of Entertaining*. New York: 1892, p. 396.
7. "The American Jewess. II. In Society," *JM,* vol. 50 (1881), no. 9, p. 1.
8. Ibid.
9. "Bowling Green, Ky.," *AI,* vol. 29 (1883), p. 234.
10. "The American Jewess. II. In Society," *JM,* vol. 50 (1881), no. 9, p. 1.
11. L. S. Harby, "Our Women and Their Possibilities," ibid., vol. 53 (1883), no. 2, p. 4.
12. "The visiting question," in ibid., vol. 53 (1883), no. 2, p. 5.
13. L. S. Harby, "Our Women and Their Possibilities," in ibid., vol. 53 (1883), no. 2, p. 4.
14. "The American Jewess. II. In Society," in ibid., vol. 5 (1881), no. 9. p. 1.
15. "The art of conversation," in ibid., vol. 53 (1883), no. 3, p. 4.
16. Ibid.
17. "The American Jewess. II. In Society." *JM,* vol. 50 (1881), no. 9, p. 1.
18. *The Epoch,* vol. 4 (1888), p. 471. "The way we get our wives. Julius Ralph."
19. *The American Jewess,* Chicago, vol. 1 (1895), p. 139.
20. "The Rambler," in *JM,* vol. 56 (1884), no. 3, p. 1.
21. "Jews and Summer Hotels," in *The American Jewess,* vol. 2 (1895), p. 532.
22. *JM,* vol. 52 (1882), no. 8, p. 1.
23. "Jews and Summer Hotels," in *The American Jewess,* vol. 2 (1895), p. 532.
24. "Watering Place Notes," in *JM,* vol. 30 (1871), no. 6, p. 6.
25. "Summer Judaism," in *American Hebrew,* vol. 11 (1882), p. 54.

NOTES FOR CHAPTER SIX:

1. *The Asmonean,* vol. 4 (1851), p. 68. Direct involvement of the Jewish press in matters of women's fashion was extremely rare but took place in the revolutionary attempt of the women's righters to reform women's dress by introduction of the bloomer:

"The New Costume for the Ladies.

We have received many letters from our lady subscribers, asking our opinion about that mighty and important subject which is now agitating the female world, viz. the Bloomer costume. . . . in New York, which is the metropolis of the Union, in fashion as well as in commerce . . . the monstrosity has been received with very great indignation and contempt. . . ."

Generally, however, the Jewish press preferred to stay out of hot water, leaving criticism to aroused readers.
2. M. E. Sherwood. *The Art of Entertaining.* New York: 1892.
3. *Harper's Bazaar,* vol. 14 (1881), p. 434, "Chaperons and Their Duties:" p. 466, "Manners at a watering place;" p. 563, "Visiting."
4. *JM,* vol. 54 (1883), no. 21, p. 4.
5. "Women Jews," in *Harper's Bazaar,* vol. 13 (1880), p. 490.
6. Ibid.
7. "Good Manners," in *JM,* vol. 53 (1883), no. 2, p. 4.
8. Ibid., vol. 50 (1881), no. 8, p. 1.
9. Ibid.
10. "Ethics for Summer Hotels," in ibid., vol. 58 (1885), no. 5, p. 5.
11. "Our Milwaukee Letter," in *JM,* vol. 58 (1885), no. 10, p. 5.
12. Ibid., vol. 51 (1881), no. 10, p. 1.

13. "Echos of the Ball," in ibid., vol. 50 (1881), no. 24, p. 4.
14. Ibid., vol. 56 (1884), no. 14, p. 1.
15. "American Notes," in *Jewish World,* London, vol. 3 (February 26, 1875), p. 3.
16. "Good Manners," in *JM,* vol. 53 (1883), no. 2, p. 4.
17. "San Francisco. Our ladies in retreat," in *AI,* vol. 29 (1882), p. 30.
18. *JM,* vol. 50 (1881), no. 15, p. 1.
19. Ibid., vol. 21 (1867), no. 7, p. 2.
20. Ibid.
21. "The Rambler," in ibid., vol. 56 (1884), no. 17, p. 1.
22. Ibid.
23. "The Rambler," in ibid., vol. 56 (1884), no. 5, p. 1.
24. *Vogue,* vol. 1 (1892/93), p. 1.
25. Ibid., vol. 1 (1892/93), p. 201.
26. P. G. Hubert Jr., "The Duty of the 'Four Hundred,'" in *The Epoch,* vol. 8 (1890/91), p. 245.
27. William H. Chambliss. *Chambliss Diary, or Society, As it Really Is.* New York: 1895, p. 365.
28. Ibid.
29. Ibid.
30. Ibid.
31. Ibid.
32. "Notes on New York Etiquette," in *Vogue,* vol. 2, Supplement, December 14, 1893.
33. *JM,* vol. 52 (1892), no. 8, p. 1.
34. "The Rambler," in ibid., vol. 46 (1884), no. 17, p. 1.
35. "On the Avenue," in ibid., vol. 29 (1871), no. 15, p. 4.
36. Ibid., vol. 50 (1881), no. 15, p. 1.
37. Ibid., vol. 21 (1867), no. 7, p. 2.
38. Ibid., vol. 31 (1872), no. 15, p. 5.
39. "Our Gossip," in ibid., vol. 50 (1881), no. 16, p. 1.
40. *AI,* vol. 29 (1882), p. 169.
41. *Daily Alta California,* vol. 5 (March 10, 1854), p. 2.
42. Ibid., March 17, 1854.
43. *AI,* vol. 27 (1876), no. 16, p. 2.
44. *The Hebrew,* San Francisco, vol. 10 (March 29, 1972).
45. Charles H. Crandall. *The Season . . . 1882-1883.* New York 1883, p. 289.
46. Alexander Francis. *Americans. An Impression.* London: 1909, p. 113.
47. *JM,* vol. 52 (1882), no. 26, p. 4.
48. Ibid., vol. 54 (1883), no. 12, p. 4.
49. "The Rambler," in ibid., vol. 55 (1884), no. 10, p. 4.
50. Ibid.
51. Mrs. Reginald De Koven, "Social life in Chicago," *Ladies Home Journal,* vol. 9 (April: 1892), p. 4.
52. "The Coming Season," in ibid., vol. 54 (1883), no. 12, p. 4.
53. "Social Debuts," in ibid., vol. 50 (1881), no. 2, p. 4.
54. "The Chaperon," in *Vogue,* vol. 5 (1895), p. 26.
55. *The American Jewess,* Chicago, vol. 1 (1895), p. 155.
56. *JM,* vol. 50 (1881), no. 2, p. 2.
57. *The Epoch,* vol. 10 (1891), p. 166.
58. *The Epoch,* vol. 11 (1892), p. 26.
59. *AI,* vol. 28 (1881), p. 66. "San Francisco."

NOTES FOR CHAPTER SEVEN:

1. F. A. Walker (1850), quoted in Arthur W. Calhoun. *A Social History of the American Family*. New York: 1945, vol. 3, p. 181.

2. Paul Bourget. *Outre Mer. Impressions of America*. New York: 1895. Quoted in Calhoun. *Social History*. p. 180.

3. *Ladies Home Journal*, vol. 13 (September, 1896), p. 4.

4. *JM*, vol. 50 (1881), no. 15, p. 1.

5. Sonneschein, Rose, "The American Jewess," *The American Jewess*, vol. 6 (February, 1898), pp. 205-209, p. 208 "Family Life."

6. *The American Jewess*, vol. 1 (1895), p. 39.

7. "San Francisco," *AI*, vol. 29 (1882), p. 160.

8. "Working women and domestic service," in *Harper's Bazaar*, vol. 20 (1887), p. 106.

9. Harriet Prescott Spofford, "The evolution of the hired girl," in the *Ladies Home Journal*, vol. 9 (September, 1892).

10. *Woman's Journal*, vol. 6 (1875), p. 166. From *JM*.

11. "Among the Israelites," *The Northern Monthly*, Newark, vol. 1 (1867), pp. 105-121, p. 121.

12. *Protokolle der Rabbiner—Conferenz abgehalten zu Philadelphia vom 3. bis zum 6. November 1869*. New York: 1870, p. 25.

The fact that under later Jewish immigrants cases of wife-desertion had occurred prompted a Jewish journalist to see them at work for the first time in his life. "The fact that of late several cases of wife-desertion have occurred among a certain class of our co-religionists, and in every instance the offending party's occupation has been a tailor, prompted a visit on Monday afternoon to a number of tailor shops on the east-side downtown, to ascertain their condition and surroundings." *JM*, vol. 56 (1884), no. 21, p. 2.

13. Ibid., vol. 22 (1867), no. 4, p. 5.

14. *Deseret News*, vol. 21 (1871/72), p. 496.

15. *Vorbote*, Chicago, vol. 2 (1875), no. 45, p. 1.

16. *Jewish Times*, vol. 4 (1873/74), p. 510.

17. "A few years past a Hebrew prostitute was a curiosity, in America at least; now such misguided and irretrievably ruined Jewesses are to be found in every large city." Kenny (1893), quoted in Arthur W. Calhoun. *A social history of the American Family*. New York: 1945, p. 211.

18. *An Hour with the American Hebrew*. By an American. New York: 1879, p. 14.

19. *Occident*, vol. 10 (1852/53), pp. 45-46, 144-153, 209-213.

There were also other legal questions of international law to be decided by American courts on the basis of Jewish marriage of emigrants. The *Jüdisches Volksblatt*, vol. 12 (1866), pp. 91/92, "Eine jüdische Trauung im Zwischendeck," deals with a Jewess from Hamburg who was married to a Bavarian Jew according to Jewish law, with Jews as witnesses, in suit over an inheritance before a New York Court.

20. *Der Israelitische Volkslehrer*, vol. 5 (1855), pp. 111-116.

21. Ibid., p. 148.

22. Metz, Jakob, "Die Juden Amerikas," *Jüdisches Volksblatt*, vol. 4 (1857), p. 171.

23. *AI*, vol. 39 (1890/91), no. 41, p. 1.

24. Ibid.

25. *Puck*, vol. 29 (1891), p. 362.

26. "New York," in *Berliner Wochenblatt*, 1857, p. 79.

27. *JM,* vol. 4 (1858), p. 93.
28. James Harwood Barnett. *Divorce and the American Divorce Novel 1858-1937.* Philadelphia: 1939, p. 30.
29. *Daily Alta California,* vol. 5 (March 20, 1854), p. 1.
30. *AI,* vol. 4 (1880), no. 4, p. 4.
31. "Divorce," in *North American Review,* vol. 136 (1883), pp. 305-325, p. 320.
32. *Life,* vol. 54 (1909), p. 241.
33. *New Yorker Handelszeitung,* 1873, no. 1288, p. 11.
34. *Philadelphia Press,* November 12, 1874; clippings from the Moss Collection of the American Jewish Historical Society.
35. "San Francisco," in *AI, vol.* 29 (1877), p. 246.
36. Ibid., vol. 29 (1882/83), p. 246.
37. Schindler, Solomon, "The Divorce Problem," *The Arena,* vol. 1 (May 1890), pp. 689-690.
38. *Woman's Journal,* vol. 11 (1880), p. 261.
39. *Die Deborah,* vol. 17 (1871/72), no. 50, p. 3.
40. *Vogue,* vol. 1 (1892/93), p. 112: "The Unmarried Woman as a Social Factor."
41. *The American Jewess,* vol. 1 (1895), p. 40.
42. *The Voice of Jacob,* vol. 4 (1845/46), London, pp. 144/145 (letter S. Solis to J. A. Franklin Esq. of March 20, 1845).
43. Ibid., p. 158.
In California, at least in the first decade of Jewish settlement, mixed marriage was a rare event. States the *Weekly Gleaner,* vol. I (1857), p. 312, in an article "Intermarriage": ". . . in this country they happen most rarely; we do not know of more than two cases in this state. . . ."

Two years later the situation began to change somewhat: ". . . Three young men of the Hebrew persuasion have within the short space of a week, offered their hands and hearts in matrimony to ladies of the Christian faith. . . ." "Hebrew Wives," ibid., vol. 3 (1859), no. 32, p. 4.
44. *Jewish World,* vol. 3 (1875), London, April 2, 1875, p. 5: "American Judaism."
45. *AI,* vol. 39 (1890/91), no. 41, p. 1.
46. Ibid.
47. *AI,* vol. 29 (1882), p. 50.
Maligning of Jewish girls with the complaint that they seek only riches in marriage dates back even to the pioneering period in the West on the occasion of the need to justify cases of an intermarriage among Jewish men, and called forth a reply from the Jewish press there:

"Hebrew young women are reproached for never marrying for love but for money. . . . fact . . . California Hebrew wives signalize themselves . . . for conjugal love. . . . After leaving a home . . . after crossing oceans and lands, with the expectations, such as California raises at a distance, some allowance must be made for extravagant hopes. . . . We never heard a Jewish husband regret having married a Hebrew wife. . . ." (*Weekly Gleaner,* vol. 3 (1859), no. 32, p. 4, "Hebrew Wives.")
48. "A Clandestine Marriage," in the *New York Times,* May 31, 1878. Moss Collection, American Jewish Historical Society.
Finally the time came when limits were set by the courts to the patria potestas over the father's marriageable daughters and public opinion was encouraged to speculate on the future of the existence of the Jews founded on Jewish family life:

"No matter what church you belong to if you have blarney enough to persuade a Jewess to marry you, you can have her to live with you notwithstanding the beak and talons of her angry father. Judge Potter of New York City, has so decided in the case of Catholic Tom Fallon and his Jewish bride. Marriages between Jew and Christian have become so common in this country and England as to make a decided tendency to amalgamation. . . ." *American Socialist,* vol. 3 (1878), p. 295.

49. *AI,* vol. 30 (1883), no. 22, p. 5.

50. Ibid., vol. 32 (1885), no. 31, p. 5.

51. Emma Wolf, *Other Things Being Equal.* Chicago: 1892, p. 177. Serious meditation on the spiritual problems of a young Jewish woman with intentions of inter-marrying are expressed in Emma Wolf's novel: "I should have little respect for a man who would give up his sacred convictions because I have come into his life. As for my religion, I am a Jewess, and will die one. My God is fixed and unalterable; he is one and indivisible; to divide his divinity would be to deny his omnipotence."

Cincinnati, Ohio. No date. *Gedichte und Scherze in jüdischer Mundart.* "So ist's jetzt," no. 21, A kind of rough popular humor within the compact Jewish communities in Germany about intermarriage found its way into print in Cincinnati: "A *shikse* some take for a wife and a good [Jewish] girl becomes a spinster for that."

52. *AI,* vol. 20 (1873), no. 24 p. 6; "Dallas, Texas," ibid., vol. 30 (1878), no. 8, p. 3. "Butte, Montana," in *The Jewish Voice,* vol. 20 (1896), no. 20, p. 1. Jacob Rader Marcus. *Memoirs of American Jews. 1785-1865.* Vol. I, "Autobiography of William Frank." Philadelphia: 1955, p. 30.

53. *Die Deborah,* vol. 17 (1871/72), no. 50, p. 3.

54. *AI,* vol. 29 (1883), p. 307.

55. Ibid.

56. "San Francisco," in *AI,* vol. 29 (1882), p. 90.

57. *American Hebrew,* vol. 20, p. 98.

58. *JM,* vol. 57 (1885), no. 6, p. 1.

59. Ibid., vol. 50 (1881), no. 9, p. 4.

60. Ibid., vol. 37 (1875), no. 21, p. 5.

61. "Matrimony," in ibid., vol. 2 (1857), p. 61.

62. Ibid., vol. 3 (1858), p. 44.

63. *Jewish World,* London, August 8, 1873, p. 2.

64. "I should like to enter a protest against the charge that the rich girl generally gives her hand to one who can maintain her in the station to which she has been accustomed, regardless of other considerations. This injustice seldom fails to attach to daughters of wealthy Jewish parents. Has the rich girl lost all capacity for love? Has her heart been replaced by a purse and its blood for blood money? Why can she not be thought to love the same as other mortals? She is but human. How many marriages are there of this kind where the first question has not been, How much? Seldom do we hear such an alliance spoken of as a love-match. And is the man always mercenary? It is a small compliment to leave him altogether out of the reckoning and certainly wrong, unles we know to the contrary, to take up the old hue and cry and immediately suspect him of an ulterior motive. That wealth is a good thing no one disputes. But there is still such a thing as love even where wealth exists. The only trouble is that the two are confounded in a manner not justified by the facts." Judicus. "The Chosen People," in *Reform Advocate,* vol. 21 (1901), pp. 133/134, p. 134.

NOTES FOR CHAPTER EIGHT:

1. There were also private schools, advertised in the Jewish newspapers as for instance in the German part of the *Hebrew Leader*:

"Dr. Minrath's private school gives instruction in six separate classes for boys and girls from five to fifteen years in the English, German and French languages. . . . Hebrew daily from three to four." *Hebrew Leader,* vol. 8 (1866), p. 31.

2. Congregation Emanuel . . . New York. Religious Instruction, School for. Year book 1898/99. Pupils of 1897-98. (Six girls' and four boys' classes had female instructors.)

3. The Teachers and Parents' Assistant; or Thirteen Lessons conveying to uninformed minds the first idea of God and His attributes. By an American Jewess. Philadelphia: 5605 (1845). Introduction.

4. Ibid., p. 1: "To the Public."

5. "Boarding and Day School for Young Ladies of the Jewish Faith. No. 97, Thomson Street, New York, conducted by the Misses Palaché," *Occident,* vol. 1 (1843/44), p. 104.

6. "The Misses Emanuel's Boarding and Day School for Young Ladies of the Jewish Faith, Linwood Seminary, Linwood, Delaware County, Penn." (*JM,* vol. 15 (1864), p. 161.)

7. Wheatly, Richard, "The Jews in New York," *Century Magazine,* vol. 43 (1891/92), pp. 323-342, 512-532, p. 518.

8. *JM,* vol. 27 (1870), no. 5, p. 5.

9. *American Hebrew,* vol. 64 (1898/99), p. 544 "Jewesses in Convents."

10. *Young Israel.* An Illustrated Monthly for Young People. New York. Vol. 1 (1871), p. 286.

11. *AI,* vol. 4 (1857/58), p. 212, "We need a Female College."

12. *JM,* vol. 10 (1861), p. 66.

"The Education of American Jewesses."

In a rare case of editorial sponsorship the *Israelite* recommends a couple for private "enlightened instruction." (*AI,* vol. 4 (1857/58), p. 190.)

13. "Eine Mädchenschule," in *Die Deborah,* vol. 1 (1855), p. 169.

14. "About our girls," in *JM,* vol. 37 (1875), no. 5, p. 5.

15. *Woman's Journal,* vol. 6 (1875), p. 79: "Jewish girls;" vol. 7 (1876), p. 244, "What becomes of them."

16. Thus Isaac M. Wise who prided himself in his autobiography and in a lecture to the *Deutscher Pionierverein* in Cincinnati to have founded a *Gesangsverein* in Albany, was one of the first to recognize the real situation.

17. "The German Language," in *The Hebrew Leader,* vol. 7 (October 4, 1865), no. 2, p. 2.

18. *The Hebrew Leader,* vol. 7 (December 1, 1865), no. 9, p. 2. "A series of meetings are now being held at the Turnhalle, in this city, at intervals of one or two weeks, for the purpose of infusing into the minds of the German residents of this city, a thorough knowledge of German literature and history."

19. *The Hebrew Leader,* vol. 7 (October 4, 1865), no. 2, p. 3. Thus "Select School for Young Ladies of the Hebrew Faith. . . . French and German languages. . . . Mrs. Henry Simons, 173 and 175, West 39th Street" [N.Y.].

20. "Philadelphia," in *Die Deborah,* vol. 4 (1858/59), p. 53.

21. "Der Jargon," in *Die Deborah,* vol. 14 (1868/69), p. 190.

22. I. J. Benjamin, *Three Years in America. 1859-1862.* Philadelphia: 5716-1956, vol. 1, p. 92.

The opinion of the intellectual German in America conformed to this opinion of the German Jewish woman and of the average Gentile woman of non-German descent, claiming superiority for German women over them.

23. *Israelitische Annalen,* vol. 3 (1841), p. 239, reports about a *Rundschreiben* of the *badische Oberrat der Israeliten* in this respect.

24. Ibid.

25. W. J. Eichborn ed. *Sammlung der die neue Organisation des Judenwesens im Grossberzogtum Posen betreffenden Gesetze. . . .* Posen: 1834, p. 26: "Die Lehr-sprache beim öffentlichen Unterricht in den jüdischen Schulen ist die deutsche."

26. Dr. A. Heppner u. J. Herzberg. *Aus Vergangenheit und Gegenwart der Juden in den Posener Landen.* Koschmin 1904-1928, pp. 603, 823, 831, 883.

27. Benjamin, vol. 1, p. 89.

28. *Hebrew Leader,* vol. 8 (October 19, 1866), p. 3.

29. In 1895 "only a few college women" were among the 1235 women preachers, 208 lawyers and 4555 doctors. Thomas Woody. A History of Women's Education in the United States. New York: 1929. Vol. 2, p. 232.

30. Woody, vol. 1, p. 482. In 1872 there already existed in the U.S. 101 female normal schools for teacher training with 11,778 students; in 1892 next to 135 public; 43 additional private normal schools, with altogether ca. 35,000 students.

About the beginnings of participation of the first Jewish girls as teachers in these schools we learn something from the Jewish press.

Young Israel, vol. 5 (1875), p. 510. "Letter file"; "The Normal College of the City of New York held its sixth annual commencement in the college on the 30th of June; one hundred forty-nine young ladies were graduated" (twenty-one Jewesses among them).

Independent Hebrew, vol. 1 (1896), p. 1 Statement of Samuel A. Lewis, President of the Board of Aldermen:

"City of New York. . . . Twenty years ago there was only one Jewess teaching in our schools, a Miss Hays, latterly there are quite a number of them, and in the training school, there are Misses Mitchel, Newstadt and Japha, selected for their merit. . . . the Normal College is well known by most young ladies of the Hebrew faith, who have attended the public schools. . . ."

On the further aftergrowth of Jewish teachers from Jewish immigrant girls we are informed already by official statistics.

31. "Mitgliederliste," p. 466; vol. 27 (1897), no. 4, p. 3. *Erziehungsblätter,* vol. 1 (Louisville, 1870), no. 1, p. 20.

32. *Erziehungsblätter* (new title *Amerikanische Schulzeitung*), vol. 3 (1872/73), pp. 177-183, "Für die Amerikanische Schulzeitung. Das Judentum in Amerika. Eine Skizze von Minna Kleeberg."

33. "Die deutsche Dichtkunst in Amerika," in *Der Deutsche Pionier,* vol. 6 (1874), p. 217.

34. *Erziehungsblätter,* vol. 3 (1872/73), p. 179.

35. *Articles and Lectures of David Einhorn,* E. G. Hirsch and others prove this.

36. "Our schools," in *JM,* vol. 41 (1877), no. 20, p. 4.

37. *Erziehungsblättter,* vol. 1 (1870), no. 1, p. 20; vol. 2 (1871/72), p. 115; vol. 27 (1897), no. 4, p. 3. Jewish names in a Milwaukee list: Jenny Benjamin, Else Cohn, Bertha Herz, Martha Schönfeld, Etta Singer, Julia Stern.

And in Cincinnati list: Nelly Adler, Valeski Danziger, Cecilia Goldberg, Rosa J. Grossmann, Minna Herzmann, Augusta Hess, Julia Hirsch, Emma Holländer, Hattie Levy, Rose Mahler, Ida Meyer, Mathilde Meyer, Martha Meyer.

NOTES FOR CHAPTER NINE:

1. The Constitution and By-Laws of the Hebrew Sunday School Society of Philadelphia. Incorporated 1858 and the Superintendent's Report of the School for 1858. Philadelphia: 1859.
2. Rev. Sol Jacobs, "Ladies Singing in Synagogue," *The Occident,* vol. 13 (1855), pp. 445, 492, 537.
3. Gustav Gottheil. *Hymns and Anthems.* New York: 1887. Penina Moise is represented in nearly all these editions of hymns.
4. "America," in *Jewish World,* London, vol. 2 (August 21, 1874), p. 5.
5. *JM,* vol. 7 (1860), p. 157.
6. Ibid., p. 156.
7. Edna Ferber. *A Peculiar Treasure.* New York: 1960, p. 183.
8. Ibid.
9. Mabel Cameron, compiler, *The Biographical Cyclopedia of American Women.* New York: 1924-1928, vol. 1, p. 283.
Maud Nathan, born in New York in 1862, of Sephardic descent, was a suffragist, and the "first woman to speak in a Jewish synagogue at the regular Sabbath evening service."
Occasionally, the results of the Jewish religious education of girls were also paraded in the synagogue:
"Cincinnati. As a curiosity, we must relate that in a synagogue of Cincinnati a young girl, not fully thirteen years old, recited the *Parasha* from the *Tora* so correctly and beautifully that everyone who listened was enraptured." *Ungarische Jüdische Wochenschrift,* vol. 1 (1871), p. 128.
10. *The Business Woman,* New York, vol. 7, no. 2 (October, 1892), p. 62. This episode even inspired a fictional account: A. S. Isaacs, "The Rabbi's Wife. Not an impossible Tale," *New Era,* vol. 2 (May, 1903), pp. 62-64.
11. "San Francisco. Israelitischer Frauenverein," in *Die Deborah,* vol. 1 (1855/56), p. 40.
12. *The Hebrew,* March 25th 1870, p. 4; *Los Angeles Star,* October 26th 1870, p. 2.
13. "Hebrew Ladies" Benevolent Society. Organized January 1870," in *Ladies clubs and societies in Los Angeles in 1892.* Reported for the Historical Society of Southern California. Compiled and Edited by Mrs. Burton Williamson. March: 1892, pp. 16/17.
14. Louis Seybold, "Akrons Deutschtum vor fünfzig Jahren und früher," *Akron Germania* December 22, 1906 (clipping) p. 63: "Schwesternbund," founded November 10, 1867.
15. *Centennial Records of the Women of Wisconsin.* Madison, Wisc.: 1876, p. 47.
16. "Madison, Ind." in *The Occident,* vol. 20 (1862/63), p. 429.
17. John St. Wilson. Atlanta as it is: . . . . New York: 1871. Pp. 22, 30, 31.
18. George H. Tinkham. *A History of Stockton.* San Francisco: 1880, p. 364.
19. Thus, in San Francisco the *"Ladies Society of Israelites"* (Der Israelitisher Frauenverein). For the purpose of assisting Hebrew women under all circumstances of want. Established August 12, 1855.
"Ladies United Hebrew Benevolent Society.—Established 1855. For the assistance of needy Hebrew women, under all circumstances of want. . . . "Crocker-Langley. *San Francisco Directory.* 1858, p. 379.
20. *AI,* vol. 2 (1855/56), p. 251.
21. "Salt Lake City, Utah, July 8, 1879," in ibid., vol. 33 (1879), no. 4, p. 5.

Salt Lake City, "The Hebrew Relief Society, and the Ladies Hebrew Benevolent Society are both in flourishing condition."

22. Thus in New York the B'nai Jeshurun Ladies Hebrew Benevolent Society. *JM*, vol. 5 (1859), p. 99.

23. *Occident*, vol. 4 (1846), pp. 394, 395. In Philadelphia the Female Hebrew Sewing Society existed already in 1846. In that year five hundred fourteen garments were given to fifty-two persons. The clients were immigrants arrived at that port.

24. Nathan M. Kaganoff, "Organized Jewish Welfare Activity in New York City," in the *American Jewish Historical Quarterly*, vol. 56 (September 1966), no. 1, pp. 27-63, p. 33.

25. Association for the Relief of Jewish Widows and Orphans. New Orleans. *Annual Report of 1860*. New Orleans: 1860, p. 20. Of the inmates, there were thirty-five women. All boys and most girls were orphans. The majority of the orphans were native-born.

26. *Occident*, vol. 4 (1846), p. 57. "The Hebrew Ladies Benevolent Society of Cincinnati . . . Purim . . . regular annual ball . . . one of the most decorous and splendid fêtes of the season."

The great times of the Fair came only much later with the demands of help for the Russian Jewish immigrant masses. In 1895 the Fair of the Educational Alliance amassed an income of $170,132.93 (one-hundred seventy thousand, one-hundred thirty-two dollars). (*Souvenir Book of the Fair in Aid of the Educational Alliance and Hebrew Technical Institute*. [N. Y.] 1895.)

The *Fair Journal* published on that occasion tells us also "The story of other fairs" from 1859 to 1886 and contains also a general evaluation of the women's work for the fairs. *The Fair Journal*, December 14, 1895, pp. 1, 3.

27. Edna Ferber. A Peculiar Treasure. New York: 1960. P. 76.

28. Brav, Stanley R., "The Jewish Woman," 1861-1865, *American Jewish Archives*, vol. 17, no. 1 (April, 1965), pp. 34-75, pp. 50-52.

29. In St. Louis existed "The Ladies' Friday Musicale" with twenty-two women as members. (A. Rosenthal. Jewish Progress in St. Louis. St. Louis 1904. Unpaginated [42]).

In Indianapolis "The Jewish Culture Club" is registered among "Woman's Literary Clubs of Indiana." (Ida A. Harper. The Associated Work of the Women of Indiana. Indianapolis: 1893. P. 7.)

30. Laura D. Jacobson, "The Pioneers. The First Literary Society of Jewish Women in America," *The American Jewess*, Chicago, vol. 1 (1895), pp. 240-243.

"A Women's Cultural Club," in *Missouri Historical Society Bulletin*, vol. 6 (1949/50), p. 109. "The society is in possession of their minutes from 1870-1949 . . . In 1880 . . . Rosa Sonneschein was assigned to write an official history . . . humorou account . . . published. . . ."

An early Jewish Literary Women's Club existed also in Leavenworth, Kansas. (Mrs. J. C. Croly. The History of the Woman's Club Movement in America. N.Y.: 1898, p. 494.)

31. Julia Richman, "The Jewish Woman of To-Day," *American Hebrew*, vol. 56 (1894/95), p. 459. "We women need the social clubs . . . if we want our girls to make happy marriages, we must raise the standard for admission to the club. . . . A dishonorable business record should bar him [the club candidate], but that his intimates are fast immoral young men, are bold, licentious women, that makes no difference. . . ."

32. "Der erste Geheime Frauen-Orden" Immanu-El Loge No. 1, New York, first meeting of the lodge on April 26, 1846, in *Ordens Echo*, vol. 14 (1897), no. 4, p. 2.

The "True Sisters" started, in their Jewish period, as we learn from the "Original Protokol" as an auxiliary to Congregation Emanu-El:

"With the prosperity of the Emanu-El congregation, as an incentive she [Henriette Bruckman] reached the conclusion that she should direct the attention of the women of this community to the formation of an organization as planned." The cooperation of the rabbi of this congregation was essential for the founding of the new organization: "Dr. Mitchels promised the ladies his help and asked them to obtain the cooperation of Rev. Dr. Merzbacher, who agreed to this on April 19, 1846. . . . Merzbacher also gave the installation speech for the first lodge of the order."

1846-1896. Goldenes Jubiläum des Unabhängigen Ordens Treue Schwestern und der Immanual Loge No. 1. T.S. New York: 1896, pp. 10, 21. This edition lists the names of all officers of the order up to 1896. These names are typically German Jewish throughout for all fourteen existing lodges of that time.

Great merit for the consolidation of the True Sisters falls to Dr. Emanuel B. Friedlein, b. 1807 in Allersheim, Bavaria, active also in the male order, B'nai B'rith, educated in the Yeshiva of Fürth, in America since 1850. Friedlein also sponsored the "Caecilia Lorsch Bildungsverein" when he arrived in 1850 in America. "Aus America," in *Österreichische Israelitische Wochenschrift,* vol. 14 (1897), p. 633.

The True Sisters strove for self-realization. "To learn and to teach, to observe and to exercise" was their motto. Their organ, *Ordens Echo,* formerly *Vereinsbote* had English and German columns side by side, with German prevailing strongly.

On August 30, 1855, Friedlein brought into the order a Frauenverein in Hartford (*Ordens-Echo,* vol. 14 (1897), no. 2, p. 3).

In 1900 the order had 15 lodges, seven in New York, one each in Philadelphia, Albany, New Haven, Chicago, Dorchester and Brooklyn and two in Newark. *Ordens-Echo,* vol. 16 (1899/1900), no. 3. The portrait of "Oberin Henrietta Bruckman, Stifterin des Ordens T.S." appears in *Ordens-Echo* vol. 17 (1900/1901), February 7, 1901, p. 1.

The order believed strongly in the virtue of good housekeeping: "Let's train our daughters to good helpers in our household." *Ordens-Echo,* vol. 15 (1898/99), November 7, 1899, p. 2. In strenuous times the True Sisters came out with programmatical declarations: "The seriousness of the time demands a serious word, our adopted country is in the midst of a bloody war. . . . To us too demand may be made. . . . The order of the True Sisters will do their duty. . . . "*Ordens-Echo,* May 7, 1898, p. 2, "Schwestern."

The True Sisters, in their later transformation into an interdenominational organization, became a point of departure from which a host of Jewish women, in time, entered the women's lodges of the mostly German lodges and auxiliaries of the Odd Fellows and Masons. As with the men's lodges there, Jewish women, too, concentrated in certain lodges' respective auxiliaries there. The volumes of the German Odd Fellows and Mason papers *Masonia* and *Der Führer* bear rich testimony to this state of affairs as also of the activities of the True Sisters, who remained essentially a body of Jewish members. Scanning the membership list of some of the Odd Fellows' and Mason's lodges shows us mainly German Jewish women's names. For instance of the Kaiserin Elisabeth Rebekka Lodge no. 125 in New York (*Der Führer,* Organ der deutschen Freimaurer and Odd Fellows, vol. 37, no. 4, March 27, 1909, p. 9) and of the "Rebekkah Witwenund Waisen-Unterstützungs-Verein." (*Der Führer,* vol. 37, April 3, 1909, p. 13). Of course, like the Jewish men in the lodges of the German Odd Fellows and Masons, Jewish women were also members in Jewish organizations. In fact, it may be truthfully stated that in the 20th century Jewish membership in German organizations was diverted to a great extent to the liberal humanistic mass organizations in the German urban milieu, mainly O.F. and Masons, German lodges. A still later development in organizational life shows us women as members of the National Council of Jewish Women who at the same time had joined the True Sisters too, as for instance Jenny Kleeberg Herz, daughter of Minna Kleeberg, b. Elberfeld, Germany. (*The Bulletin,* National Council of Jewish Women, New York Section, vol. 1 (October, 1915), p. 9.)

33. Edward E. Grusd. B'nai B'rith. The Story of a Covenant. New York [1966]. Pp. 46, 98, 106, 115.

34. Ibid.

35. *Woman's Journal,* vol. 22 (1891), p. 129.

36. *Woman's Journal,* vol. 3 (1872), p. 403.

"B'nai Jeshurun. . . . they frequently transact their business more quickly than their husbands and sons. . . ."

Rather the most speaking example of such independent women's administration of an old-style Jewish institution was the battle of the administration of the Home for Aged and Infirm Hebrews in New York against voting rights for men: ". . . There is much excitement among the Jewish people of this city about an effort to introduce certain changes in the Management of the Home for Aged and Infirm Hebrews. . . . Mrs. P. J. Joachimsen, President. . . . At present the management of the Home is vested exclusively in the lady members, the gentlemen being allowed no vote. . . . action . . . enfranchisement of the male honorary members. . . ." (*Woman's Journal,* vol. 8 (1877), p. 392.)

37. Goldie Stone. *My Caravan of Years.* New York: 1945, p. 143.

The fashionable arrangement of bridal processions caught on quickly also in smaller communities and male critics let off steam in the Jewish press.

As to the ball-like atmosphere of socials and their entertainments, the fun-playing with the wedding ceremony could create problems where negligent persons used the full legal ritualistic form of concluding marriage ceremonies spoken over couples as a mockery: ". . . . Great consternation among the members of Jewish society at Yonkers has been the outcome of the recent Purim ball. During the evening, one hundred couples went through a mock marriage ceremony. . . ." *Southwestern Jewish Sentiment,* vol. 3 (1902), no. 13, p. 2. "Mock Weddings are claimed binding."

The precautions of the Yiddish stage in performing theatrical marriages in traditional style were surely not known to the Purim practical jokers.

There were also protests in public against throwing out the beloved traditional forms of wedding by Reform synagogues as the following recorded by the Gentile press: "A fashionable Jewish wedding in the Washington synagogue was interrupted the other day by the groom's father, who refused to let the ceremony go farther, as no canopy was held over the bridal pair which the "Orthodox" Hebrews, of whom he is a rabbi, hold to be essential. The synagogue belonging to the "Reformed" faith would not allow a canopy, so the wedding had to take place at the residence of the bride's father." *Sporting Times and Theatrical News,* vol. 7 (1870), no. 169, July 23, 1870, p. 4.

38. *American Hebrew,* vol. 11 (1882), p. 64.

39. [*Association for the Advancement of Women.*] Papers. Nos. 2-18, 1874-1891.

40. *Woman's Journal,* vol. 24 (1893), p. 172.

41. *American Hebrew,* vol. 54 (1893/94), p. 410.

42. *American Hebrew,* vol. 56 (1894/95), p. 323. (In a Friday night address by F. de Sola Mendes.)

43. Program of the National Council of Jewish Women for 1895/96, pp. 8-10: "Topics—Papers and Study."

188   *The Jewish Woman in America*

44. National Council of Jewish Women. *First Annual Report. 1894-1895,* p. 5. "All Jewish educational organizations have pledged us their support."
45. Ibid., p. 35, p. 9.
46. *American Jewish Year Book 5661* (1900-1901), p. 77.
47. *Proceedings of the First Convention.* . . . Philadelphia: 1897, p. 29.
48. Leopold Kist. *Amerikanisches.* Mainz: 1871, pp. 115, 117: "The Jewish girls, to be sure, participated in the service on deck on August sixteenth [ninth of Ab] reading very devoutly in their prayer books."
49. *Voice of Jacob,* vol. 4 (1845), p. 145. Letter of S. Solis.
50. *JM,* vol. 1 (1857), p. 18.
"The future of Israel. By Mirjam, a New York Jewess." The *Messenger* expresses its admiration for this lady: "We feel a degree of national pride in introducing Miriam. . . . We hope to see many Miriams in the field." (Ibid., p. 21, "Miriam, a New York Jewess.")
51. *Occident,* vol. 20 (1862/63), p. 429. (Madison, Indiana.)
52. *JM,* vol. 50 (1881), no. 15, p. 1.
53. *AI,* vol. 29 (1877), p. 244, "Lone Star Flashes. By Koppel von Vloomburg."
54. *JM,* vol. 55 (1884), no. 10, p. 4, "The Rambler."
55. *JM,* vol. 50 (1881), no. 4, p. 4, "The American Jewess."
56. *JM,* vol. 51 (1881/82), no. 13, p. 5, "The Jewess and the Synagogue."
57. Isaac M. Wise. *Reminiscences. Cincinnati:* 1901, p. 212.
58. Mary M. Cohen, "Hebrew Women," *Good Company,* vol. 3 (1879), pp. 620-624.
59. Rose Sonneschein, "The American Jewess," *The American Jewess,* vol. 6 (February, 1898), pp. 205-207: "The Jewess of to-day . . . Communal activity."
60. Emil G. Hirsch, "The Modern Jewess," *The American Jewess,* vol. 1 (1895), pp. 10-11.
61. Dr. Adolph Moses, "The Position of Woman in America," *The American Jewess,* vol. 1 (1895), pp. 15-20.
62. *Atlantic Monthly,* vol. 73 (1893), p. 137. Review of *The Rebel Queen,* by Walter Besant.
63. Madame Blanc. The condition of women in the United States. . . . Boston: 1895. P. 66.
64. Mary M. Cohen, "Hebrew Women," *Good Company,* vol. 3 (1879), pp. 620-624.
65. *Proceedings of the National Council of Jewish Women,* 1897, p. 224.

NOTES FOR CHAPTER TEN:

1. Annie Wittenmyer. *History of the Woman's Temperance Crusade.* Philadelphia: 1878, p. 772.
"The nationality of those engaged in the business in this city was as follows: Chinamen 2, Jews 2, Italians 18, Spaniards 140, Welsh 160, Americans 205, Africans 265, Frenchmen 285, Scotts 497, English 568, German 2,179, Irish 3,041, unknown 672, total, 8,034."
2. *Chicago Commons,* vol. 1 (1897), no. 15, p. 15.
"Social Value of the Saloon," reporting on an article of E. C. Moore, in the *American Journal of Sociology,* July 1897, which is a "clear exhibit of the fact that the saloon, with all its evils, does supply real social needs. . . ." and November 1900, no. 52, pp. 1-9: "Social Function of the Saloon in Chicago. Ethical Substitutes for It."

From the Report to the Committee of Fifty of a Six Months Investigation. By Royal Loren Mclendy.

3. Wittenmyer, p. 140, on a liquor dealer in Alliance, Ohio, who went around "accompanied by a very small Jew for protection. . . ."

4. Wittenmyer, p. 280.

5. Mother Hubbard [Stewart, Eliza]. *Memoirs of the Crusade.* Columbus, Ohio: 1888, p. 499.

6. Mother Hubbard, p. 501.

7. Ibid., p. 500.

8. Catharine E. Beecher. *Educational Reminiscences and Suggestions.* New York: 1874. P. 247.

9. *Woman's Journal,* vol. 11 (1880), p. 252 signed, "Narcisse Cyr."

10. Ibid., p. 100.

11. Ibid., vol. 16 (1885), p. 345.

12. "Woman's Rights among our German Citizens." Three lectures of Clara Neyman from New York in Milwaukee, in ibid., vol. 4 (1873), p. 148.

13. "Dr. S. Lilienthal on Women Physicians," in ibid., vol. 8 (1877), p. 63; and Kate N. Dogget, "Letter from Illinois," *Woman's Journal,* vol. 3 (1872), p. 113.

14. *The New Cycle. . . .* Official Organ of the General Federation of Woman's Clubs, vol. 8 (1895), pp. 637-640.

15. "New York," in *Die Neuzeit,* vol. 14 (1874), p. 187.

16. *Overland Monthly,* New Series. Vol. 21 (1893), p. 555.

17. Dr. Thomas L. Nichols. *Forty Years of American Life.* London: 1864, vol. 2, p.. 22. Ida Tarbell, "The American Woman," in *American Magazine,* vol. 69 (1909/10), p. 449.

18. *Woman's Herald of Industry and Social Science Cooperator,* San Francisco, vol. 2, no. 8 (August 1883), p. 1.

19. Kate Field, "Polygamy Unveiled," *Woman. A Monthly Magazine,* New York, vol. 1 (1888), pp. 296-305; "A high old time," in *The Ishmaelite,* Indianapolis, vol. 5 (1899), p. 149; "The Utah Election—Woman Suffrage vindicated," in *Woman's Journal,* vol. 3 (1872), p. 96.

20. "Salt Lake City," in *The Jewish Voice,* vol. 16 (1894, no. 3, p. 7.

21. *The Free Church Circular,* Oneida Reserve, vol. 4 (1851), p. 88.

22. "Henriette Herz," in *Woman's Journal,* vol. 26 (1895), p. 299.

There was, for instance, bland admiration for the secular Jewess in Germany's literary salons with her knowledge even of Hebrew, as for instance in the full-page biographical sketch of Henriette Herz: "Her Hebrew was made use of to teach the Humboldts to write Hebrew, as in the Hebrew letters a long correspondence was kept up between them." (*Woman's Journal,* vol. 2 (1871), p. 407.

23. *Woman's Journal,* vol. 5 (1874), p. 50.

Chivalry on New York's busses proved a matter of perpetual debate. Still in 1882, *Judge* answers a Jewish lady: ". . . . little girl we have noticed that when we rose to give you a seat . . . a Jew plumped into it. . . ." (Judge, vol. 2, no. 51 (October 14, 1882), p. 12. "Front seats in the synagogue.")

24. *Woman's Journal,* vol. 5 (1874), p. 50.

25. *Woman's Journal,* vol. 5 (1874), p. 84 "The Rabbis and Woman;" vol. 11 (1880), p. 261, "Woman in the Talmud. Not the aesthetic, but the ethic power and importance of Woman is it which finds recognition in the Talmud."

The argument runs here in the same way as with the Fundamentalists in respect to the Biblical woman.

26. Elisabeth Cady Stanton, "The Woman of the Bible—Deborah and Jael," in *The Revolution*, vol. 3 (1869), p. 311.

27. Thus the *Woman's Journal* takes over without any critical thought the panegyric of the *Jewish Messenger* on the status of the Jewish women in their community: "The women, too, have been ennobled, not degraded, by being thrown on themselves and on their families for their sphere of thought and action. They are almost always instructed in business and capable of taking a part in great affairs; for it has been the custom of their race to consider the wife the helpmate—the sharer in every transaction that establishes the position, or enhances the comfort, of the family. Leisure, activity of mind, and the desire to hand on the torch of instruction from the women of one generation to those of another, inspire Jewesses with a zeal for education, a love of refinement, and a sympathy with art. Homes of the best type are of course to be taken as the standard, when it is inquired what are the characteristics of a race as seen at its best; and European family life has few things equal to show to the family life of the highest type of the Jew."*Woman's Journal*, vol. 3 (1872), p. 160.

28. Ibid., vol. 1 (1870), p. 167.

29. Ibid., vol. 6 (1875), p. 244.

30. Andrew Sinclair. *Better Half*. New York: 1965, p. 159.

31. *Woman's Journal*, vol. 5 (1874), p. 59.

32. Ibid., vol. 6 (1875), p. 244.

33. Ibid., vol. 12 (1881), p. 9.

34. Ibid., vol. 17 (1886), p. 188.

35. "Women in the Church," in ibid., vol. 23 (1892), p. 242.

36. "Women in the Churches," in ibid., vol. 25 (1894), p. 413.

37. "Letter from Germany," in *Woman's Journal*, vol. 11 (1880), p. 8.

38. Ibid., p. 180.

39. Ibid., vol. 12 (1881), p. 9.
On the other hand, there was a sharp eye for a keen deviation of a rabbinical daughter from Jewish tradition:
"Miss Adler, daughter of the venerable Dr. Samuel Adler, and sister of Professor Felix Adler, has created not a little discontent among the faithful disciples of Judaism in New York by marrying during Atonement week. . . ." *Woman's Journal*, vol. 9 (1878), p. 337.

40. *Woman's Journal*, vol. 5 (1874), p. 13.
Mrs. Mary Rachel and Mr. Alexander Jonas; p. 100 "Mrs. Mathilde C. Weil as the principal speaker. . . . Mr. A. A. Oppenheim took the chair."

41. "Our New York Letter," in *Woman's Journal*, vol. 25 (1894), p. 101.

42. "Notes and Views," in *Woman's Journal*, vol. 25 (1894), p. 341.

43. "Jewish Women's Council," in *Woman's Journal*, vol. 25 (1894), p. 339.

44. "Progressive Jewish Women," in *Woman's Journal*, vol. 27 (1896), p. 262.

45. *Woman's Journal*, vol. 3 (1872), p. 69.

46. "Jews in Hotels, Negroes in White Churches," in *Woman's Journal*, vol. 11 (1880), p. 180.

47. "The Proscriptions of Jews," and "Judae-Phobia," in *Woman's Journal*, vol. 7 (1877), p. 204, 317.
A later case like this touched a Gentile woman married to a Jew: "Mrs. Jacobi, the wife of Dr. Abraham Jacobi of New York, was refused last week accommodation in St. Mark's Hotel, Staten Island, because her husband was a Jew. . . . Dr. Jacobi does not belong to any synagogue or profess to be a Jew in his religious convictions. He is a descendant of the Jewish race, but by birth and associations a German." "Jews in Hotels, Negroes in White Churches," in *Woman's Journal*, vol. 11 (1880), p. 180.

The still later case of a Jewess, wife of the American Ambassador in Vienna, snubbed there in society, aroused accusing voices which certainly drew also the attention of gentile women: "Let Mr. Keily draw his salary at home until his commission shall expire. By no means let him be handled in Austrian or Italian fashion." *The Current,* vol. 4 (1885), p. 3.

48. *Woman's Journal,* vol. 5 (1874), p. 135, "Jews and Women."

49. *The Revolution,* vol. 3 (1869), p. 165.

50. "Let the Jews alone," in ibid., p. 220.

51. "Jewesses and the Gospel," in *Woman's Journal,* vol. 31 (1900), p. 179.

52. Ibid., vol. 30 (1899), p. 237.

53. Ibid., vol. 10 (1879), p. 324.

54. "Concerning Women," in ibid., vol. 3 (1872), p. 289.

55. *The Condition of Women in the United States.* By Madame Blank. Boston: 1895, p. 145.

56. *Papers of the Jewish Women's Congress.* Held at Chicago, September 4, 5, 6, and 7, 1893. Philadelphia: 1894, p. 41. From the address of Helen Kahn Weil, Kansas City, Mo." Jewish Women of Modern Days."

On intercourse of Jewish with gentile women in the Chicago club see: Herma Clark. *The Elegant Eighties.* Chicago: 1941, pp. 58, 59 ("Kaffeeklatsch.")

57. *Proceedings of the First Convention of the National Council of Jewish Women* held at New York, November 15, 16, 17, 18 and 19, 1896 and 1897: Philadelphia, p. 177.

58. Ibid., 1897, p. 193.

59. Ibid., p. 230.

60. Ibid., p. 233.

61. Ibid., p. 180.

62. *The American Jewess,* Chicago, January 1898, p. 193.

NOTES FOR CHAPTER ELEVEN:

1. Of non-immigrants the poetess Penina Moise, of old Sephardic stock, belonged completely to the nineteenth century.

2. Rachel Frank, b. San Francisco, April 10, 1866, teacher in mining camps in Nevada, first woman preaching to Jews; Mrs. Lee C. Harby, born Charleston, September 7, 1849; Mary M. Cohen, b. Philadelphia, February 26, 1849. (Francis Elisabeth Willard. *A Woman of the Century.* Buffalo: 1893, pp. 299, 357, 388.) Henrietta Levy, b. Bristol, England, 1868; Alice Moritz Lowenstein, b. Paris, France, January 1869; Clara Damrosch Mannes, b. Breslau, December 12, 1869; daughter of Leopold Damrosch; Selma Oppler Münsterberg, b. Germany, June 1, 1867. (*Woman's Who's Who in America. 1914-1915.* N.Y. [copyr. 1914].) Mary Fels, b. Sembach, Germany, March 10, 1863. (Mabel Ward Cameron comp. *Biographical Encyclopedia of American Women.* New York: 1924, vol. 1, p. 121.)

3. *The Revolution,* vol. 2 (1968), p. 201. Leo Shpall, "Adah Isaacs Menken," *Louisiana Historical Quarterly,* vol. 26 (1943), no. 1, pp. 162-168. Artisten Lexikon. Düsseldorf, p. 134.

4. "The Bernhardt Boom in New York," p. 202, "Actresses and Advertising," *Puck,* vol. 8 (1880/81), p. 134.

5. Clare Lipman Mann was a success in *Telephone Girl.*

6. Bime Abramowitch arrived in America in 1886, Sarah Adler in 1883, Jenny Atlas in 1884, Bessie Tomaschefsky in 1885, Kenny Lipzin in 1887, Berta Kalisch in 1896, Annie Tomaschefsky acted in children's roles already in the nineteenth century.

Zalmen Zylbercwaig *Leksikon fun yidishn teater.* New York: 1931-1969, vol. 1, pp. 33, 47; vol. 2, pp. 840, 847, 1108; vol. 4, p. 2425.

7. In the Jewish press appear: Rebecca Hynemann, Rose Sonneschein, Caroline Harby and others.

8. Nahida Remy, "Ray Frank in synagogue pulpit." in *The Jewish Woman.* Cincinnati: 1895, pp. 221-226. Mary Fels was also known as reformer.

9. Maud Nathan. The story of an epoch making movement. Garden City, N.Y. 1926.

10. Yuri Suhl. *Ernestine L. Rose and the Battle for Human Rights.* New York [1959], p. 244.

11. Ibid., pp. 220-224.

12. Ibid., p. 288. "If your house were on fire, and an atheist should offer to carry a pail of water, could you spurn his kindness because your religious opinions might receive a "violent shock" to have your house saved by heretical hands. . . ."

13. Richard Drinnon. *Rebel in Paradise. A Biography of Emma Goldman.* Chicago: 1961, pp. 61, 202, 204 on prisons; p. 304 on Spanish anarchists' educational institutions.

14. "Our Girls," in *AI,* vol. 24 (1875), no. 4, p. 5.
"I venture to make the assertion that of the few really educated women of Israel of this country not one is born in America or has received that education in this country. Not an authoress of our faith, not a contribution of any note (perhaps none at all) to any of the many popular magazines or weeklies. . . ."

15. *Woman's Journal,* vol. 13 (1882), p. 137.

16. Josephine Lazarus. *Madame Dreyfus.* New York: 1899, p. 8.

17. Josephine Lazarus. *The Spirit of Judaism.* New York: 1895.

18. Dr. H. Pereira Mendes, "The Spirit of Judaism," in *American Hebrew,* vol. 58 (1895/96), p. 227.

19. Ibid., pp. 229-231. "Dr. Emil G. Hirsch's Opinion of the Work."

20. Helen Brent. M.D. New York: 1893.

21. *It's Been Fun.* New York: 1951, pp. 11-13.

22. Dora Askowitz. *Three Outstanding Women.* New York: 1949, pp. 27-49.

23. Emma Wolf. *Other Things Being Equal.* Chicago: 1894.

24. *The American Jewess.* Chicago: 1895, vol. 1, p. 294.

25. Mary Antin. *From Plotzk to Boston.* Boston: 1899.

26. Gertrude Stein's respect for the Jewish religion "on account of its concern with life on earth" is recorded in Elisabath Sprigge. *Gertrude Stein.* New York: 1957, p. 10. A talk with Stein "about how impossible it was for a Jewish woman to marry a Gentile" is noted by her biographer. Hutchins Hapgood. *A Victorian in the Modern World.* New York: 1939, p. 539.

27. Edna Ferber. *A Peculiar Treasure.* New York: 1960, p. 60: "Jewish Ladies' Aid Society"; Fanny Hurst. *Anatomy of Me,* Garden City, N.Y.: 1958, p. 24; "The Pioneers," a literary society of Jewish ladies in St. Louis.

28. "The Jewess in San Francisco," in *The American Jewess,* vol. 4 (October 1896), pp. 10-12.

29. Abram S. Isaacs, "The Jewess in authorship," *Ladies Home Journal,* vol. 9 (October 1892), p. 17.

30. Born in 1876 in Kovno, Anna Rappaport published her first poem in the *Arbayter Tsaytung* in 1893 and later in the *Tsukunft.* (*Anthology of Jewish Poetesses.* Ed. E. Korman. Chicago: 1928, p. 353. Yiddish.)

31. *Der Deutsche Pionier.* Vol. 10 (1878), pp. 472, 473.

32. *Amerikanische Schulzeitung,* vol. 3 (1872/1873), pp. 177-183 "Das Judentum in Amerika. Eine Skizze von Minna Kleeberg."

33. Minna Herrman, Cincinnati, "Eine Schwedin. Charakterbild," in *Jahrbuch des Deutschen Lehrervereins. . . . Ohio: 1895;* pp. 52-58.

34. Few women wrote in the *Deborah* with their given names, and only in later volumes; even the earlier articles on woman's rights are written by men in this man-made woman's paper, although not signed by these men. Nevertheless we have to assume that certain articles showing intimate knowledge of, and insight into woman's life were written there by women.

The poem "Das Gottesreich (God's realm) Ein Schebuoth Gedicht (A Shebuoth poem) von Anna Salzberger" appeared in vol. 27, no. 1 (July 1, 1881), p. 1. In 1883 a frequent contributor was Frida Schellitzer, represented with a novel "Schicksals-wende (turn of fate)" during the last quarter of that year, and also with a series of "New Yorker Plaudereien (chattings)" at the same time. On December 14, 1883, p. 2, this lady contributed "Die Hahnkrähe. Sage aus Breslau's Vorzeit." (The rooster crow. A legend from the early times of Breslau.) Furthermore, in vol. 29, no. 19, p. 4, a notice says: "The lecture of Mrs. Frida Schellitzer on the education of children pub-ilshed in the *Deborah* was reproduced in two European newspapers."

As to woman's rights the article "Frauenrechte," in its entirely conservative atti-tude, represents the thoughts of I. M. Wise on that matter, and to conclude from its style was written by him (vol. 15 (1869/70), no. 44, p. 2).

Eight years later (vol. 29 (1877), no. 18, p. 2), "Eine friedliche Umwälzung (A peaceful revolution)" already deals with the changed position of the Jewish woman in America. The article is written in an entirely peaceful and conceding manner.

35. These activities are surveyed in regular periodical reports of the secretaries of the lodges and grand lodges of the order and a "Logenkalender" of current and coming events is given. *Ordens Echo,* vol. 14, no. 5 (1897), p. 4, "Logenkalender" reports on all 15 German lodges in New York.

Of the themes dealt with in the paper woman's wages take an important place. Thus we find (vol. 14, no. 6, p. 1), Louise Mary Simon "Woman as wage earners," and vol. 15, no. 2 (September 3, 1898), p. 3) Emma Schlesinger's article under the same title. But in time articles of general knowledge also came to the fore; thus for instance (vol. 16, no. 3 (October 7, 1899), p. 3) Jenny Kleeberg Herz, "Primitive Culture."

36. Some of the more characteristic may be given by their titles: "Ein Gruss aus Sharon Springs" (A greeting from . . .) signed Marie Obermeier, (vol. 14, no. 4, p. 2); "Trost" signed Deborah Kleinert Janowitz (Ibid., p. 3) and the telling "Be-trachtungen über den Kaffeeklatsch" (Considerations . . .) characteristically not signed. (vol. 14, no. 8 (February 1898), p. 3).

37. Minna Kleeberg. Gedichte von Minna Kleeberg. Louisville: 1877. The volume was reviewed in *Der deutsche Pionier,* vol. 10 (1878), pp. 472-474;

Minna Neuer. Am Wage gepflückt. Gedichte. Washington, D.C.: 1889.

38. Isaac M. Wise. Hymns, Psalms and Prayers in English and German. Cincinnati: 1868. Minna Kleeberg is the only authoress in this compilation and her contribution consists of:

No. 19, p. 53, "Sabbath;"
No. 27, p. 77, "Die Tora;"
No. 32, p. 91, "Der Mensch" (Man);
No. 37, p. 103, "Gottvertrauen" (Trust in God);
No. 38, p. 105, "Hannukah;"

No. 64, p. 167, "Pesach;"
No. 68, p. 185, "Shabuoth;"
No. 74, p. 213, "Sukkoth;"
pp. 239-243, "Hymne zur Einweihung eines israelitischen Tempels" (hymn on the occasion of the consecration of an Israelitic temple).
pp. 243-246, "Purim,"
39. *The American Jewess*, vol. 1, no. 1 (April 1895), pp. 10-11, Hirsch, Emil G., "The modern Jewess;" Ibid., pp. 15-20, Moses, Dr. Adolph, "The position of woman in America," were the tributes to the new organ by the male spiritual leaders of the new organ; the thoughts of the editor, Rose Sonneschein, on the place of the Jewess in American womanhood are given in her article "The American Jewess." (*The American Jewess*, vol. 6 (February 1898), pp. 205-209). According to her, the Jewess is on a par with the American woman and "nevertheless she is loyal to her faith and race and is not favorably disposed to intermarriage. . . . Even the Sabbath has lost much of its sanctity, and the American Jewesses congregate in later numbers at the matinees than at the temples . . ." (p. 207), confirming with this last passus the world's opinion about the onward march of secular incentives holding the Jewish community together.
39a. Professor J. H. Ingraham. *The Clipper-Yacht; or Moloch, the Money-Lender! A Tale of London*. Boston: 1845, p. 5. Nathaniel Hawthorne even speaks of "wonderful hair, Jewish hair," *Complete Works*. Boston: 1902, vol. 8, *English Note Books*, p. 228.
40. *The Oregonian*, February 26, 1853, p. 2. Another version of the same theme can be found in "The Jewesses," *Ladies' Companion*, vol. 7 (1837), p. 306.
41. *The New York Visitor, and Parlour Companion*. New Series, vol. 1 (1840/1841), p. 139: "Jewesses."
42. *The Knickerbocker*, vol. 54 (1859), p. 51.
43. *JM*, vol. 13 (1863), p. 37.
44. Arthur Kyle Davis. *Traditional Ballads of Virginia*. Cambridge, Mass.: 1929, pp. 400-415: "Sir Hugh or the Jew's Daughter."
45. "California. Story of a Jewess," *Christian Work*, March 1, 1867, pp. 139/140. On the same level stands the motif of the willingness of the Jewess to throw aboard her faith on the appeal of the Christian soldier to join him:
"The Hebrew Maiden's Answer.
Christian Soldier must we sever?
Does the creed our fates divide?"
Mrs. Crawford, "To the Hebrew Maiden," *Ladies Companion*, vol. 4 (1835/36), p. 235.
In reverse, parents forcing a gentile girl to marry a rich Jew, may be a literary theme too:
"I will not—I must not—I *cannot* marry a *Jew!* She passionately exclaimed . . ." *Ladies Companion*, vol. 6 (1836/37), p. 258 ff. "The Jew of Marburg, or the Effect of a Monopoly, p. 259.
46. *The Complete Works of N. P. Willis*. New York: 1846, p. 596.
47. J. H. Ingraham. *The Clipper-Yacht*. Boston: 1845, p. 24.
48. "The Rachel Mania Continues Unabated" in *The Spirit of the Times*, vol. 9 (1839), p. 48.
49. "The old guitar," *Folio*, Boston, vol. 9 (1873), p. 163.
50. Feaste of Wit. . . . Philadelphia: 1821. P. 62, "The Mosaic Mother."
Albert I. Spencer. *Spencer's Book of Comic Speeches*. . . . New York: 1867. P. 121, "The Jewess and her son."

51. "The Jewess," *Shamrock*, 1817, p. 136. The story appears in another version in *The Spirit of the Times*, vol. 11 (1864/65), p. 349.

52. "The Jewess of Cairo," *Ladies' Companion*, vol. 15 (1841), pp. 270-281; "Queen Esther," *Ladies' Companion*, vol. 18 (1843), pp. 270-281; "The Heroism of Queen Esther," *Ladies' Companion*, vol. 10 (1839), p. 20; "The Heroism of Deborah," *Ladies' Companion*, vol. 10 (1839), p. 233; "The Heroism of Miriam," *Ladies' Companion*, vol. 10 (1839), p. 270.

53. *Spirit of the Times*, vol. 93 (1877), p. 526; *Wilke's Spirit of the Times*, vol. 9 (1863/64), pp. 3, 61. "Racing in Canada . . . Mr. Stevenson's . . . Jewess by Bob Logic." P. 61, "New Orleans Races. . . . The Jewess."

54. *The Spirit of the Times*, vol. 9 (1839), p. 42.

"The Jewess" as a title of popular stage performance is also favored. "New Drama of the Jewess," *Spirit of the Times*, vol. 6 (February 20, 1836), p. 8; and "The Jewess is still drawing good houses" (at the Bowery), *The Spirit of the Times*, February 27, 1836, p. 36.

55. "Cigars vs. Clothing," *Life*, vol. 4 (1884), p. 94.

56. Keppler Scrapbook. N.Y. Public Library. Vol. 2, *Puck*, April third 1881, cartoon "A. T. Stewart Frauen-Hotel."

57. *Life*, vol. 53 (1909), p. 79.

58. "Biographical Sketches of Jewish Communal Workers in the United States," in the *American Journal Year Book* 5666 (1905/06), pp. 32-118.

59. Ibid.

60. Exceptions to this rule may be found in ibid.

61. Eckhause, Emma, b. September 3, 1857 in Kokomo, Ind. educated in Convent Sacred Heart and English-German Academy, Rochester.

Jacobs, Minnie M. see note 60.

Mordecai, Laura. b. Philadelphia, educated in Washington and Philadelphia French Schools.

62. To this type of schools belong:

Miss Lucretia Brown's Academy, Philadelphia; Mrs. Frölich's School, New York; Bonnay, Dillaye Academy, Philadelphia; West Walnut Street Institute, Philadelphia; Academy School, Columbus, Ga.; Packer Collegiate Institute, Brooklyn, N. Y.; New Orleans Hebrew English College; Rayen School, Youngstown, O.; Collegiate Institute, Rollstone House, Toronto, Canada; New York Chartier Institute.

Eshner, Julia Friedberger, b. Philadelphia, Graduate Girls' Normal School; Miller, Fanny S., b. October 4, 1857, Cincinnati Normal School; Steinem, Pauline, educated in Memmingen, Bavaria, "Holds Teachers Diploma conferred by Teachers Seminary, Memmingen."

63. Lubitz, Bertha, M.D. 1891; Levy, Kate, b. New York, Medical Education at Woman's Medical School, Northwestern University, M.D. 1899.

64. Lillian Wald, b. 1866 in Cincinnati, O., educated in private schools in Rochester, "Special course N.Y. Women's Medical College and New York Hospital."

65. Other graduates and graduates of special courses:

Baldauf, Minnie L., b. July 7, 1872, in Louisville, Graduate, 1890, Henderson Female Seminary; Goldberg, Jeannette Miriam, courses Vassar College, A.B. Rutgers College; Hays, Rachel M., b. April 10, 1854 in Utica, N.Y. Graduate Normal College; Schönfeld, Julia, b. April 19, 1878 in Bellaire, O., A.B. 1897, Allegheny College; Bamber, Golde, b. January 5, 1869, Boston, Boston University, School of Oratory; Davis, Jeannette Isaacs, b. November 1, 1857 in New York, Jersey City Normal School, was teacher in Jersey City three years; Friedenthal, Hattie S., b. May 3, 1867 in New

York, visited Denver University; Greenbaum, Selina, b. June 6, 1866 in New York, Training Department Normal College, Normal College; Israels, Belle Lindner, b. October 5, 1878, New York. Horace Mann and Teachers' College; Stone, Rosetta, b. July 20, 1875 in New York, Normal College.

66. Einstein, Hanna Bachman, b. Jan. 28, 1862, in New York, Auditor Criminology and Sociology, Columbia University; Rosenberg, Pauline, b. in Pittsburgh, special courses University of Western Pennsylvania; sociology Columbia University.

67. Einstein, Hannah, Graduate Summer School of Philanthropy, Philadelphia; Krombach, Beatrice de Lack, b. April 9, 1874 in New York, graduate school of Philanthropy.

68. Weinschenker, Esther, graduate Chicago Business College; Newman, Hannah, b. February 23, 1848 in Cincinnati, Public School, Talmud Yelodim, Cincinnati.

Bibliography

Allgemeine Zeitung des Judentums. 1837-1900.

American German Review, The. Vol. 1 (1898/1899).

American Jewess, The. Vol. 1-6 (1895-1898).

American Jewish Historical Quarterly, vol. 57 (September 1966), no. 1, pp. 27-63.

American Jewish Year Book.

American Magazine. Vol. 62-75 (1900-1913).

Anderson, Margaret. My thirty year's war. An autobiography. London 1830.

An hour with the American Hebrew. By an American. New York 1879.

Antin, Mary, From Plotzk to Boston. Boston 1899.

Arena, The. Vol. 1 (1890).

Ariel, The. Philadelphia. Vol. 5 (1831).

Artistenlexikon. Düsseldorf 1895.

Askowitz, Dora. Three outstanding women. New York 1949.

Association for the Relief of Jewish Widows and Orphans. New Orleans. *Annual Report 1860.* New Orleans 1860.

[Association for the Advancement of Women] *Papers.* No .2-18. 1874-1891.

Atlantic Monthly. Vol. 1-106 (1857-1910).

Barnet, James Harwood. Divorce and the American divorce novel. 1858-1937. Philadelphia 1939.

Beecher, Catharine E. Educational reminiscences and suggestions. New York 1874.

Benjamin, J[oseph] I[srael]. Drei Jahre in Amerika. 2 vols. Hannover 1862.

Berliner Wochenblatt. 1857.

Besant, Walter, "The Rebel Queen," reviewed, *Atlantic Monthly,* vol. 73 (1893), p. 137.

"Biographical sketches of Jewish Communal Workers in the United States," *American Jewish Year-Book* 5666 (1905/6). Page 32-118.

Blanc, Madame. The condition of women in the United States. Boston 1895.

Bourget, Outre mer, quoted in Calhoun, Arthur W. Vol. 3, p. 180. See Calhoun.

Boyd's Business Directory of Essex, Hudson and Union Counties, N. J. . . . New York 1859.

Brav, Stanley, R., "The Jewish Woman, 1861-1865," *American Jewish Archives,* vol. 17, no. 1 (April 1865), pp. 34-75.

Bulletin, The. Vol. 1, 2 (1915, 1916).

Business Woman's, The. Vol. 7 (1892).

Calhoun, Arthur W., A social history of the American family. New York 1945. 3 vls.

Californischer Staats-Kalender auf das Schalt-Jahr . . . 1860.

Cameron, Mabel *comp.* The Biographical Cyclopedia of American women. New York 1924-1928. 3 vls.

[Campbell, Monroe] The First Fifty Years. A history of the National Council of Jewish Women. 1893-1943. [1943]

Centennial records of the women of Wisconsin . . . Madison, Wisc. 1876.

Century Magazine. Vol. 43 (1891/1892).

Chambliss, William H., Chambliss's Diary; or Society, as it really is. New York 1895.

Chicago Commons. Vol. 1 (1897).

Child, Maria L. Letters from New York. New York 1843.

Christian Work. 1867.

Clark, Herma. The Elegant Eighties. Chicago 1941.

Club Life. Vol. 4, 5 (1899-1900).

Club Woman's Magazine, The. New York. 1899.

Cohen, Mary M., "Hebrew Women," *Good Company,* vol. 3 (1879), pp. 620-624.

Congregation Emanuel. . . . New York. School for Religious Instruction. Year book 1898/99.

Constitution, the, and By-Laws of the Hebrew Sunday School Society of Philadelphia. Incorporated 1858 and the Superintendent's Report of the School for 1858. Philadelphia 1859.

Crandall, Charles H., The Season. . . . 1882-1883. New York 1883.

Croly, J. C. S. Mrs., The history of the Woman's Club Movement in America. New York [1898].

Daily Alta California. Vol. 5 (1854).

Davis, Allen M., "The Women's Trade Union League: Origins and organization," *Labor History,* vol. 5 (1964), pp. 3-17.

Davis, Arthur Kyle. Traditional Ballads of Virginia. Cambridge, Mass. 1929.

Der deutsche Pionier. Vol. 1-18 (1869-1886/1887).

Der Führer. Organ der deutschen Freimaurer und Odd Fellows. Vol. 37 (1909).

Der Israelitischer Volkslehrer. Vol. 5 (1855).

Der Nayer Gayst. Vol. 1 (1897).

Der Orient. Vol. 7 (1846).

Der Zeitgeist. Vol. 1 (1880).

Deseret News. Vol. 9 (1859), 18 (1869), 20 (1871), 21 (1871/1872).

Deutsche Monatshefte. Vol. 7 (1856).

Deutsche Schnellpost, 1843, No. 41, May 24, 1843.

Dexter, Elisabeth Brown. Career Women of America. Francestown 1960.

Di Arbayter Tsaytung. The Workman's Paper. Vol. 1 (1890/1891).

Die Deborah. Vol. 1-45 (1855-1900). Neue Folge,. Vol. 1, 2 (1900-1901).

Die Neuzeit. Vol. 14 (1874).

Die Wahrheit. Prag. Vol. 2 (1872).

Doehla, Johann Konrad, "Amerikanische Feldzüge," *Deutsche Amerikanisches Magazin,* vol. 1 (1887), p. 398.

Drinnon, Richard. Rebel in Paradise. A Biography of Emma Goldman. Chicago 1961.

Eberhard, Kurt von. Respectlosigkeiten über New York. Wien 1910.

Eichborn, W. J. *ed.* Sammlung der die neue Organisation des Judenwesen im Grossherzogtum Posen betreffenden Gesetze. . . . Posen 1834.

1846-1896. Goldenes Jubilaum des Unabhangigen Ordens Treue Schwestern und der Immanuel Loge No. 1. T.S. . . . 1896, New York.

1898-99. *Report of the Woman's Association of German Teachers. Additional reports up to 1909.*

Ellington, George. The Women of New York or Social Life in the Great City. New York, 1870.

"Emil G. Hirsch," *Reform Advocate,* vol. 23 (1902), p. 37.

Encyclopedia Judaica.

Epoch, The. Vol. 4, 8, 10, 11 (1888, 1890/91, 1891, 1892).

Erziehungsblätter, later *Amerikanische Schulzeitung,* vol. 1-27 (1870-1897).

Evening Post, 1896.

Facts by a woman. Oakland, Cal. 1881.

Feast of Wit. . . . Philadelphia 1821.

Ferber, Edna. A peculiar treasure. New York 1960.

Field, Kate, "Polygamy unveiled . . ." *Woman,* Vol. 1 (1888) pp. 296-305.

Filler, Louis. Crusaders for American liberalism. New York 1939.

Finkelstein, Louis. Jewish self-government in the Middle Ages. New York 1924.

First annual report of the Jewish Foster Home Society of Philadelphia. Philadelphia 1856. Constitution and bylaws. . . . Philadelphia, 1855. Later reports up to 1915.

Folio. Boston. Vol. 9 (1873).

Francis, Alexander. Americans An impression London 1909.

Free Church Circular, The. Oneida Reserve. Vol. 4 (1851).

Goldberg, Jacob. Attitudes to the New York Kehilla. New York 1937.

Gottheil, Gustav. Hymns and Anthems. New York, 1887.

Gottheil, Gustav, Dr. "The Jewess as she was and is," *Ladies Home Journal,* vol. 15 (1897/1898), December, 1897, p. 21.

Grunwald, Max. Die moderne Frauenbewegung und das Judentum. Wien 1903.

Grusd, Edward E., B'nai B'rith. The story of a covenant. New York [1966].

Hapgood, Hutchins. A Victorian in the modern world. New York 1939.

Harby, L. S., "Our Women and their possibilities, *"Jewish Messenger,* vol. 53 (1883), no. 2, p. 4.

Harper, Ida A., The associated work of the women of Indiana. Indianapolis, 1893.

Harper's Bazar. Vol. 13, 14, 20 (1880, 1881, 1887).

Hawthorne, Nathaniel. Complete Works. . . . Boston, 1902.

Hebrew, The. San Francisco. 1870, 1872.

"Hebrew Emigrant Society" der Vereinigten Staaten . . . Bericht . . . Für das Jahr 1882."

Hebrew Leader. Vol. 8 (1866).

Hebrew Sheltering and Immigrant Aid Society. *Reports,* 1909-1911.

Hebrew Standard. Vol. 4 (1900).

Hebrew Watchword, The. Devoted to the Interests of the Hebrew Sunday Schools of Philadelphia. Vol. 1 (1896).

Heppner, Dr. A. u. J. Herzberg. Aus Vergangenheit und Gegenwart der Juden in den Posener Landen. Koschmin 1904-1928.

Hirsch, E. G. A tribute to the memory of Liebman Adler. Chicago 1892.

Hirsch, Emil G. "The modern Jewess," *The American Jewess,* pp. 10-11.

Hubert, P. G., Jr. "The duty of the 'Four Hundred,'" The Epoch, vol. 8 (1890/1891), p. 245.

Hurst, Fanny. Anatomy of me . . . Garden City, New York 1958.

Independent Hebrew. Vol. 1 (1876).

Ingraham, J. H., Professor. The Clipper-Yacht; or Moloch, the money-lender! A tale of London. . . . Boston 1845.

Isaacs, Abraham S., "The Jewess in authorship," *Ladies' Home Journal,* vol. 9 (October, 1892), p. 17.

Isaacs, S. M., "The Reform Agitation," *Occident,* vol. 2 (1844/1845). p. 283.

Ishmaelite, The. Vol. 5 (1899).

Israelite, American Israelite, The.

Israelitische Annalen, vol. 1 (1839).

Jacobs, Sol, Rev., "Ladies singing in Synagogue," *Occident,* vol. 13 (1855), pp. 445, 492, 537.

Jewish Forum. Vol. 8, 9 (1925, 1926).

Jewish Messenger.

Jewish Times. Vol. 4 (1873/1874).

Jewish Tribune. Vol. 4 (1904).

Jewish Voice. Vol. 16 (1894).

Jewish Woman's Home Journal, The. Froyen Yournal. 1922.

Jewish World. London. Vol. 3 (1875).

Jewish World. London. Vol. 2 (1874).

Judaism. New York 1895.

Judge. Vol. 2 (1882).

Jüdisches Volksblatt. Vol. 4, 6, 12 (1857, 1859, 1866).

Kaganoff, Nathan M., "Organized Jewish Welfare activity in New York City," Keppler Scrapbook. New York. [1893].

Kist, Leopold. Amerikanisches. Mainz 1871.

Knickerbocker, The. Vol. 54. 1859.

Kober, Adolph, "Jewish Emigration from Wuerttemberg to the United States of

America," *Publications of the American Jewish Historical Society,* vol. 51 (March, 1952), pp. 225-273.

Kohut, Rebekah. Jewish Women's Organisations in the United States. New York 1931.

Konopka, Otto, "Das Privatschulwesen der Stadt Posen unter besonderer Berücksichtigung der Erziehungsanstalten für das weibliche Geschlecht," *Zeitschrift . . . Provinz Posen,* vol. 26 (1911), pp. 243-309.

Korman, E. *ed.* Jewish poetesses. Anthology. Yiddish. Chicago 1928.

Koven, Reginald de, Mrs., "Social life in Chicago," *Ladies Home Journal,* vol. 9 (April 1892), p. 4.

Ladies Companion. Vol. 3-6, 15 (1835-1837, 1841).

Ladies Home Journal. Vol. 9, 13, 15 (1892, 1896, 1897/1898).

Ladies Repository. Vol. 25 (1865).

Langley San Francisco Directory. 1858.

Laubhütte, Die. Vol. 1 (1866).

Lazarus, Josephine. Madame Dreyfus. New York [1899].

Lazarus Josephine. The spirit of Judaism. New York 1895.

Life. Vol. 4, 53 (1884, 1909).

Lily, The. New York. Vol. 1-6 (1849-1854).

Logan, Mrs. John A. The part taken by women in America. Wilmington 1912.

Los Angeles Star. 1851-1877.

Marcus, Jacob R., Memoirs of American Jews. 1755-1855. Philadelphia 1955.

Metz, Jacob, "Die Juden Amerikas," *Jüdisches Volksblatt,* vol. 4 (1857), p. 171.

Missouri Historical Society Bulletin. Vol. 6 (1949/1950).

Missouri State Gazetteer and Business Directory. . . . St. Louis 1860.

Mitgliederliste des Vereines Deutscher Lehrerinnen in Amerika. 1902.

Mormon, The. Vol. 1 (1855/1856).

Moses, Adolph, Dr., "The position of woman in America," *The American Jewess,* vol. 1 (1895), pp. 15-20.

Mother Hubbard [Stewart, Eliza]. Memoirs of the Crusade. Columbus, O. 1888.

Nachrichten von den vereinigten Deutschen Evangelisch-Lutherischen Gemeinen in Nordamerika, absonderlich in Pensylvanien. . . . D. Johann Schulze, Halle 1787.

Nathan, Maud. The story of an epoch making movement. Garden City, N.Y. 1926.

Nation, The. Vol. 41 (1885).

National Council of Jewish Women. *First Annual Report.* 1894-1895. National Council of Jewish Women. Proceedings of the First Convention. . . . Philadelphia: 1897.

National Socialist, The. Cincinnati. Vol. 1 (1898).

New Cycle, The. . . . Official Organ of the General Federation of Woman's Clubs. Vol. 8, (1895-1897).

New York Visiter and Parlour Companion. New Series. Vol. 1 (1840-1841).

New Yorker Handels-Zeitung. 1855, 1859, 1865-1880.

New Yorker Staatszeitung. 1870.

•Nichols, Thomas L .Forty years of American Life. London 1864. 2 vls.

Niles Weekly Register. Vol. 1-75 (1811-1879).

North American Review. Vol. 1-131 (1881-1900).

Northern Monthly, The. Vol. 1 (1867).

Occident, The. Vol. 1-25 (1843-1868).

Ordens Echo, New York. Vol. 14-17 (1897-1901).

Overland Monthly. Vol. 1-10 (1868-1873).

Overton, Grant. The women who make our novels. New York 1928.

Papers of the Jewish Women's Congress. Held in Chicago, September 4, 5, 6, and 7, 1893. Philadelphia: 1894.

Philadelphia Press. November 21, 1874.

Philippson, Ludwig, Dr., Wie sich der Statistiker, Staatsrat etc. Dr. I. G. Hoffman verrechnet! Leipzig 1842.

Philippson, Martin. Neueste Geschichte des judischen Volkes. Leipzig 1907.

Play Bill, The. Vol. 2 (1865).

Porter's Spirit of the Times. Vol. 1-4 (1856-1859).

Proceedings of the First Convention of the National Council of Jewish Women held at New York, Nov. 15, 16, 17, 18 and 19, 1896. Philadelphia 1897.

Program of the National Council of Jewish Women for 1895/1896.

Program of Work. Council of Jewish Women. December, 1909.

Protokolle der Rabbiner—Conferenz abgehalten zu Philadelphia vom 3. bis zum 6. November 1869. New York 1870.

Puck. Vol. 8, 29 (1880/1881, 1891).

Ralph, Julius, "The way we get our wives," *The Epoch,* vol. 4 (1888), p. 471.

Recollections of Life and Doings in Chicago. Chicago 1945.

Reform Advocate, The. Vol. 7-24 (1894-1903).

Report of the Executive Committee Presented at the First Annual Convention of the Jewish Community (Kehilla). New York, February 26 and 27, 1910. Second Annual Report, 1911. Fifth Annual Report, 1914.

Revolution, The. Vol. 1-7 (1868-1871).

Riley, Thomas James. A study of the higher life of Chicago. Chicago 1925.

Ripley, William Z., "Race factors in labor unions," *Atlantic Monthly,* vol. 93 (1904), pp. 299-308.

Rosenthal, A., Jewish Progress in St. Louis. St. Louis 1904.

Schindler, Solomon, "The Divorce Problem," *The Arena,* vol. 1 (May 1890), pp. 689-690.

Schlesinger, Arthur. Learning How to Behave. A historical study of American etiquette books. New York 1947.

Schnee, Heinrich. Die Hochfinanz und der moderne Staat. Berlin 1953.

Scouller, Mildred Marshall. Women who man our clubs. Philadelphia 1934.

Season, The.

Seybold, Louis, Akrons Deutschtum vor Fünfzig Jahren und Früher," *Akron Germania,* December 22, 1906.

Shamrock. . . . 1817.

Sherwood, M. E., The art of entertaining. New York 1892.

Shoe and Leather Reporter. Vol. 3 (1860).

Shosteck, Robert, "The Jewish Community of Washington, D. C. 1861-1865," *American Jewish Historical Quarterly,* vol. 56, no. 3, March, 1967.

Shpall, Leo, "Adah Isaacs Menken," *Louisiana Historical Quarterly,* vol. 26 (1943), no. 1, pp. 162-168.

Silverman, Morris, Hartford Jews. Hartford 1970.

Sinai. Erlangen. Vol. 2 (1847).

Sinclair, Andrew. The Better Half. The Emancipation of the American Woman. 1965.

Smith, Helen. *ed.* With her own wings. Portland, Oregon 1948.

Sonneschein, Rose, "The American Jewess," *The American Jewess,* vol. 6 (February, 1898), pp. 205-209.

Sonneschein, Rose, "The Jewess of to-day. . . . Communal activity," *The American Jewess,* vol. 6 (February, 1898), p. 207.

Southern Business Directory, The. Vol. 1. Charleston 1854.

Souvenir Journal . . . 25th Anniversary of the Seligman Solomon Society Alumni of the Hebrew Orphan Asylum Terrace Garden. March 10, 1912.

Spencer, Albert I. Spencer's Book of Comic Speeches. . . . New York 1867.

Spirit of the Times, The. Vol. 6-87 (1836-1874).

Spoffort, Harriet Prescott, "The evolution of the hired girl," *Ladies Home Journal,* vol. 9 (September, 1892).

Sprigge, Elisabeth. Gertrude Stein. Her life and work. New York 1957.

Stein, Mrs. Oswald, *ed.* Leading Women in Social Service, 1915. n.p.

Stenographischer Bericht über die Delegierten-Versammlung zur Beratung der Hilfsaktion für die Russischen Juden. Berlin, 20. und 21. Oktober, 1891.

Stone, Goldie. My Caravan of years. New York, 1945.

Suhl, Yuri. Ernestine L. Rose and the Battle for Human Rights. New York [1959].

Sulamith. Vol. 2 (1809).

Sutro, Florence Clinton, "Woman's Work and Influence," *The American German Review,* vol. 1 (1898/99), pp. 63-72.

Taenzer, A., Die Geschichte der Juden in Jebenhausen and Göppingen. Berlin, 1927.

Tarbell, Ida, "The American woman," *American Magazine,* vol. 69 (1910), p. 449.

Teachers and Parents' Assistant, The, or Thirteen Lessons conveying to uninformed minds the first ideas of God and His attributes. By an American Jewess. Philadelphia, 5605 (1845).

Thompson, Grace Gallatin Seton. A Woman tenderfoot. New York, 1900.

Tinkham, George H., A history of Stockton. San Francisco, 1880.

Treue Schwestern. Vol. 38 (1910).

Trow Business Directory of New York City. 1851-1860.

Twentieth Century. New York. Vol. 1-5 (1888-1890).

Ungarische Jüdische Wochenschrift. Vol. 1 (1871).

Vogue. Vol. 1-2 (1892-1893).

Voice of Jacob. Vol. 4 (1845).

Vorbote. Chicago. Vol. 2 (1875).

Wheatley, Richard, "The Jews in New York," *Century Magazine,* vol. 43 (1891/1892), pp. 323-342, 512-532.

Willard, Frances Elisabeth. A woman of the century. Buffalo, 1893.

Williamson, Burton, Mrs., Ladies' Clubs and Societies in Los Angeles in 1892 . . . March, 1892.

Willis, N. P. The complete works. New York, 1846.

Wilson, St. John, Atlanta as it is: . . . New York, 1871.

Wilson's Business Directory of New York City, 1852.

[Wisconsin State Historical Society] "Four Episodes in Wisconsin Pioneering." Recollections of a Pioneer Woman of La Crosse. By Augusta Levy. Pp. 201-215.

Wittenmyer, Annie. History of the Woman's Temperance Crusade. Philadelphia, 1878.

Wolf, Emma. Other things equal. Chicago, 1894.

Woman. New York. Vol. 1 (1888), pp. 296-305.

Woman Suffrage Leaflets. 1899, 1900.

Woman Suffrage Year Book, The. 1917.

Woman's Association of Commerce, Chicago. Membership Book 1919/1920.

Woman's Herold of Industry and Social Cooperator. San Francisco. Vol. 2 (1893).

Woman's Illustrated World. New York. Vol. 1, 2 (1889).

Woman's Journal. Boston and Chicago. Vol. 1 (1870), 11 (1880), 24 (1893).

Woman's Literary Union. Portland, Maine. Year Book. 1894-1895. (1899-1900).

Woman's Magazine, The. Brattleboro, Vt. Vol. 11-13 (1887-1889).

Woman's Magazine, The. St. Louis. Vol. 10-21 (1904-1910).

Woman's Municipal League of the City of New York. Yearbook. 1910-1914.

Woman's World and Jennes Miller Monthly. New York. Vol. 10 (1897), 22 (1906).

Woodhull a. Clafflin's Weekly. Vol. 2 (1870), 3 (1871), 5-10 (1873-1875).

Woody, Thomas. A history of Woman's Education in the United States. New York, 1929. 2 vls.

Year Book, The. New York Section. Council of Jewish Women. New York, 1917-1918, 5678. 1920-1921. 1922-1923. 1923-1924.

Yezierska, Anzia. Red ribbon on a white horse. 1950.

Young Israel. An Illustrated Monthly for young people. New York. Vol. 1 (1871).

Zeichen der Zeit. Chicago. Vol. 1 (1863).

Zeitschrift für die religiösen Interessen des Judentums.

Zylbercwaig, Zalmen. Leksikon fun yidishen teater. New York, 1931-1969. 6 vls.

Index

abolitionist sentiment 18
Abramovitch, Bime 191
"academy, hohere Töchterschule," Miss Lucretia Brown, Mrs. Fröhlich, Eschner, Julia Friedlinger, Miller, Fanny S. 195
Adler, Felix 190
Adler, Liebman 2, 171
Adler, Miss 190
Adler, Nelly 183
Adler, Samuel, Dr. 190
Adler, Sarah 191
Africa, barbaric 61
agunah—situation 87, 88
Akron, Ohio 125
Albany 134
Allersheim, Bavaria 186
American, Sadie, Miss 152
"American and Foreign Papers please copy" 76
American Israelite 98, 113
American Jewess 165
American Jewish literature 161-164
American Jewry 1
American sporting scene 51
American Yearbook 171
Amram, Esther 171
anecdote 49
anomalies, in Jewish women's life 84, 85
anti-saloon movement, Christian Temperance Movement 137-139
Antin, Mary 163, 192
arbiter elegantiarum 63
Armen-Mädchen Anstalt (poor girls' institute) in Berlin 12
articles of value to gentlemen, gloves, suspenders, studs, dress suits and ulsters 41
Askowitz, Dora 192

Association for the Advancement of Women 130
At Home 24, 25
Atlantic migration 2
Atlas, Jenny 191
attire, of woman 74
Aufhausen, Württemberg 171
Avery, Rachel Foster 152

Baden, duchy of 10
Baldauf, Minnie L. 195
ball, wallflowers at 49
balls, charity, Purim 57, 65
 fairs 127
Baltimore 8
Baltimore Society News 64
Bamber, Golde 195
Barnett, James Harwood 180
bathing suit 61
Baum, Esther 171
Bavaria X, emigration from 8, 9
Bavarian government 9
Beecher, Catharine E. 189
beer saloon 137
belle 67
Bellson, R. Rev. 172
Benjamin, I. J. 182
Benjamin, Jenny 183
Bermudas 75
Bernhardt, Sarah, the "Jewess" 191
Besant, Walter 188
best men, group of, at balls 50
biblical models of women, Sara, Esther, Miriam, Deborah, Rahab, Ruth, Abigail 143
Bienstock, Sarah 171
bigamy 88
billiards 41
blackballing 175
Blanc, Madam 188, 191

205

deserted woman, desertion, of wives 20, 84
diamonds 154
divorce 79, 85-92
and social decline,
in fictional literature and drama,
in California, Illinois, Indiana, Western states,
in popular humor,
procedures 79, 85-92, statistics 91, 93, 94
status, legal 93
Doehla, Johann Konrad 175
Dogett, Kate N. 140, 189
domestic hearth 18
life 21, 22
servants, female, housemaids 81
German 81
Irish 81
Negro 81
Chinese 81
dress 64, dresses, display of, and good manners 56, sleeveless 58
Dreyfus, Madame 154, 162, 192
drink 41, drinking among Jews 138, 139, drinking places, saloons 137
Drinnon, Richard, 172, 192
drummers 68, 148
dry goods 148
dude 52
Dürkheim am Haad, Rhenish Bavaria 171

East, of Europe 20
East Side of the Chicago River 171
Eckamn, Dr. [Julius] 90
Eckhause, Emma 195
economic adjustment and achievement XII
education, female, girls' 109-120, elementary schools of Jewish communities 109, Sunday schools 110, academy, "höhewe Töchterschule" 110, private instruction 112, 113
Eichhorn, W. J. 183
Einhorn, David 183
Einstein(s) 111
Einstein, Hanna 196
Einstein, Hanna Bachman 196
Ellwangen 7
elopement 103

Emanuel, Misses 182
Emanu-El sisterhood 128, 129
Emigrant Aid Societies 129
emigration, immigration, after-pull of 10, preparation of 11, German Jewish 15, Russian Jewish 15
engagements 81
England XIII
English language 110
English model, of the Society Page 76
engraver, of capital 10
enlightenment 2
Ephraim, Benjamin Veitel 171
Erziehungsblätter 164
ethnic groups VIII
etiquette, of social life 44, 62-65
Eufaula, Ala. 68
examination in public, of orphan homes, inmates 118
exclusion from the visiting list, of the Jewess 27

family-building IX-XI, 79
after-pull of family members 10
celebrations, weddings
founding
German Jewish, Russian Jewish life 16-20
pew 148
fashion, dictates of 58
Fels, Mary 191
Felsenthal, Rabbi 140
feminine appeal, sphere and social intercourse 26-29
Ferber, Edna 125, 163, 184, 185, 192
Feustman, Rosalia 171
fidelity, marital 83
Field, Kate 189
Fifth Avenue [New York] 59, promenade on 65
finger-bowls 63
Finkelstein, Louis 176
folk-language, old Jewish 2, 25
formal visiting 32
forms of social entertainment, reception, "kettle drum," social dance, midnight supper 32
foundlings 84
"Fountain House," Waukesha 57
Four hundred, The, in San Francisco 63
Francis, Alexander 178

Howe, general 175
Hubert, P. G., Jr. 178
Hunt, Florence 153
Huntington, Mr. 63
Hurst, Fanny 163, 174, 192
Hymns, singing of in synagogue 122, hymn books 122
Hyneman, Rebecca 192

ice cream parlor 67
Ichenhausen, Wuerttemberg 6
immigration, female, Jewish VII, VIII
new, Russian VII, VIII
independence, economical, of women 3
Indianapolis 77
industrial school 113
Industrieschule, industrial education 11, 12
infant's mortality 23
Ingraham, J. H., Professor 194
intermarriage 96-98, statistics of 98
Isaacs, Abram S. 184, 192
Isaacs, S. M., Rev. 173
Israelite 175
Israels, Belle Lindner 196

Jacobi, Abraham, Dr. 190
Jacobi, Mrs. 190
Jacobs, Mrs. 190
Jacobs, Sol, Rev. 184
Jacobson, Froecken 174
Jacobson, Laura D. 185
Jaffe, Miss 96
Janowitz, Deborah Kleinert 193
Japha, Miss 183
jargon 116
Jassy, Rumania 171
Jebenhausen, Wuerttemberg 7
Jenkinsisms 77
"Jesuitism and Woman" 140
"Jew clothing establishment" 19
jewelers, jewelry, cheap, fondness for 60
Jewess, beauty of 166, 167
Jewess, converted 167
Jewess, in American folklore and popular literature 165-169
Jewess, "little" 167
Jewish Labor Movement in Palestine 160
Jewish Messenger 84, 113, 145-149, 153

Jewish Radicalism 162
Jewish Reformer 149
Jewish schools, instruction in German language 117
Jewish Times 85
Jewish Women's Congress in Chicago 1893, 155
Jewish World, London 174
Jewry, German 2
Joachimsen, Caroline J. 149
Joachimsen, P. J. Mrs. 187
Jonas, Alexander 190
Jordan, Dr. 154
Joseph, Annie 171
Joseph, Sadie, Miss 154
Judenedikt of 1813 (Jewish statute of June 10, 1813, in Bavaria).
Judenfeind 66
Judge Hilton 28
Judicus 181
"Judisch Schreiben" X, taught in Germany's Jewish schools 117
"Judith in the Apocrypha" 143

"Kaffeeklatch" 67, 157
Kaganoff, Nathan M. 185
Kalisch, Berta 191
Karl-Schule in Frankfurt/Main 12
Kaschau, Hungary 171
"kasher" in households 133
Keily, Mr. 191
Keppler 195
"kettledrum" 32
Key of Haven 175
Kist, Leopold 173, 188
"Kitchen-Judaism" 21
klatsch corner, of the women 30
Kleeberg, Dr. L. 119
Kleeberg, Minna 119, 123, 165, 183, 187, 193
Kober, Adolph 8, 172, 173
Kohut, Rebekka 171
Koppel von Vloomburg 188
Korman, E. 192
kosher board 80
Kovno 192
Kramer, Simon 172, 174
Krombach, Beatrice Lack 196

Ladies' Friday Musicale 185
Ladies' Hebrew Benevolent Society 125

210   *Index*

Moore, E. C. 188
Morais, Nina 150, 159
Mordecai, Laura 195
Morgenstern, Lina 150
Mormons 18, 91, 147
Mosaic faith 6
"Mosaic Mother" 168
Moses, Dr. Adolph 165, 188
Mother Hubbard [Stewart Eliza] 189, 194
muckraker 25
Münsterberg, Selma Oppler 191
Murdock, Miss Marian 150
Murphy, Mr. 98

Nashville, Tenn. 131
Nathan, Maud 159, 184, 192
National Council of Jewish Women 14, 130, 131, 150, 151
Negro, ostracized 153
Neuburg 13
Neurer, Minna 165, 193
New Orleans 123
Newman, Hannah 196
Newstadt, Miss 183
New Year's visits 34
New York 8, 99, 139, White Garden in 100
Normal College 183

Oakland 98
Oberdorf 7
Oberfranken 13
Obermeier, Marie 193
Oberpfalz 13
Occident 110
"*on dits* of the day" in conversation 49
Open house, on Purim 32, 33
Oppenheim, A. A. 190
Oppenheim, Germany 172
Oppenheimer[s] 8
Ordensecho 164
orders, female 14, masonic 14
O'Reilly, John Boyle 140
orphan asylum 46, 118 (New York), German language, instruction in 118
orphan bride 106, 107
Otterbourg, Judge 93
oyster saloons 67

painting, ladies' of faces 55, 61
Palaché; Misses 182
Palestine, Jewish labor movement in 160, parents, cared for 19
parent, care for daughters 104
Paris 191
Party, The 38-41
Parvenue Advertising Agency 63
Parvenuecracy 63
peddling 83, 95
perijah v'rebiya 24
Pfalz 13
Philadelphia 121
Philippson, Ludwig, Dr. 171
Philippson, Martin 172
Phillips, Lewis, Mrs. 69
Pilsen, Bohemia 171
Pine Lake 74
Pinne 9
"Pioneers," St. Louis 128
Plain Dealer, Cleveland 150
pogroms, Russian 1
Police Headquarters 85
popular humor, Jewish woman in 168, 169
Portuguese congregation 115
Portuguese synagogue in Philadelphia 150
Posen, Poseners IX, X
Posen province, emigration from IX, X, schools in X, German language in in 117
Prague 12
pregnancy, avoiding of 23, 24
press, Jewish 55, society news treated in 77, 78
processions, bridal 129
promenade 65-67
prostitution 85
Prussia X
public places 65-67
pulpit 125, 192
Pulpit, Chicago 153
Purim 34, Purim Association 58, in New York 1883, 70

rabbinical authorities, in Europe 86
rabbinical courts 86
rabbinical literature, responsa 86
Rachel, actress 167
Rachel, Mary, Mrs. 190